David Lodge

Twayne's English Authors Series

Kinley Roby, Editor

Northeastern University

TEAS 553

DAVID LODGE
Photo compliments of Curtis Brown

David Lodge

Bruce K. Martin

Drake University

Twayne Publishers
New York

Twayne's English Authors Series No. 553

David Lodge
Bruce K. Martin

Twayne Publishers
1633 Broadway
New York, NY 10019

Library of Congress Cataloging-in-Publication Data

Martin, Bruce K., 1941–
    David Lodge / Bruce K. Martin.
        p.   cm. — (Twayne's English authors series ; TEAS 553)
    Includes bibliographical references and index.
    ISBN 0-8057-1671-8 (alk. paper)
    1. Lodge, David, 1935 –   —Criticism and interpretation.
I. Title.   II. Series.
PR6062.036Z76   1999
823'.914—dc21   99-11814
                                                                CIP

This paper meets the requirements of ANSI/NISO Z3948-1992 (Permanence of Paper).

10 9 8 7 6 5 4 3 2 1

Printed in the United States of America

For Glenn Skoy and Ted Stroud

Contents

Preface

Since the mid-1970s, David Lodge has emerged as one of the principal novelists in Britain as well as one of the most popular British writers among American readers. Today he has few serious rivals for the generally middle-class, college-educated readership to which his fiction seems to appeal most, and especially for those readers at all aware of developments in humanistic disciplines during recent decades. This is not to say that the readership with which Lodge has found favor is solely an academic one. Rather, those of his novels that first gained wide attention and that continue to be his best known—*Changing Places* (1975), *Small World* (1985), and *Nice Work* (1989)—have succeeded in part by appealing, in a decidedly nonthreatening manner, to the curiosity of middlebrow, nonacademic readers about developments and controversies within universities—developments and controversies international in scope and implication and widely publicized and discussed in newspapers and popular newsmagazines. The Anglo-American emphasis in the first two of these novels, as well as Lodge's satirical scrutiny of academicians and their ways in all three, also have contributed to their appeal throughout the English-speaking world.

As a result, not only these three but almost all of Lodge's other novels have achieved considerable prominence. While for many years they routinely appeared in paperback editions after the normal interval following hardcover publication, it seems significant that three of his earlier titles—*The British Museum Is Falling Down* (1965), *Out of the Shelter* (1970), and *Souls and Bodies* (first published in Great Britain, as *How Far Can You Go?*, in 1980)—were not published in this format until many years later. Their belated paperback publication in the late 1980s, when Viking Penguin issued the entire list of Lodge's books—some for the first time in America—suggests the degree of popularity his three "academic" novels have achieved. Today all of David Lodge's novels—even his first, *The Picturegoers* (1960)—are in print, and several titles normally are stocked in British and American bookstores. An additional sign of his increasingly secure place with a wide readership, particularly in the United States, is that each new novel since the early 1980s has been reviewed not only in literary quarterlies such as the *Yale Review* or *Hudson Review* or in the standard reviews for serious readers, such as *TLS* and the *New York Review of Books,* but also in the newsmagazines intended for a mass audience, notably *Time* and *Newsweek.*

Despite such evidence that more and more people are finding David Lodge's fiction appealing in many ways, his audience and appeal are not unlimited. Perhaps more than most writers in recent decades who have enjoyed critical acclaim and commercial success, Lodge writes particular kinds of novels for particular kinds of readers. Determining and describing as precisely as possible the categories into which his novels and readers fall (as well as the apparent reasons for his success—reasons found both in his writings and in the reading publics to which they have appealed) becomes the central challenge of a study such as this. What exactly do the terms usually applied to Lodge's fiction—such as *literary novels* or *social comedies*—mean, and how well do they serve as descriptors? What characteristic concerns, techniques, and strategies seem to mark his writing? How do his novels relate to other recent fiction of the same type or to their precursors? What shift in categories—in his fiction and its readership—is evident in the four decades during which he has been writing novels? How does whatever place in literary history one might even tentatively assign David Lodge's writings relate to the niche they have achieved in the postwar and contemporary literary markets?

Such questions require first some consideration of the relevant historical and social forces and developments that have helped form the kinds of fiction David Lodge has written and to which, in turn, his writings have contributed. For this reason the first chapter discusses the period in which Lodge came to writing, as well as key events in his personal development. It looks closely at the two early novels (*Out of the Shelter,* 1970, and *Ginger, You're Barmy,* 1962), which are his most openly autobiographical fiction and, interestingly, the only writing he has revised extensively for later editions. Chapter 2 examines Lodge as a satirist of contemporary academic life in England and the United States, with special attention to the three "academic" novels mentioned previously.

Much of the richness and force of Lodge's fiction, especially the academic satires, rests on a deep awareness of the tradition of the English novel and of the vicissitudes of recent literary theory. Even those novels unconcerned with academia seem to participate self-consciously in literary history and literary theory and point to Lodge's parallel career as longtime literature professor at the University of Birmingham and writer of academic books. Any serious consideration of his total career must confront the interplay between the "two Lodges"—the novelist and the literary theorist-critic-historian—as well as their separateness.

In what ways do his critical and theoretical writings provide a gloss for his practices as a fiction writer, and in what ways do the novels challenge, and sometimes even repudiate, theoretical or critical stances Lodge may have taken? Chapter 3 considers these and related questions in describing Lodge's work as theorist and critic.

Chapter 4 concerns yet another strain of David Lodge's writing, one that is in some ways the most persistent. It reaches back to his earliest published fiction (*About Catholic Authors*, 1957) and forward to his latest, *Therapy* (1995). Lodge's infrequent but regularly appearing novels about English Catholics and the difficulties of being both Catholic and English in the rapidly changing social and religious environment in the latter half of the twentieth century represent some of his most compelling writing and a valuable reflection on the uneasy place of traditional institutions in an age paradoxically wary of traditions and institutions yet hungry for stability. It is the paradoxical spirit of these seemingly parochial novels that reaches beyond their obvious audience to address Americans and non-Catholics as well and that accounts in part for their belatedly wide acceptance.

Chapter 5 looks at Lodge's most recent work—novels, critical writings, and other projects (film scripts, television adaptations of his own fiction, and drama)—undertaken since he abandoned his academic career at Birmingham to write full-time. It examines changes in the kind of work, even the kind of critical work, Lodge has done since then as well as the consolidation and different directions his latest fiction possibly suggests. The concluding chapter considers the totality of David Lodge's career and writing thus far for both its symptomatic and its distinctive qualities. Further, it speculates on his work's impact and on implications for similar writing in the twenty-first century, as well as on the possible ways in which Lodge may be received by future readers and literary historians.

Acknowledgments

Many individuals and institutions have helped me in writing this book and preparing it for publication. First I must acknowledge David Lodge's kindness in granting me permission to quote from his novels and other books and in answering my questions. Elizabeth Harrison generously and unfailingly shared from the bibliographical data on Lodge that she has been gathering for publication. Mike Shaw of the Curtis Brown agency was helpful to me when we visited in London. The Cowles Library of Drake University and its staff made it possible to secure material and information vital to this study, as did the libraries and staffs of Illinois Benedictine University, the University of Minnesota, the British Film Institute, and the University of London. The Center for the Humanities at Drake University provided support for research in London. Finally, I must thank my wife, Barbara, not only for her encouragement on this project but for reading and commenting on drafts of all of its parts and for helping with various tasks attendant to its completion.

Permission to quote from the following works has been kindly granted by Curtis Brown on behalf of David Lodge: *After Bakhtin* © 1990 David Lodge; *The Art of Fiction* © David Lodge, 1992; *The British Museum Is Falling Down* © David Lodge, 1965, 1981; *Changing Places* © David Lodge, 1975; *Ginger, You're Barmy* © David Lodge, 1962, 1982; *Language of Fiction* © David Lodge, 1968; *The Modes of Modern Writing* © David Lodge, 1977; *The Novelist at the Crossroads* © David Lodge, 1971; *Nice Work* © David Lodge, 1988; *Out of the Shelter* © David Lodge, 1970, 1985; *The Picturegoers* © David Lodge, 1960, 1963; *Paradise News* © David Lodge, 1991; *The Practice of Writing* © David Lodge, 1996; *Souls and Bodies* © David Lodge, 1980; *Small World* © David Lodge, 1984; *Therapy* © David Lodge, 1995; *The Writing Game* © 1991 by David Lodge; *Write On* © David Lodge, 1965, 1968, 1969, 1971, 1975, 1976, 1978, 1980, 1981, 1982, 1984, 1985, 1986; *Working with Structuralism* © David Lodge, 1981.

Chronology

1935   David John Lodge born 28 January in Dulwich, south London, to William Frederick Lodge and Rosalie Marie Murphy Lodge.

1939   Beginning of World War II, during which Lodge and his mother evacuate to Surrey and Cornwell.

1945   End of war; returns to London and enrolls at St. Joseph's Academy in Blackheath.

1952   Graduates from St. Joseph's and enrolls in University College, London.

1955   Receives B.A. in English (with honors) from University College; is drafted into Royal Armoured Corps and spends two years as clerk at Bovington Camp in Dorset.

1957   Discharged from army; begins postgraduate study at University College.

1958   *About Catholic Authors* published.

1959   Marries Mary Frances Jacob on 16 May; receives M.A. degree in English.

1959–1960   Teaches English and literature to foreign students for British Council in London.

1960   Appointed lecturer at University of Birmingham; *The Picturegoers* published.

1962   *Ginger, You're Barmy* published.

1963   "Between These Four Walls," coauthored review, produced in Birmingham.

1964–1965   Lives and travels with his family in the U.S. on Harkness Commonwealth Fellowship.

1965   "Slap in the Middle," coauthored review, produced in Birmingham; *The British Museum Is Falling Down* published.

1966   *Language of Fiction* and *Graham Greene* published.

1967   Receives Ph.D. from University of Birmingham for work done in connection with *Language of Fiction*.

1969   Appointed visiting associate professor at University of California, Berkeley.

1970   *Out of the Shelter* published.

1971   Appointed senior lecturer at University of Birmingham; *The Novelist at the Crossroads* and *Evelyn Waugh* published.

1972   *Twentieth-Century Literary Criticism: A Reader* published.

1973   Appointed Reader in English Literature at University of Birmingham.

1975   *Changing Places* published and awarded Hawthornden Prize and *Yorkshire Post* Fiction Prize.

1976   Appointed professor of modern English literature at University of Birmingham.

1977   *The Modes of Modern Writing* published.

1980   *How Far Can You Go?* published (published as *Souls and Bodies* in U.S. in 1982) and awarded Whitbread Book Prize of the Year.

1981   *Working with Structuralism* published.

1984   *Small World* published and short-listed for Booker Prize.

1986   *Write On* published.

1987   Retires from University of Birmingham and is appointed honorary professor of modern English literature; November: *Big Words: Small World* broadcast by Channel Four.

1988   *Nice Work* published and chosen *Daily Express* Book of the Year; *Modern Criticism and Theory: A Reader* published.

1989   April–May: Adaptation of *Nice Work* broadcast by BBC.

1990   May–June: *The Writing Game* produced in Birmingham; *After Bakhtin* published.

1991   *Paradise News* and *The Writing Game* published.

1992   *The Art of Fiction* published.

1994   November–December: Adaptation of *Martin Chuzzlewit* broadcast by BBC.

1995   *Therapy* published and short-listed for 1996 Common-
        wealth Writers Prize.

1996   *The Practice of Writing* published.

1997   Lodge is made a *Chevalier dans l'Ordre des Arts et Lettres*
        by French Ministry of Culture.

1998   February–March: *Home Truths* produced in Birmingham.

Chapter One

Postwar England and the Autobiographical Impulse

The period that led to the beginning of Lodge's writing career was especially striking for the degree to which public events impinged on the private lives of ordinary people. While there can be considerable debate over the importance to everyday existence of political developments and political leaders as described by traditional historians, probably no event in human history changed the lives of so many people so drastically and so immediately as the Second World War. Certainly its effect on civilian life was unprecedented in England, which faced its first serious threat of foreign invasion since the Norman Conquest and suffered the destruction of large parts of London and other cities.

Because Lodge was only four years old when the war began and because he and his family experienced fully the discomfort and dislocation wartime Londoners faced from early 1940 until the German surrender five years later—including several years of relocation to the countryside—the prewar period held but a slight place in his memories of childhood. Perhaps this is why the tensions of postwar England occupy so significant a place in his writing, while the contrast between the 1930s and wartime England is scarcely mentioned. Lodge's age no doubt also helps explain why, though he sometimes appears to share the largely apolitical stance that many of the so-called Movement writers took in the 1950s (a stance conditioned in part by relief at the shift to civilian normalcy in an England wrecked by war), he has at no time reverted to the nostalgia about England's former greatness or the regret over England's postwar decline that marked the later work of so many Movement writers, including Philip Larkin and Kingsley Amis. Neither has Lodge embraced the political and social conservatism that inform much Movement writing. Instead, he seems to satirize both the left and the right in fairly equal measures.

While the details of both the wartime and early postwar British experience are familiar to people in Great Britain, even many Americans know at least the broad patterns. They know of Churchill, the blitz, and

1

Dunkirk and of the hardships and heroics of the "people's war" waged
by British civilians, and they know of welfare measures put in place by
the postwar Atlee government, notably the National Health Service,
and of the rationing and general economic austerity marking British life
until well into the 1950s.

It was during this postwar period (one historian has described it as
"rock-hard and grey"[1]) that Lodge, his family resettled in London,
received the sustained schooling and undergraduate education that
would lead to an academic career. During this time, too, he began to
write fiction. Not surprisingly, his novels have continued to return to
this formative period of his life. Also not surprisingly, they offer a
thoughtful and often detailed reflection on British life during this
period. Two Lodge novels set during these years, *Out of the Shelter* (1970)
and *Ginger, You're Barmy* (1962), are especially rich in such detail and
reflection and seem particularly driven by autobiographical concerns.
Indeed, they center, respectively, on two memorable events of this
period for Lodge: his vacation trip to West Germany in 1951 and his
National Service experience from 1955 to 1957.

Out of the Shelter

In his afterword to the revised edition of *Out of the Shelter,* Lodge recalls
traveling as an unaccompanied 16-year-old to Heidelberg, where he
spent a summer vacation under the supervision of his mother's sister, a
civilian secretary for the United States Army. Lodge calls this venture
"one of the formative experiences of my life," in that it strengthened his
self-confidence and "opened new horizons for future aspiration."[2] He
gratefully remembers his Aunt Eileen, to whom the novel is dedicated,
as "[a] vivacious and attractive lady, who always looked at least fifteen
years younger than her real age" (*OS*, 273), and he recalls the ease with
which she made friends and otherwise took advantage of the "personal
liberation" that living and working in Europe offered her. This opportunity to go beyond the "limited means and possibilities" of postwar
England—to venture among what he later recalled as "this rather afflu-
ent and euphoric American expatriate community, which was really having a ball in post-war Germany"[3]—gave the young David Lodge "a
privileged foretaste of the hedonistic, materialistic good life that the
British, and most of the other developed or developing nations of the
world, would soon aspire to, and in some measure enjoy" (*OS*, 276). It

was a preparation not only for the change in status and lifestyle that the succeeding decades would bring him but also for many of the concerns and issues that would inform his writing.

Lodge's counterpart in *Out of the Shelter* is Timothy Young. The novel's first section ("The Shelter") describes the situation of Timothy and his family early in the war and just after it. While Lodge relies mainly on memories of his own childhood, the opening chapters, in the details of air raids and various restrictions on everyday life, resemble other accounts of wartime England. Specifically, such details recall first-hand reports and vivid memoirs, such as Vera Brittain's *England's Hour* (1941) and John Lehmann's *I Am My Brother* (1960), as well as fiction—not only the many novels written during the war, such as Graham Greene's *The Ministry of Fear* (1943), but even those written afterward, including Elizabeth Bowen's *Heat of the Day* (1949) and Greene's *End of the Affair* (1951), which make integral use of such material.

Lodge departs significantly from this wartime genre, however, in the perspectives and related styles he employs: he uses the 5-year-old Timothy's point of view in the first two chapters and that of Timothy at age 12 in the third and final chapter of "The Shelter"; for the second and third sections ("Coming Out" and "Out of the Shelter," which together comprise three-quarters of the novel), he uses the perspective of Timothy the 16-year-old. While presenting everything from Timothy's point of view, the novel's narrative method involves what Lodge terms a " 'covert' authorial voice" (*OS,* 282). Like the viewpoints of the 5-year-old and the 12-year-old, that of the adolescent is rendered through "a slightly more eloquent and mature style than Timothy himself would have commanded" (*OS,* 282). In presenting this "naive consciousness" at various stages, Lodge has acknowledged the influence of James Joyce's *Portrait of the Artist as a Young Man* and some of the *Dubliners* stories and also of Henry James's *What Maisie Knew* (*OS,* 273); he has also recalled his "conscious imitation" of Joyce's *Portrait* in writing the early part of *Out of the Shelter.*[4]

The novel begins in London, with Timothy and his mother sheltering with a neighborhood family during an air raid. For the little boy, the war offers limitless pleasure and excitement:

> a Mickey Mouse gasmask that steamed up when you breathed and his father getting a tin hat and a whistle and Jill crying because her Dad was going away to join the Air Force and the wireless on all the time and black paper stuck over the front-door windows and sirens going and get-

ting up in the middle of the night because of the raids. It was fun getting
up in the middle of the night. (*OS*, 3)

But when German bombs damage the shelter's interior, Jill (the
other family's little girl) rushes out, her mother goes in search of her,
and both are killed by further explosions. After Timothy and his mother
are removed to the country for a time—during which he begins board-
ing school—they return to London. For the balance of the war they are
visited periodically by his much-older sister Kathleen, who has finished
school and wants a more exciting life than London and her home situation promise. Eventually she goes to work for the United States Army,
and by the end of the war she has been transferred to Paris.

The immediate postwar years for Timothy and his parents are
marked by signs of seemingly permanent economic privation in Britain
and of Kathleen's increasingly rich lifestyle. Now transferred to Germany, Kathleen gets home only occasionally and then not at all after
Christmas 1947. The three following years pass uneventfully, as the
increasingly restless Timothy grows into adolescence and as the absent
Kathleen, her letters full of interesting new friends and exciting travel,
becomes an object of increasing speculation for her parents as well as for
Timothy. The novel's second section ("Coming Out") focuses on the
family's preparations in response to a sudden invitation from Kathleen
that Timothy join her in Heidelberg for a holiday and on his trip there
and their reunion.

All of this prepares us for the extensive account of Timothy's four
weeks away from England and from the ordinary controls of home. During this time he is, above all, an impressionable observer. The observation process begins, of course, during his travel, as he observes intently
the sounds, sights, and protocols of the foreign people and places to
which he is introduced, and continues until he falls asleep his first
evening in Germany. That evening ends with Timothy, who is lodged in
a room in a women's hostel offered by a friend of Kathleen's, keenly
aware of a couple having sex in the room next door. By this point, he has
begun to observe Kate (as Kathleen's friends call her) and, as she introduces him to Heidelberg, to wonder more concretely about her life
there. He notices especially the Americans he meets: Don Kowalski, a
teacher recently released from the army who befriended him on the train
to Heidelberg, and Kate's two friends, Vince and Greg, who to Timothy
seem typically American in their brashness, their flashy cars, and their
secretive work in postwar Germany.

Ten days after arriving in Heidelberg, Timothy recalls the flood of impressions and discoveries he has experienced on his own, in the company of Kate and her many friends, and with Don, with whom he soon met up again. Lodge has described *Out of the Shelter* as a generic combination of the bildungsroman and the Jamesian "international" novel of conflicting ethical and culture codes, citing *The Ambassadors* and *A Portrait of the Artist* as its "most obvious literary models" (*OS*, 275). The wonder with which Timothy first encounters the goods and services available to American military personnel illustrates the force with which his entire outlook is being rapidly altered; we see the "orgy of curiosity and covetousness" of his daily visits to the PX and his sense that the trunks of American cars "opened greedily like the jaws of whales until they were gorged with paper bags and cartons" (*OS*, 125). His initiation into the postwar consumerism not yet available in England in the early 1950s defamiliarizes many things well known even to English readers by the time the novel was written, as when at an ice-cream parlor he asks about the purpose of "the small metal boxes, fitted with buttons and knobs, that were fixed on the wall above each table" (*OS*, 178).

Such details help to sustain the feel of Timothy's entering a larger world from which the war and its aftermath, plus his English upbringing generally, had separated him and to establish the credibility of his quite rapidly changing perspective. Although Lodge had previously published three other novels, *Out of the Shelter* was the first to turn on international travel, a feature of most of his later fiction. While Timothy is under Kate's watchful care during his time in Heidelberg, and while he has a number of guides in this strange environment, no one interests him as much—and no one comments as knowledgeably on contemporary events—as Don Kowalski. Through this device, Lodge spells out some of broader implications of what Timothy is witnessing. Don's many discussions with Timothy—which Lodge places sporadically throughout the novel's main section, as a counterpoint to the boy's meetings with other people—relieve the narrative of what otherwise might have been a weighty load of political and historical background and represent the first of the many cultural exchanges between Britons and Americans that characterize Lodge's fiction.

As perhaps the first self-proclaimed intellectual Timothy has known, Don presents an unconventional way of thinking that especially challenges the boy's sheltered upbringing. He alerts Timothy to McCarthyism, the excesses of Allied bombing of German cities, and the parasitic aspect of the American presence in postwar Germany. He suggests that

the 1945 election defeat of Churchill, which Timothy learned from his
parents to deplore, constituted a victory of "politics over patriotism" and
proof of the British people's immunity to dictatorship (OS, 146). From
the beginning of their relationship, Timothy's sense of Don's singular
attitude toward the war is confirmed as the American reveals his wartime status as a conscientious objector and his obsession with postwar
Eastern Europe stemming from his Polish-Jewish background. Over the
course of their brief time together Timothy's outlook is dramatically
complicated by the older man's, as when, after viewing the devastation
of civilian life in Frankfurt, he remembers his earlier romanticizing of
British airmen and their sacrifices but now wonders "how it would be to
discover, in the total knowledge that came after death, that your terror
and pain had been entirely futile?" (OS, 222).

But for all of its merits as a corrective to the boy's limited background,
Don's outlook is in some ways as narrow as Timothy's. By the time
Lodge began to write Out of the Shelter, he had been teaching at the University of Birmingham for several years and had visited the United States
for six months on a fellowship. Before completing the novel, he would
serve a stint at Berkeley as a visiting faculty member. The character of
Don, therefore, reflects considerably more contact with Americans, and
particularly with American academics and intellectuals, than either Timothy or the teenage Lodge had in 1951. It is significant that Don aspires
to enter graduate school and eventually becomes a professor, as Lodge's
characterization of him represents an implicit critique of the attitudes
and behaviors that academic life often reinforces—a critique Lodge
would pursue more explicitly, though more amusingly, in later novels.

Despite Don's intelligence and the keenness of his observations, and
despite his importance in drawing Timothy out of the shelter, Don's
viewpoint appears inadequate in that it involves a smug readiness to
judge and dismiss the values of others. This is why for Robert Morace
the character of Don "invites both approval and dismissal."[5] It is also
why, for example, Don's encouragement of Timothy to study architec-
ture strikes an intolerant, patronizing note:

> —If you were an architect, what would you want to build?
> —I dunno. Churches, maybe.
> —Churches? Don seemed amused.
> —What's wrong with churches? Timothy said defensively.
> —Nothing. Nothing at all. I just wonder whether we need any more
> churches?

—We do in England—Catholic ones, anyway. The ones we've got are crowded out.

—If I were an architect, I'd go in for building schools and universities—they're the churches and cathedrals of our age. (OS, 145)

The certainty with which Don counters Timothy's observations about a situation the boy may understand at least as well as he weakens his position and typifies the arrogance and relentless pedagogic urge of his approach to human problems. These are the things Kate remembers most about Don many years later: "There were times when I'd say something about the news, or a book, or a movie, and he'd sort of look at me, as if he was wondering whether to set me straight or let it pass" (OS, 267). More than a difference in age accounts for the fact that while Don advocates an open mind, Timothy seems more open minded.

Although Timothy's experience with Don helps him to see postwar (and Cold War) realities in a clearer light and ultimately moves him beyond his lower-middle-class beginnings to the rewards of upward social mobility—including an academic career he cannot even imagine until many years later—his personal growth centers at least as much on the emergence of his adult sexuality. Significantly, Lodge frames the story of Timothy with sexual incidents: the first is the five-year-old's sex play with little Jill in the air-raid shelter; the last is Timothy's sexual initiation with a pretty American teenager living in Heidelberg. These, plus the many related incidents in between (including an older woman's attempt to seduce him) and the way such incidents merge with Timothy's moral and religious sensibility, transcend the claims made on him, as well as on the reader, by the more public and impersonal issues of politics and nationality.

Lodge's tracing of Timothy's sexual development represents the novel's most Joycean element. The brief business with Jill contributes to the entire effect of an opening chapter that, in its emphases and style, many critics have linked to the opening of *Portrait of the Artist*.[6] Later, in his shyness and naiveté, in his persistent curiosity, and in the series of epiphanies that define his developing awareness, Timothy resembles the young Stephen Dedalus, though Lodge's portrayal of Timothy's sexual longings—at an English beach resort with his parents, in a train with a group of English schoolgirls, in the women's hostel, and amid various groups of young people in Heidelberg—takes on an increasingly comic tone more similar to Kingsley Amis, with whom Lodge has admitted a "strange community of feeling," than to Joyce.[7] Park Honan has further refined the Joycean connection by acknowledging the "limpidity, the naiveté and the symbolic quality" of Timothy as Lodge portrays him yet noting—and praising—the absence of "artificial bravura" in that portrayal. Indeed, Honan maintains, *Out of the Shelter* explores "more convincingly than any other postwar novel" the "complex innocence of sexuality."[8]

Timothy's most telling—and most amusing—sexual discoveries come, significantly, in the company of Americans. In this the novel's major concerns merge nicely, to produce what one reviewer in 1970 described as "a kind of Anglo-American encounter very remote from anything ever envisaged by Henry James, yet central to the English experience of the past twenty-five years" ("Encounter," 1155). Timothy's culture shock stems primarily from witnessing the lifestyle Kate has taken on among her American expatriate friends, a lifestyle especially identified in his mind with the sexual frankness of Vince, Greg, and the others. The mixture of adventure and inadequacy he feels among them increases in his encounters with American teenagers, who seem so much more socially advanced and self-assured, and it often produces amusing results, as when he responds to an American boy's macho remark about a girl they see ("She shows her tits to guys for a dollar") by countering, "Seems expensive. . . . You can see quite a lot for nothing" (*OS*, 179).

For much of the novel, though, it is sister Kate who unwittingly fuels Timothy's most intense speculations, sexual and otherwise. And it is through his relationship with her—a relationship the novel's epilogue extends to America many years later—that the terms of his maturation are defined. Having been deputized by his parents to find out why Kate will not come home and spurred by their wild imaginings, he assumes that sexual license prevails among her group of friends, wonders initially whether Vince and Greg are married, and even imagines, when Kate takes him to visit an orphanage, that she has been hiding an illegitimate child.

Gradually he learns the less sensational but no less compelling truths about his sister and her situation, especially her determination to escape the drabness and limited opportunities of English life and to go eventually to the United States. She tells him of her sexual innocence on first arriving in Europe ("I was still a good Catholic girl in those days" [*OS*, 166]), of her disillusionment at the chance discovery that the one man she had come to love was married, and of her intention now to have a bit of fun and avoid being hurt further. She also tells of having lapsed from her previously strict religious practices and shocks Timothy with the family secret her parents would never admit, that she was born six months before their marriage.

Timothy's growing understanding and respect for his sister as they move down this "endless slope of disclosure" contribute to his sense of leading a full life: "There were times when he thought it must be the fullest life in the history of boyhood" (OS, 167, 168). They contribute, too, to the complex of conflicting loyalties he is experiencing—such as the conflict between absolute belief in the war against Hitler and skepticism about its methods and outcomes, between dislike of the Germans as "the enemy" and personal sympathy for the German people he meets, between the morality of home and religion and his desire for sexual pleasure, between his mission to bring Kate back home and his respect for her wishes, and between the urge to condemn her relationship with Don when he finds them making love and the strange pleasure he feels at what is happening between them.

Robert Morace sees this preoccupation with Timothy's being "poised between two worlds, two sets of values, two meanings" as one of the novel's key reflections of Joyce's writing and argues that in this work, as in Lodge's other novels, the choices his characters face are "dialogically presented rather than monologically distinct" (Morace, 145). At the end of the epilogue, Timothy—now 30, with a wife and children he loves and a promising career—reflects on his extraordinary good fortune:

> He was so lucky it was almost a scandal, he thought to himself. . . . Don, divorced, Vince and Greg driven out into the wilderness, his parents growing dully old, shedding one human interest after another. . . . When one thought of all the thwarted, broken, cramped lives . . . and the deaths. The unnumbered dead of the war, of his war and all the wars, lives cut off unseasonably, at random, with no reason. (OS, 270)

But suddenly his thinking shifts to "the familiar fear that he could never entirely eradicate—that his happiness was only a ripening target [and] that somewhere, around the corner, some disaster awaited him, as he blithely approached" (OS, 270). Morace links this shift to "similarly dialogical endings" at earlier points in the novel: "[Timothy] remains discontented," Morace argues, "not because he has failed to mature but because the process of 'coming out of the shelter' . . . is, as Lodge defines it, continual. His desire for shelter and his counter desire for freedom cannot be reconciled, only dialogized" (Morace, 154). Such a reading may represent a forcing of Bakhtinian concepts, or at least Bakhtinian terms, onto the novel. Rather than discontentment, Timothy's momentary entertainment of this "familiar fear" seems to represent what Lodge has termed "a temperamental cautiousness" (Haffenden, 151).

Of course, the entire epilogue device has been criticized, notably by Dennis Jackson, who judges it "an awkward and contrived effort to tie up some of the plot's loose ends" (Jackson, 475)—an observation not unrelated to Jackson's view that the novel as a whole lacks intensity. For Morace, these and other problems are contained in the novel's "literary recidivism," principally the failure of its narrative method and, frequently, its language to sustain the heightened realism it intends (Morace, 144–45). Recalling his attempt to write "a really ambitious socio-cultural novel, in the form of a *Bildungsroman,*" Lodge has remarked that "it didn't quite come off," and he has conceded that had he later taken on the kind of project *Out of the Shelter* represents, he would have employed "more stylistic variety, more differences of perspective" (Haffenden, 151). Given his considerable personal investment in this, his most autobiographical novel, Lodge recalls the "crisis of faith in myself" he felt at its commercial failure ("[F]rom the publishing point of view it was a total flop") and the small number of reviews it received (Haffenden, 150).

Even so, initial responses to *Out of the Shelter* did offer some consolation, such as the *TLS* reviewer's observation that the novel's "bringing together of individual consciousness and public history is extremely well done, in a way that is rare in contemporary fiction" ("Encounter," 1155) and Park Honan's assessment of it as "Lodge's latest and finest novel" (Honan 1972, 172). The *TLS* reviewer of the revised edition 15 years later was similarly untroubled by the problems noted in academic commentary on the novel. Instead, he praised the "fine sense of pace" and "tone of the narrative" with which Timothy's development was represented.[9] Indeed, *Out of the Shelter* provides a valuable and convincing account of postwar England and Germany, and of the contrasts between the British and American outlooks at this time—accounts and contrasts that still resonate in contemporary Anglo-American relations. And while a current reader might criticize the novel's harsh treatment of Kate's friends Greg and Vince—who, ironically counter to Timothy's initial suspicions, turn out to be homosexuals—the numerous references to the 1951 Burgess-MacClean spy scandal help contextualize such a perspective. That all of this is seen through the eyes of a sensitive English boy makes Lodge's novel all the more remarkable, if not unique.

Writing such a novel in the late 1960s reinforced Lodge's sense of separation from younger people who did not remember World War II (he admits to "feeling myself on the other side of the wall from every-body who came afterwards"): "I wanted to recover that sense of growing up through the war and into the period of austerity, being a meritocrat, and so on" (Haffenden, 150). He built into *Out of the Shelter* his later recognition of 1951 as a year of "crucial transition" in British life between austerity and growing prosperity, represented in the conserva-tive party's defeat of the Atlee government (*OS,* 276). Particularly useful in rendering this and other transitions is Timothy's unfolding relation-ship with Rudolf, a young German slightly older than he who spent time in a British war camp and who takes Timothy home with him. As much as anything else, talking with Rudolf about life in Germany dur-ing the war and meeting Rudolf's ex-Nazi father ("the first certified specimen Timothy had met") move Timothy beyond the "distorting lens of a wartime childhood" and help concretize his worldview generally (*OS,* 187, 274). This more complex attitude is reinforced on a more per-sonal level when, many years later, he compares his situation with that of Kate, who is nominally successful in the new life she has chosen in America yet unhappy at not being married.

Out of the Shelter *is a rich book, and it is clearly even richer for the hundreds of changes (deletions, restorations, additions, and transposi-tions, most of them minor but virtually all of them careful and judi-cious) that Lodge made for the revised edition—among them the replacement of quotation marks and related conventions of third-person narrative with the more direct Joycean dashes to indicate dialogue. No doubt the original publisher's mishandling of the manuscript and its botched printing, amusingly described in Lodge's afterword to the revised edition, contributed to the novel's failure in 1970. And no doubt his success with later novels, especially *Changing Places,* accounts in part for *Out of the Shelter*'s being reissued in the mid-1980s and gaining a more favorable reception then. Regardless, *Out of the Shelter,* even in its original published version, reveals Lodge's considerable command of the tech-niques of traditional realism as well as of Joycean counters to them and represents an interesting treatment of many of the same concerns and issues central to his later writing.

Ginger, You're Barmy

In a 1990 essay entitled "Fact and Fiction in the Novel," Lodge observed that "Novels burn facts as engines burn fuel, and the facts can come only from the novelist's own experience or acquired knowledge." "Not uncommonly," he added, "a novelist begins by drawing mainly on facts of the former kind" (*PW,* 27). In an interview several years earlier, Lodge had criticized his own "[tendency] to work rather cautiously within the limits of experience and particularly environments that I know" and described the novel he was writing at that time as "a more ambitious one than I've tried before," one he hoped would mark "some development" in terms of this problem.[10] That novel-in-progress was *Out of the Shelter,* while the one Lodge cited as particularly exhibiting his overreliance on personal experience was *Ginger, You're Barmy.*

More even than the other pair of novels he published in the 1960s (*The Picturegoers* and *The British Museum Is Falling Down*), these two explicitly reflect Lodge's autobiographical impulse. But whereas with *Out of the Shelter* that impulse was nurtured over a much longer period of time—the actual writing did not begin until almost two decades after the personal experiences on which it is based and after two return trips to Heidelberg, one for research on the book—with *Ginger* he had to stifle the temptation to record immediately his impressions and experiences. Recalling the considerable resentment fueling this desire to describe peacetime military life as he had seen it and describing *Ginger, You're Barmy* as "almost an act of revenge" (Bergonzi 1970, 112) and "a personal settling of scores,"[11] Lodge comments, "I hope its anger is controlled, for I deliberately delayed writing it for some years after completing my National Service" (*GB,* 217).

Written almost 10 years later than *Ginger, You're Barmy, Out of the Shelter* seems both more personal and more impersonal, and in many ways more impressive—with its broad and sometimes intense tracing of Timothy's impressions from infancy through adolescence (and many years beyond, if the epilogue is considered), its singular deployment of the various devices of realism (including free indirect discourse) in depicting the naive consciousness at various stages, its links with a number of grand literary traditions, and its serious exploration, unlike anything in Lodge's other novels, of broad political and social issues, international as well as domestic. Given such intentions and the considerable time and energy they exacted, and given Lodge's hope that this novel would transcend what he had come to see as the parochialism of his earlier fiction, one can well understand his discouragement at its failure with readers.

And yet one can understand, too, how *Ginger, You're Barmy* would appeal to a larger audience and seem a stronger novel to a certain kind of reader. To be sure, it covers a much shorter period of time (only the two years its protagonist, Jonathan Browne, is in the army—plus the following three years quickly passed over in the epilogue), and it does so more selectively. But perhaps it is just this narrower scope that helps create a sense of sharper focus and intensity than in *Out of the Shelter.* While by definition *Ginger,* in its critique of the postwar National Service in place in Great Britain from 1948 to 1960, appeals to a more local interest, its greater topicality no doubt contributed to its greater success with British readers. Lodge has cited the immediate recognizability of Browne's experience in the novel ("one which most young men born between, say, 1928 and 1941, underwent") and the small number of novels dealing with the National Service ("especially if you discount those set in places where conscript soldiers were involved in actual combat . . . [which] belong to the literature of war") as significant factors in *Ginger's* success (*GB,* 212). Even its relative lack of the intensely realistic detail and sense of locale often so striking in *Out of the Shelter* becomes excusable in terms of the broadly comic shape that emerges in this antimilitary novel.

To describe *Ginger, You're Barmy* as comic is to counter Lodge's insistence that, though the work contains "a note of humour and incidental comedy," it was intended to be "serious, even sombre" (Bergonzi 1970, 111). To be sure, this novel has its dark side. Among its most serious elements is the story of a hapless recruit named Percy Higgins, who midway through the novel shoots himself after particularly rough treatment on the firing range by a sadistic officer who insulted and humiliated him throughout his time in camp. (Whether Percy kills himself intentionally or accidentally is never established.) Lodge surrounds Percy's story with other similarly grim material, such as one recruit's recollection of how his pacifist brother-in-law was transformed into a bloodthirsty warrior type by his superior officers, or Jonathan Browne's account of a medal-laden corporal given to anecdotes more about his wartime sexual exploits than about his military heroics. For Browne such behavior epitomizes "the paradox of military courage":

> This was the man we had decorated for valour; the man to whom we owed our freedom. And yet what had carried him through innumerable bloody campaigns was a fundamental barbarism, an utter disregard for human life and human decencies. He was not even proud of his military achievements. He was just a fighting, rutting animal in uniform. (*GB,* 165)

Similar reflections punctuate the novel and obviously relate to the critical view of World War II suggested in *Out of the Shelter.* But where there is little to mitigate the seriousness with which the teenager Timothy Young views such matters, here it is relieved and complicated by other attitudes and perspectives. As one of only two narrator-protagonists in all of Lodge's novels, Jonathan Browne himself is the principal means by which Lodge attempts to influence our feelings. Browne's account of army life invites laughter through its biting wit (comparable to that of Amis or Waugh, two of Lodge's special favorites), as when he describes one of his fellow recruits as "squat and powerfully built, with short legs and a great pear-shaped head ravaged by what I took to be the legacies of venereal disease" or compares the camp breakfast to "the leftovers of a nasty operation" or when his friend Mike Brady insists that the shepherd's pies they are served are made from "real shepherds" (*GB,* 30, 54, 145).

While Jon Browne tells us initially that his narrative will compress two tedious years in the army—and thus will address the peculiar challenge of "convey[ing] some sense of the drag of days, the endless sameness, the routine, without this quality being conferred on the novel" (Bergonzi 1970, 113)—the narrative itself hardly concentrates consistently on serious issues. Repeatedly Browne takes time out to develop the comic potential of persons and incidents he encounters, as when he describes how one recruit nearly breaks the patience of the typing instructor in the army Clerks Course: "He wrecked three typewriters in as many days, and on the fourth day managed to inflict a ghastly wound on his hand by thrusting it into the bowels of his machine and pressing the tabulator key" (*GB,* 144).

Such digressions from strict seriousness are Lodge's way of conveying, in a nontedious fashion, the tedium inherent in Browne's situation and the countless absurdities defining army life. While they function to establish and reinforce a sense of setting (partly analogous to Timothy's often-detailed descriptions of Heidelberg and the other locales in *Out of the Shelter*), they also help establish an absurdist, darkly comic tone and invite overall anticipations in the reader different from those in the other, more realistic novel. Thus Lodge's efforts to show how the military perpetuates the class-based injustices of civilian life—and thus subverts the egalitarian claims for the postwar welfare state in Great Britain—include the same comic impulse to ridicule and caricature evident elsewhere in the novel. Similarly, the developing relationship between Browne and Mike Brady's girlfriend Pauline—Jonathan's longings and fantasies after Mike introduces them to each other and his sexual frustration after he succeeds in winning her away from Mike—is amusingly rendered, in contrast with the way adult relationships, and often even Timothy's discomforts and mishaps, are portrayed in *Out of the Shelter*. Not even the grim story of Percy Higgins is entirely without such comic touches.

Because Lodge here uses a double narrative, alternating Jonathan's account of his last week in the army with his earlier experiences in basic training—a technique Lodge claims to have borrowed unwittingly from Graham Greene's *The Quiet American* (*GB*, 215)—we know in a broad sense that things will turn out reasonably well for Browne. We know, for example, that his longing to be with Pauline will not go unsatisfied—which focuses attention on the questions of exactly how and why such satisfaction goes to him—and that by the end of his army duty he is enjoying an easy tour of duty as a clerk (as did Lodge himself) and looking forward to a relatively comfortable civilian life with Pauline. We know, too, that army service does not go nearly so well for Mike Brady, who ultimately is sentenced to prison for trying to right the wrong of Percy's death with an attack on Corporal Baker, who had humiliated him.

Jonathan tries to dissuade Mike from this and several other risky ventures. In fact, the contrast in attitude and behavior between the risk-taking Mike Brady and the more cautious Jon Browne constitutes a principal concern of the novel. Almost from the beginning of their army life together, when they find each other on the train to the same camp, Jon surveys the fundamental differences that separate him from Mike, whom he knew slightly in the university course they just finished. Proud of his first-class degree, he compares it with Mike's failure in examinations and recalls not only that Mike did no work but that "[i]n his soiled and neglected clothing he had always stood out from the calculated and self-conscious bohemianism of college like an authentic cowboy on a dude ranch" (*GB*, 21). This issue of authenticity continues to hound Jonathan as he realizes that Mike worked during vacations, whereas he has had a "protected life" of study during such periods, and that Mike's Irish roots seem to include "a violent, dramatic family life" quite unlike his own relatively spoiled existence as an only child (*GB*, 32). Whatever disapproval Jon feels toward Mike's numerous acts of insubordination and resistance against army procedures—and whatever disdain he has felt for such a loser in the university system—is tempered by a growing recognition of something commendable in Mike, something he himself lacks. Even though he often finds the specific terms of Mike's rebelliousness excessive, Jon senses in it a completion of himself and comes to consider the prospect of army life without Mike unbearable.

From their discussions about such matters, and especially from their
disagreement over the proper response to Higgins's death, the difference
between the two characters emerges as the classic philosophical and psychological distinction, variously labeled idealist-realist, spiritualist-
materialist, active-passive, emotional-rational, theoretical-practical, and
the like. Perhaps the most appropriate labels here refer to Jonathan's
self-styled agnostic outlook and Mike's Catholic faith. Anxious to pro-
tect Percy, also a Catholic, from further derision after what he suffered
when alive, Mike reacts angrily to Jonathan's suggestion that it makes
little difference whether Percy committed suicide: "Of course not, from
your point of view. . . . To you he's just dead" (*GB,* 100). Later, as they
discuss the senseless drills and humiliations of army discipline, Jonathan
remarks that he obeys to avoid punishment, which Mike calls "the very
worst reason" for doing something without purpose. "I mean, I know I
wasn't put on this earth to wear army boots and put one foot in front of
the other just because somebody tells me to, and to stop because he tells
me to" (*GB,* 150), Mike goes on, working himself up to an angry
denunciation of conscription as a violation of his free will. Jonathan then
notes his own objection to conscription on tellingly different grounds: "I
objected to having my studies interrupted, my liberty curtailed, my
comforts removed. . . . The theoretical questions of war and conscience
which Mike raised scarcely touched me" (*GB,* 150).

In his afterword to the 1981 reissue of the novel, Lodge tells how
Jonathan and Mike related to his own response to the army, which
shifted "from an indignant moral resistance to its values . . . to a pragmatic determination to make myself as comfortable as possible and to
use my time as profitably as possible":

> For the purpose of *Ginger,* I split these reactions into characters, and set
> them interacting. To heighten the contrast between them I gave the
> rebel an Irish Catholic republican background (and flaming red hair) and
> made the conforming pragmatist an agnostic. And to give additional
> interest to the see-saw of their fortunes, I put a girl between them.
> (*GB,* 214)

Several commentators, including Lodge himself, have noted the links
between this agenda and that of Graham Greene in *The Quiet American.*
While since adolescence Lodge had been strongly influenced by Greene's
novels, that influence was reinforced by the postgraduate research on
English Catholic fiction writers he did at University College, London,
between leaving the army and beginning to write *Ginger, You're Barmy.*

The Greene segment from his London M.A. thesis would be revised and published separately in 1966. For many reasons, then—including the fact that when Greene's last major novel, *A Burnt-Out Case* (1961), was published, his reputation had never been higher—Lodge's recourse to him as a model is scarcely surprising.

As already noted, the narrative scheme of *Ginger, You're Barmy* (the final stage of Jonathan's army service alternating with the first stage) closely resembles that of *The Quiet American,* though Lodge employs it more systematically. Also, there is a similar difference between the two principal characters in each novel. Greene's narrator, an English core spondent in Saigon named Fowler, resembles Jonathan Browne in his self-regard and his indifference toward the idealism and enthusiasm of the title character (and analog to Mike Brady), a newly arrived American attaché named Pyle. Finally, the two novels share an element of "betrayal" (a preoccupation of Greene's fiction), as in each the "agnostic narrator" (Lodge's phrase to describe Fowler)[12] turns the idealist over to adversaries while winning the woman who has stood between them.

However, the differences even within these resemblances suggest that Lodge's novel is less serious or somber than he perhaps realized and considerably less so than Greene's. Following Mike Brady's escape from the camp jail after attacking Corporal Baker, Jonathan is given a clerk's posting at a different camp for the duration of his service time. Over two years later, on the final night before his release, he foils an I.R.A. raid and attempted robbery at the camp. On learning that Mike has led that raid and will now surely go to prison, Jonathan is filled "with horrified fascination at the fact that I, of all people, had unwittingly betrayed Mike, in the one act of my military career that had exceeded the minimal performance of duty" (*GB,* 201). But where this "betrayal" is unintended, though all the more ironic for being so, in Greene's novel Fowler willfully conspires to bring the trusting young American to his death at the hands of Communists. Additionally, while Lodge delays revealing the one comparably grim event in *Ginger,* the death of Percy Higgins, until midway through the novel—mostly by having Jonathan amusingly describe the absurdities of basic training—Greene has Fowler tell us of Pyle's death in his opening pages and keeps it in view until the very end, when the full measure of Fowler's betrayal is revealed.

The theater of operations in *The Quiet American* is by definition much broader and the stakes much more extreme. This is classic Graham Greene territory: Vietnam in the early 1950s, where the French are still fighting to stay on, where corruption and intrigue are everywhere, and

where death is an hourly occurrence. The world of Lodge's novel, by
contrast, is a contained and orderly one, so much so that the exciting—
or even mildly interesting—event is exceptional. The resentment that
Lodge and most other National Service recruits felt related to the fact
that "any kind of positive or constructive meaning" that attached to service in the hot spots of the 1950s, such as Korea, the Suez, or Malaya—
or even Vietnam, where, as Greene shows, young French soldiers were
defending their nation's colonial interests—was wholly missing (GB,
212). Things are not as serious in Lodge's novel because they cannot be.
In this context, Lodge's insistence that The Quiet American is "far from
being a purely secular novel" requires little demonstration (GG, 3). The
cosmic issues of Good and Evil seem much more evident in the tangle of
innocence and guilt marking international and personal relations as portrayed by Greene than in the relatively inconsequential civilian and
domestic concerns of Lodge's territory (which, as he says, are "trans-
posed into a homelier, more suburban key").[13]

Even so, Ginger, You're Barmy does manage to suggest some larger
questions, though its way of doing so points to its broadly comic structure. Perhaps the most striking aspect of Jonathan Browne is not that he
does anything particularly wrong but that he fails to do anything particularly right and still enjoys a more comfortable existence than most of
his fellow recruits. As the novel nears its end, Jonathan is anticipating
an even more comfortable civilian life. In addition, Jonathan is sensitive
enough to wonder occasionally at his relatively good fortune and even to
feel sheepish about it, particularly compared to what seems to be happening to Mike Brady. When Mike is facing imprisonment for having
attacked Corporal Baker, Jonathan struggles to account for their different situations: "Mike had got himself into this mess, it was nothing to
do with me, and yet his misfortune gnawed at my sense of relative com-
fort and security like a worm of conscience" (GB, 163). Even though
Brady's courage in defending Percy Higgins and his indignation at
Higgins's death lead him to the foolish attempt to square things with
Corporal Baker (not to mention the pointless I.R.A. raid), so that
Jonathan's negative virtues take on some solidity, the basic difference in
moral character between the two is never allowed to disappear entirely,
especially not from Jonathan's mind. Just as the question of Pyle's death
hangs over The Quiet American from beginning to end, the question of
Jonathan's luck hangs over Ginger, You're Barmy.

At the very end of his National Service duty, this question comes
crashing down on him. On the day after the ill-fated I.R.A. raid, his ela-

tion at his impending discharge is tempered by the news that Mike has been the ringleader and is in jail. This news also dampens any enthusiasm Jonathan might have felt for the perfumed letter he receives from Pauline that morning, in which she assures him that Mike means nothing to her and promises long-deferred sexual pleasure on their holiday to Majorica, which will begin the next day. "Some people 'ave all the luck," the camp mail clerk comments as he sniffs the letter, but Jonathan suddenly sees recent fortunate events as some sort of providential "double treachery: to Mike himself, and to that code of contempt for the Army which we had once shared" (*GB*, 201). He even wonders whether he might not have been guilty of intentionally betraying Mike by winning Pauline and securing an easy army life. Assurance of his blamelessness from Mike ("You were only doing your duty") when he visits him in the camp jail only makes Jonathan wonder what Mike really means ("Reassurance? Dismissal? Benediction? Would I ever know?"[*GB*, 203, 204]).

After leaving camp for the last time, as he rides the train back to London and Pauline, Jonathan first sees in his prospects "as heavy a sentence as that which awaited Mike" but then immediately rejects this as "mere sentimental hyperbole" in favor of the pragmatism that informed his earlier choices:

> [S]uccess was bound to be more pleasant than detention in a military prison. . . . Even the wild idea of renouncing Pauline had to be rejected as soon as it occurred; for Pauline wanted me, not Mike. And one could not blame her. Mike was no hero, he was barmy, and there was no place for him. . . . Was Lazarus distressed because he could not moisten the parched tongue of Dives with a single drop of water? (*GB*, 205)

Like the character in Philip Larkin's "Self's the Man"—though from a standpoint opposite from that of Larkin's confirmed bachelor—Jonathan thus weighs the practical advantages of his course in life, ascribes them to personal merit, and concludes that neither guilt nor self-sacrifice serves any useful purpose. But despite arriving at so logically tight a conclusion, Jonathan seems not entirely convinced. Again like Larkin's character, he retains a residue of uncertainty ("Questions, questions. . . . [O]ne could not forbear to ask them, tossing the pennies in the air, crying 'Heads' or 'Tails' ") even as he leaps into civilian life again (*GB*, 205).

Lodge has written of the "unamiable traits—envy, selfishness, conceit" with which he drew Jonathan Browne in the main narrative of *Ginger, You're Barmy,* adding that "[t]o mitigate this effect I bracketed the main narrative with a prologue and epilogue in which Jonathan shows some inclination to moral self-appraisal and self-renewal" (*GB,* 214). (Or, as he explained in 1970, the epilogue was intended to show the novel's narrator "as developing some generosity of spirit" [Bergonzi 1970, 113]). Some critics, however, have found such a change in Jonathan "less than convincing" (Jackson, 472), and Lodge himself admits, "I am not sure, now, whether this was not a failure of nerve" (*GB,* 214). The prologue, of course, identifies the main narrative about to unfold (with its alternating strands) as a novel written by Jonathan Browne—a highly concentrated and highly revised version of his life as a National Serviceman. Morace interestingly argues that by having Jonathan introduce the main part of *Ginger* as "an agreeable exercise in the manipulation of bits of observed life" (*GB,* 10), Lodge places in doubt the status and reliability of everything in the text, particularly those elements that work at all in Browne's favor. To complicate matters further, Morace points out, "[O]ur reading of the framed story's two textual levels cannot be separated from the fictive author's (Jonathan's) commentary on them in the appended frame and, for readers of the third edition, from Lodge's commentary on them in his introduction" (Morace, 118). The result, whether intended by Lodge or not, is a sense of Jonathan himself as "a series of images in a funhouse mirror" (Morace, 119).

If a principal function of the prologue is to destabilize the status of Jonathan as both character and narrator, that of the epilogue is to reveal the present situation from which the main story of three years earlier is being viewed and presented. Even if Lodge's intention to "mitigate" the earlier, ambivalent view of Jonathan does not succeed—and even if Morace shows why—the epilogue does succeed in showing Jonathan's ongoing discomfort and its sources, and it does so without creating sympathy for him. In capsule fashion it brings us up to date about him and Pauline—beginning with their disappointing holiday trip and the resulting pregnancy that hastened their marriage ("I succeeded in rupturing her hymen, and planted in her the sperm which became the small boy now emitting such an offensive odour at my feet") and ending with the present moment, as they await a visit from Mike, just out of prison: "Now he is free, and I am shackled,—by a wife and family I do not greatly love, and by a career that I find no more than tolerable" (*GB,* 209, 210).

No more likable than before—neither his visits to Mike in prison nor his stated intention to teach prisoners suffices to make him so— Jonathan appears simply to feel more terminally trapped, and the trap, or at least the feeling, seems the appropriate consequence of what he has done and become. Like Larkin's bachelor, he realizes that the opportunistic, self-serving bargain he struck is proving less than satisfying. Timothy Young, too, wondered at his luck. But his wonder, unlike Jonathan's, was without cynicism or claims of personal merit. The more Jonathan tries to justify his situation—either in terms of minor adjustments or rationalization—the more he is doomed to discontentment. Hardly comparable to any of Greene's guilt-ridden sinners—either in terms of his "sin" and its consequence to others, or his suffering—he likely will stumble on, no wiser or happier but no more unhappy, ultimately defined by the shallowness of his egocentricity.

It surely is of more than autobiographical significance that for much of the novel Lodge has Jonathan anticipate returning to the university to do research and pursue an academic career, an intention he has not abandoned entirely even at the end. On his last night in the army, as he reads William Empson's *Seven Types of Ambiguity* while the others on guard duty read pulp novels or nothing at all, one of them asks him about his career plans and presses, "What use is literature?" Rather than offering the stock Arnoldian response about cultural and moral values, rather than responding at all, he considers his true objectives: "I was not eager to return to the university because I thought my research would be of any use, to myself, or to others. All human activity was useless, but some kinds were more pleasant than others" (*GB*, 185–86)

Such an attitude toward the academic life is not unrelated to how Jim Dixon feels throughout much of Kingsley Amis's *Lucky Jim* (1954). And to judge from the final chapter of Lodge's first critical book, *Language of Fiction* (1966)—a chapter titled "The Modern, the Contemporary, and the Importance of Being Amis"—during the time he wrote *Ginger* Lodge was much aware not only of *Lucky Jim* but also of the other comic novels Amis wrote in the wake of its extraordinary success. If, as Lodge then argued, the main source of comedy in *Lucky Jim* is "the contrast between Jim's outer world and his inner world" (*LF*, 251), then surely such a contrast figures heavily in our attitude toward Jonathan Browne. But where Jim takes some risks to get out of his funk and in the process realizes that authentic "luck" consists of renouncing an existence he regards as hypocritical (so that the comedy featuring him turns into romantic triumph), Jonathan does nothing. *Ginger, You're Barmy* never becomes simply the British equivalent of Ira Levin's *No Time for Sergeants* (1956) or of other situational comedies with peacetime military settings. The comedy of *Ginger* becomes—and remains—caustic and punitive.

Chapter Two

Academic Comedy and the Central Style

Out of the Shelter was David Lodge's fourth published novel. While this and the earlier ones (especially *The British Museum Is Falling Down,* 1965) had received some critical and popular recognition, only with his fifth novel, *Changing Places* (1975), was Lodge's reputation as a writer of fiction firmly established. And only by writing *Changing Places* did he resolve certain problems and uncertainties that, by his own admission, had plagued his earlier efforts and did he secure the repertoire of attitudes and techniques—collectively, a central style—that in large part have characterized his fiction ever since. *Changing Places* and the two later, related novels—*Small World* (1984) and *Nice Work* (1988)—won literary prizes for Lodge, gained him an international reputation, and aroused new interest in his earlier work. Satirical comedies concerned with academic life, these three novels draw on social history after the Second World War, on David Lodge's personal and professional life as it was unfolding, and on certain postwar literary developments. But however much they may resemble similar writings by others during this period, in tone and outlook they remain very much Lodge's own.

"I was a classic product of the 1944 Education Act," he told an interviewer in 1984 (Haffenden, 148), referring to the legislation that set in motion a pattern of educational reform and expansion in Britain after World War II. Popularly known as the Butler Act (after its principal architect, R. A. Butler), this legislation signaled the wartime coalition government's intention to redress long-standing inequities in British education. In the 40 years between its enactment and Lodge's reminiscing about his educational experiences, secondary schooling in Britain became available to all children for the first time, the official school-leaving age was raised, several new universities were established (including, in 1969, the Open University, designed especially for nontraditional students), and postsecondary enrollment increased significantly.

Of course, such developments in the universities were part of the larger welfare-state agenda designed to make life more secure for all

British citizens and to offer opportunities to everyone who might benefit from them. And to a degree they succeeded, as the proportion of post-secondary students from the working class and lower middle class grew, thanks to dramatic increases in student grants and in government subsidies of university budgets that exceeded prewar levels. Lodge calls attention to such developments in this exchange between Don Kowalski and Timothy Young in *Out of the Shelter:*

> —Are you planning to go to college?
> —I might. Or I might do an apprenticeship. I'm waiting to see what my O-Level results are like.
> —But it's free, isn't it—college education in England?
> —If you can get in. (*OS*, 85)

Although the headmaster at Timothy's school has been encouraging him to pursue A-level work—which contradicts his father's class-related skepticism about the benefits of university education—it is only after exposure to Don's American attitudes regarding higher education that Timothy determines to capitalize on his academic record and good test scores by seeking university admission.

Timothy's initial hesitancy to pursue his educational ambitions (and perhaps to a lesser extent, his father's doubts as well) may reflect a reality obscured by the euphoria attending the postwar educational boom in Britain and by the statistical data accompanying it. To be sure, as early as 1947 parliamentary grants-in-aid had tripled from their prewar level, and in 1951 (the year in which *Out of the Shelter* is set) 73 percent of the students in British universities were receiving state aid.[1] By 1983, almost five times as many students would be enrolled in British universities as in 1938. Even so, as late as 1968 only about six percent of young people in the 18–21 age range were participating in full-time education, compared with 50 percent in the United States.[2] As one historian comments, "The tradition of elitism in higher education was proving hard to shake off."[3] Despite indisputable progress toward opening up British universities to all deserving students, a "classic product" of educational reform such as David Lodge was in some respects still improbable even in 1951.

As Lodge tells it, academic success in a time of expanding educational opportunity "propelled me out of my class into the professional middle class" (Haffenden, 148). Among the very first students from his Catholic grammar school in London even to seek university admission, he enrolled in University College, London, in 1952. Like Jonathan Browne in *Ginger, You're Barmy,* he took a first-class honors degree in English at London and received a scholarship to do postgraduate research. In 1960, after completing his M.A., he began his long career in the English department at the University of Birmingham, where he soon began to win recognition for his scholarly and critical work.

Lodge's academic life from his postwar schooling through his first decade or so at Birmingham thus encompassed the era of greatest educational expansion in British history, particularly at the university level. One historian claims that "academics had really never had it so good" as in the early 1970s, when *Changing Places* was written.[4] But Lodge's somewhat singular background—his family upbringing, to be sure, but also his ambition to be a writer, which predated his intention to become an academic and which, obviously, he never abandoned—prepared him to view academic life and academic institutions with some skepticism even as he joined them. Such skepticism—readily evident in *Ginger, You're Barmy* and *Out of the Shelter,* though less so in his other two early novels—came to full fruition only with *Changing Places.*

Of course, a skeptical view toward academics and toward university life had become very much a part of the literary climate by the time Lodge wrote his first campus novel. His interest in Amis's *Lucky Jim,* which became enormously popular on both sides of the Atlantic, has been noted. The 1950s and early 1960s saw an explosion of campus novels by such diverse talents as C. P. Snow (*The Masters,* 1951, plus other titles in his Strangers and Brothers series), Mary McCarthy (*The Groves of Academe,* 1952), Randall Jarrell (*Pictures at an Institution,* 1954), Malcolm Bradbury (*Eating People Is Wrong,* 1959), and Bernard Malamud (*A New Life,* 1961)—plus many others. By the 1980s the field of campus fiction was so dense that, according to Bradbury, the genre had grown "elaborately self-allusive."[5] Continuing interest in such writing today is evidenced by the recent success of Jane Smiley's *Moo* (1995).

The initial postwar burst of campus fiction in the United States and Great Britain reflected the fact that higher education was figuring in the lives of more citizens of both societies than ever before—which is why Don Kowalski compares that "fine institution called the G.I. Bill" to the state scholarships increasingly available to deserving English schoolboys like Timothy Young (*OS,* 86). However, though expansion raised university enrollments in both countries to levels unimaginable before World War II, because in Britain this involved the elevation of some institutions and the wholesale creation of others, it was to the promise and the perceived shortcomings of these new universities (or "redbricks," as the

first wave was popularly known) that much British campus fiction
turned its attention. As one historian notes, "This being Britain, the
rapid 50 percent increase in numbers produced its own version of the
later 'more means worse' controversy."[6] And of course, the campus novels in both countries dealt with contemporary problems and developments in the larger society even as they purported to be concerned with
the seemingly insular concerns of the academy.

Malcolm Bradbury suggests a distinction between the fiction coming
out of the redbrick universities and that connected with the older
Oxbridge tradition (Snow, Waugh, and others), which he links to D. H.
Lawrence, *Jude the Obscure,* and even Hawthorne's *Blithedale Romance*
(Bradbury 1967, 50–51). He traces, too, the trajectory of his own campus writing, from the more conventional *Eating People Is Wrong* to the
more indignantly satirical *History Man,* which appeared in the same year
as *Changing Places.* It is significant that Bradbury taught at Birmingham
during David Lodge's first years there (1961–1964), that they were
(and have remained) close friends, and that Bradbury encouraged Lodge
to develop and utilize his comedic gifts—the most immediate results
being the two satirical reviews ("Between These Four Walls" and "Slap
in the Middle") on which he collaborated with Bradbury and others at
Birmingham, and *The British Museum Is Falling Down,* which Lodge
regarded as his first comic novel and which he dedicated to Bradbury.
Perhaps more to the point, though, during their time together at Birmingham, while Lodge was writing *The British Museum,* Bradbury himself
was writing a novel about an Englishman going to teach in an American
university, which became *Stepping Westward* (1965). Lodge's first treatment of the Anglo-American theme that had so captivated him would,
of course, be the decidedly noncomic *Out of the Shelter.* But as he settled
into his own academic career, as he honed his skills as a comic writer,
and as he prepared to write his own campus fiction, he was hardly ready
to abandon that subject.

Changing Places

David Lodge's ongoing fascination with American society and with the
differences between American and British cultures took other forms
besides writing fiction. In 1964 he visited the United States on a Harkness Commonwealth Fellowship, which allowed him to spend six
months at Brown University studying American literature and then, in
early 1965, to drive across the United States with his family to San

Francisco, where they spent the summer. During his time at Brown he completed *The British Museum Is Falling Down.* Five years later, Lodge and his family returned to the Bay Area, where he served for two academic quarters as a visiting associate professor of English at the University of California at Berkeley. His experience and observations during the turbulent spring of 1969 on the Berkeley campus were to form the basis of *Changing Places.*

Lodge's interests in American society and in American literature obviously fed each other. In a 1970 interview he pronounced American novelists "more exciting from the point of view of the literary critic" than their British counterparts, citing Malamud, Salinger, Nabokov, and Bellow as examples (Bergonzi 1970, 114). These views had been anticipated in a 1965 essay—presumably reflecting his study at Brown—titled "Anglo-American Attitudes: Decorum in British and American Fiction," which concludes by expressing a preference for Bellow's *Herzog,* with its characteristically American weaknesses, to "most 'successes' in contemporary British fiction" (*WO,* 87). Furthermore, his first critical book, *Language of Fiction,* included a discussion of *The Ambassadors,* as Henry James combined a number of Lodge's interests, including Anglo-American relations. The essays making up his next critical book, *The Novelist at the Crossroads* (1971), almost all of which were published separately between his first visit to the United States and the time he began to write *Changing Places,* include pieces on Burroughs, Hemingway, and Updike (with whose writing Lodge's would have much in common) and refer, sometimes extensively, to Hawthorne, Faulkner, Barth, McCarthy, and other American writers—including James. In addition, the 1970s would see *TLS* essays by Lodge on Salinger, Mailer, and Fitzgerald plus many book reviews on American authors written for other publications.

Recalling his early disappointments as a novelist and the patience they instilled in him, Lodge told one interviewer, "I don't think I really made it as a writer until *Changing Places,* when I was 40" (Haffenden, 150). *Changing Places* was awarded the *Yorkshire Post* and Hawthornden Prizes, was reviewed widely and positively, and significantly, was read widely by Americans (so much so that Penguin issued an American paperback edition in 1978). Its appeal to Americans no doubt stemmed in part from its premise: a transatlantic faculty exchange featuring a stereotypical English academic from a redbrick university and an American high roller from a thinly fictionalized Berkeley.

Lodge's two academics, dear to his loyal readers, are named Philip Swallow and Morris Zapp. *Changing Places* shows what happens when, during the winter and spring quarters of 1969 (the same period Lodge spent at Berkeley), Swallow is transplanted to Zapp's institution (Euphoric State, as Lodge calls his fictionalized version of Berkeley, located in the town of Plotinus, not far from the larger city of Esseph [S.F., or San Francisco]). Zapp, meanwhile, takes up residence at Rummidge University, located in an industrial city of the same name somewhere in the English midlands. Though they are both 40 years old and have been university teachers for approximately the same length of time, Swallow and Zapp are, at least superficially, a study in contrasts. An entrepreneurial careerist given to large cigars, loud remarks, and libidinous conquests, Zapp seems the antithesis of the shy, unambitious Swallow (Lodge calls him "a mimetic man; unconfident, eager to please, infinitely suggestible.")[7] Similarly, Zapp's wife, Désirée, a brash woman's liberationist determined to divorce Morris, is the opposite of Hilary Swallow, who stays in Rummidge to attend to her and Philip's children and maintain their home.

Although Zapp and Swallow never cease to be distinguishable, in the course of the novel they exhibit characteristics and behave in ways that challenge the simplicity of their initial contrast. Once settled into the nonthreatening atmosphere of Rummidge's English department, Zapp—the author of four books on Jane Austen and determined to outdo other Austen scholars by writing the last word on her in his fifth—becomes much less interested in academic gamesmanship. He emerges as a voice of moderation within the department and as a mediator favored by the university administration in its struggles with an increasingly contentious student body. By the end of his time at Rummidge, he is seriously considering the offer of an academic chair there. Furthermore, once out of the macho atmosphere of Euphoria, where he has made his reputation as a womanizer, Zapp is able to confront without rancor the fact that not only his best scholarship but also his sexual venturing may be behind him. As he tells Hilary Swallow, "At a certain age a man can find satisfaction in one woman alone" (CP, 234).

The seeming metamorphosis that Philip Swallow undergoes back in Euphoria is no less remarkable (though the metamorphosis is somewhat nebulous because in large part it represents more the emergence of latent or repressed desires than any fundamental change of character). While in England, Morris Zapp discovers in himself a vein of goodness that his life and work in America kept hidden; at one point not long after his arrival in Rummidge, he "wondered what had come over him. Some creeping English disease of being nice, was it? He would have to watch himself"(*CP,* 93). Similarly, and at the same time, Swallow begins to seek out pleasures and experiences he has shunned in his role as husband, father, and British academic and in the process becomes at least somewhat "Americanized" (not necessarily a bad thing in Lodge's scheme). Unconstrained by the obligations and inhibitions of his ordinary identity and inspired by the relaxed hedonism of his new environment, he manages not many weeks after his arrival at Euphoric State to engage in party games with the pot-smoking young people living in his apartment building, to have sex with the prettiest of this group (who turns out to be Morris Zapp's daughter from an earlier marriage), to patronize a strip club, and to begin an affair with Désirée Zapp.

This last turn of events stems from Philip's arrest and jailing when he unwittingly gets caught up in a confrontation between students and the police. Neither such political involvement nor his other seemingly uncharacteristic activities are developments he would have predicted for himself before coming to Euphoria. And all are accompanied by characteristic uncertainty and guilt. But even on the plane to America he had thought of the absence of his family (and presumably, of the limits on pleasure they would enforce) as "a rare treat . . . one which, though he is ashamed to admit it, would make him lightsome were his destination Outer Mongolia" (*CP,* 22). As time passes, he learns to manage his guilt and to keep it at a sufficient distance so that he can enjoy himself as never before. In fact, guilt over the affair with Désirée turns to pragmatic concern about how to inform his wife back in Rummidge—a concern comically resolved when he appears on a talk show to discuss politics and ends up fielding a call from an indignant Hilary, to whom he announces the affair in a decidedly nonconfessional manner.

David Lodge also ended up appearing on the radio (and on television, too) when he visited the United States, though this occurred during his 1964 visit and he talked much more about the just published *Ginger, You're Barmy* than about politics (*PW,* 11). (During this trip he also took to smoking cigars, like Morris Zapp.) In general *Changing Places* demonstrates Lodge's increasing skill at drawing on personal experiences without self-consciousness and at reshaping and deploying them strategically. In this respect it moves beyond *Ginger, You're Barmy,* in which, according to Lodge, "there is scarcely a minor character or illustrative incident or detail of setting that is not drawn from the life " (*GB,* 213). Although the author's note to *Ginger* does little more than assure the reader that its characters and actions, rather than referring to the lives of actual persons, are "fictitious" (*GB,* 6), the note preceding *Changing*

Places (which, according to Lodge, was "carefully worded" [*PW,* 13]) invokes a much subtler distinction in characterizing that novel's two locales. Rummidge and Euphoria, we are told, are "places on the map of a comic world which resembles the one we are standing on without corresponding exactly to it, and which is peopled by figments of the imagination" (*CP,* 6).

To illustrate the disparity between his novel and the life experience on which it was based (and between "resemblance" and "correspondence"), Lodge has pointed out that he did not go to Berkeley on an exchange program and that, unlike both Swallow and Zapp, he took his wife and family with him (*PW,* 33). In this and other respects Philip Swallow is not David Lodge, at least not the David Lodge of 1969. However, Lodge's account of his 1964–1965 visit to America suggests that the portrayal of Philip in *Changing Places* combines that experience with his time at Berkeley in 1969, at least to the extent of grafting aspects of his emotional development during his earlier American stay onto the political and social realities of Berkeley that he observed five years later. Interestingly, Lodge even casts Philip's exchange trip to Euphoric State as his second journey to the United States, the first having occurred several years earlier, when he and Hilary are said to have spent their honeymoon traveling from the East Coast to the West, ending up in Esseph, thanks to a generous fellowship Philip had received. (Lodge, of course, spent his fellowship year with his wife and children, but in its broad outlines Philip's earlier venture resembles Lodge's own.)

Philip Swallow is thus prepared, on returning to the United States, to enjoy the consumer amenities he earlier learned to associate with living there. He is said to have become "relaxed, confident, happy" during his original visit. In fact, "[h]e learned to drive, and flung the majestic Impala up and down the roller-coaster hills of Esseph with native panache, the radio playing at full volume" (*CP,* 20), this last note echoing Lodge's memory of "[driving] fast with the radio playing rock music" during his own first visit to San Francisco (*PW,* 33). Despite such resemblances, though, there is no indication that in his earlier time on the East Coast—he spent several months at Harvard in miserable solitude as he worked on his M.A. thesis ("the last major project he ever finished" [*CP,* 20])—Swallow ever became acclimated to life in American academe in the same way that David Lodge did. During his months at Brown, Lodge soaked up American literature and culture and developed long-term relationships, such as with the journal *Novel,* then being launched. Neither does Swallow seem to approach his stint at Euphoric

State with the perspective on both British and American cultures that
Lodge exhibited in the essay "The Bowling Alley and the Sun," published not long before he went to Berkeley.

Of course, in more important ways Lodge constructs Swallow and his
experiences to exceed, and even parody, himself and what he experienced in 1969. He noted recently that "[the] fictitious and jokey place
names licensed me, I hoped, to exaggerate and deform reality for literary purposes," going on to discuss how the Rummidge of his novel (both
town and university) was intentionally "more dourly provincial" than
Birmingham, and Euphoria "more 'far out' " even than Berkeley and the
Bay Area as he observed them (*PW,* 11). "Exaggeration and deformity"
also drove Lodge's decision to bring Swallow to Euphoria without
Hilary, so that the novel's premise of changing places—the confrontation with an unfamiliar environment, which this novel shares as a central subject with Lodge's previous ones—is compounded. In this respect
Philip Swallow is closer to Timothy Young in *Out of the Shelter* than to
Jonathan Browne in *Ginger, You're Barmy* (who, after all, enters a more
constraining environment when he enters the army). Even so, "exaggeration and deformity" move *Changing Places* outside of both the seriousness of Timothy's story and the broad realism of *Ginger.*

This greater flexibility in appropriating and transforming personal
experience combines with other narrative strategies to create the kind of
comic fiction with which Lodge has felt most comfortable. In this
instance perspective is a most important factor, a perspective established
for the reader by the introduction of Philip Swallow and Morris Zapp.
With epic sweep, yet with a keen sense of the contemporary, the novel
begins: "High, high above the North Pole, on the first day of 1969, two
professors of English Literature approached each other at a combined
velocity of 1200 miles per hour" (*CP,* 7). The first pages play on this
image of the two travelers suspended in midair and on how the technology of modern air travel ironically prohibits their greeting each other (or
even knowing of each other's proximity) as they might were they traveling on ocean liners. The narrative insists on a flight of fancy ("Imagine,
if you will . . .") that posits a sort of umbilical cord connecting each professor with his native land. These cords then become thoroughly entan-
gled through a series of reciprocal "criss-crossing, diving, soaring and
looping" by the two planes as they pass:

> It follows that when the two men alight in each other's territory . . .
> whatever vibrations are passed back by one to his native habitat will be

felt by the other, and vice versa, and thus return to the transmitter subtly modified by the response of the other party. . . . It would not be surprising, in other words, if two men changing places for six months should exert a reciprocal influence on each other's destinies, and actually mirror each other's experience in certain respects, notwithstanding all the differences that exist between the two environments, and between the characters of the two men and their respective attitudes towards the whole enterprise. (*CP*, 8)

Here Lodge gives us the principle by which the novel will unfold—not just a way of writing or of organizing material but a way of reading that material, a way of regarding the people and events in the narrative. Having termed *Changing Places* a "duplex chronicle" (and having noted the technical meaning of *duplex* from the *O.E.D.*: "systems in which messages are sent simultaneously in opposite directions" [*CP*, 7]), he challenges the reader to consider the ways in which the two principal narrative strands are reciprocally linked in a relationship that can be seen as dialectic, dialogic, symbiotic, and the like. Besides the premises of the novel already noted (the other "what-ifs"), he asks us to suspend not so much our disbelief as our primary attention to the emotional appeal of the insular "characters" promoted by traditional realism and modern psychology. Lodge is not interested in a type of reciprocity caused only (or simply) by the gross elements of society and institutions—which, after all, traditional realism fully recognizes as pressures on the individual. Instead, he asks us to attend to the reciprocity caused by the subtler lines of mutual influence that, interestingly, become activated in circumstances (two strangers exchanging ordinary situations at a great distance, and with no direct contact in the process) that might seem to preclude their very operation.

Such reading requires the sort of suspended vantage point assumed (literally) at the beginning of the novel; the reader must be ready to change places much more frequently than the two characters do. This suspension is encouraged not only by the acrobatics of Lodge's narrative opening but by the schematic sense imparted throughout the novel, a schematic that mitigates against both the seriousness of *Out of the Shelter* and the darkly comic realism of *Ginger, You're Barmy*.

During the late 1960s, David Lodge began to study intensively some manifestos of what he termed "the foreign territory loosely known as 'structuralism' " (*PW*, 34) because it seemed to address many theoretical and critical questions that had interested him for some time. Despite

difficulties in obtaining writings by Barthes and other prominent structuralists (especially in English) and in comprehending them, Lodge was
led by them to Roman Jakobson's distinction between metaphor and
metonymy. "Lightning—and enlightenment—struck," he recalled later,
for he sensed in Jakobson's distinction "the possibility of an all-embracing
typology of literary modes" as well as a key to understanding structuralism and the literary and linguistic movements allied to it.[8]

The first of his pronouncements in this direction was a 1974 essay
titled "The Language of Modern Fiction: Metaphor and Metonymy."[9]
No doubt Jakobson's basic distinction as Lodge interprets it in that
essay is considerably applicable to *Changing Places,* since the novel was
written during the very same period when Lodge was formulating his
version of structuralism, a version that would inform the influential
essays of his next two critical collections, *The Modes of Modern Writing:
Metaphor, Metonymy, and the Typology of Modern Literature* (1977) and
Working with Structuralism (1981). But perhaps even more important to
Changing Places than the metaphor-metonymy distinction is the distanc-
ing from the ideology of realism that Lodge's immersion in structuralism during this period seems to have legitimized for him. While clearly
he would retain a repertoire of realistic devices and would appropriate
them frequently in his later writings, never again—not even in his novels of the 1990s, which some readers have seen as representing a return
to realism—would he use them with the same commitment as in *Out of
the Shelter* or without an accompanying mix of antirealist devices. Having confirmed the artificiality of realism through his absorption of structuralist ideas, Lodge evidently felt freer to admit metafictional artifice
into his own writing.

If a pervasive air of schematic design contributes centrally to the kind
of comedy Lodge was seeking in *Changing Places,* it is the novel's "mirroring" element that is most important in this regard. Of course, the
exchange premise itself—the superimposition of an American double
(though by no means a clone) onto the autobiographical "facts" behind
Lodge's narrative—invites a monitoring of difference-within-similarity
(and of the reverse). This pattern is established early and pursued relentlessly. The introductory comparison of the personal and professional
backgrounds of the two flying academics gives way to an ongoing
description of how each fares with a particular aspect of his new location, especially compared with how the other is faring at the same time
with the same aspect.

Such patterning sacrifices verisimilitude and emotional attachment for frequent (and immediate) mirroring opportunities even beyond those that the virtually identical university calendars of England and America afford. Philip meets Morris's wife at a party at about the same time (and at about the same point in the narrative) that Hilary Swallow first comes upon Morris at Philip's office. Philip spends the night with Morris's daughter Melanie at about the same time that Morris behaves with uncharacteristic "niceness" to two young women he has met in Rummidge (even to the point of refusing the offer of one of them, his landlord's niece, to repay him with a nighttime visit to his bedroom). Philip's visit to the Pussycat Go-go coincides with Morris's to a Soho topless club—even in the immediate aftermaths of these visits (Philip meeting up with Melanie outside the Pussycat and Morris discovering the Soho topless dancer to be the other young woman he has befriended) and in the similar ways they further befriend the young women. Given this pervasive pattern and the established probability of its continuation, the affair between Morris and Hilary, when it finally ensues, seems but a necessary part, an almost obligatory parallel to the Philip-Désirée.

What is almost as notable about this pattern as its pervasiveness is the way it keeps the reader suspended between the two narrative strands and precludes serious concern with the problems or outcomes of either. Robert Morace may be right in claiming that "whether intentional[ly] or not" Swallow receives more of the narrator's time, to offset the stronger presence of the more flamboyant Zapp (Morace, 169). However, given the way in which that time is parceled out, the difference is negligible. Within the scant 50 pages of the novel's second section (which describes the lively manner in which each character settles into his new situation), no fewer than 18 shifts of viewpoint and locale occur. Not that the two characters and their stories are always compartmentalized by this method; sometimes they are allowed to bleed into each other. As Morace remarks, "Not content to narrate Zapp's and Swallow's stories in merely parallel fashion, Lodge runs them together as best he can in the absence of the film director's split screen and short of resorting to Derrida's coupling of columns in *Glas* or Nabokov's coupling of text and commentary in *Pale Fire*" (Morace, 163). Not until the fifth section, two-thirds of the way through the novel, does either Swallow or Zapp receive much uninterrupted attention. (In between, the third section offers letters between Swallow, Zapp, and their wives, while the fourth, reminiscent of the "Aeolus" section of Joyce's *Ulysses*, alternates newspaper clippings and other public documents from Euphoria, mostly about student political activities, with those from Rummidge—documents that, Lodge has noted, Swallow and Zapp are supposed to be reading.)[10]

The variation of formats among the sections of *Changing Places* (a technique that is anticipated, though less spectacularly and for a different effect, by stylistic parody in *The British Museum Is Falling Down* and that is also linked to Joyce [*WO*, 68]), plus the self-reflexive gestures accompanying such variation, contributes to the novel's emotional distance and reaches its peak, appropriately, in the sixth and final section, which takes the form of a film script. Earlier, in the letters section (titled "Corresponding"), Hilary writes to Philip about a book called *Let's Write a Novel,* which he has asked her to find, and observes, "There's a whole chapter on how to write an epistolary novel, but surely nobody's done that since the eighteenth century" (*CP*, 130). At a later point Philip reads from the same book: "Flashbacks should be used sparingly, if at all. They slow down the progress of the story and confuse the reader" (*CP*, 186)—an ironic note in a novel replete with flashbacks (including a fairly long one, completed just before this point, that recounts the origins of Philip's affair with Désirée Zapp).

This "running metafictional joke" begins much earlier, when Morris finds *Let's Write a Novel* in Philip's office, which he is temporarily occupying, and happens to read that "[t]he best kind of story is the one with a happy ending; the next best is the one with an unhappy ending, and the worst kind is the story that has no ending at all" (*WO*, 229; *CP*, 88). The question of novelistic endings reappears in the concluding section of *Changing Places,* the title of which ("Ending") is itself part of the joke— "noun, participle and gerund: this is the end of the book, this is how it ends, this is how I am ending it" (*WO*, 229). During this dramatized New York meeting of the two couples to sort out their affairs and determine their futures, an exasperated Hilary complains to Morris and Philip, "You sound like a couple of scriptwriters discussing how to wind up a play" (*CP*, 245). And on the final pages, where (as Lodge even has Philip point out) the end is literally in sight for the reader, issues of narratology and film theory compete with more personal concerns. Morris and Philip argue about whether the novel is dying and film supplanting it as a more meaningful medium, while the women ask that they attend to what Hilary terms "something a little more practical . . . [l]ike what the four of us are going to do in the immediate future" (*CP*, 250). The reader sees the phrase "The End" approaching at the bottom of the last page and reads the final speech, in which Philip declares that unlike the novel, the film ("especially nowadays") doesn't announce that it is ending. As he says, "The film is going along . . . and at any point the director chooses, without warning, without anything being resolved, or explained, or wound up, it can just . . . end." The novel ends right there, with nothing settled about the future: "[T]he camera stops, freezing [Philip] in mid-gesture" (CP, 251).

According to Let's Write a Novel, this is the worst kind of ending. According to Morace, it constitutes a final step in Lodge's mediation, evident throughout Changing Places, "between life and art, between the liberal tradition and postmodern innovation, narrative drive and verbal texture, verbal muscle and quiet conversation" (Morace, 169). And according to Lodge himself, it represented a way of remaining neutral: "I did not want to have to decide, as implied author, in favour of this partnership or that, this culture or that." The shift in the novel's final section to a film-script format—with its greater impersonality, externality, and cultivation of "the Surface"—was intended, Lodge says, to help legitimize an ending of "radical indeterminacy" to a plot that until then had been "as regular and symmetrical in structure as a quadrille" (AF, 228).

To the extent that it succeeds and to the extent that it amuses, such an ending cooperates with the more conventionally comic elements in the novel. More than in Ginger, You're Barmy, the narrative here abounds in humorous surface touches, mostly (but by no means exclusively) conveyed from Morris Zapp's point of view. Thus the Rummidge English Department's bulletin board ("a thumb-tacked montage of variegated scraps of paper") is said to be reminiscent of the early work of Robert Rauschenberg, concrete evidence that "[t]he end of the Gutenberg era was evidently not an issue here: they were still living in a manuscript culture"(CP, 59). At one point Zapp decides that the BBC weather forecast, like everything else he hears on British radio, must be "some kind of spoof, predicting every possible combination of weather for the next twenty-four hours without actually committing itself to anything specific, not even the existing temperature" (CP, 71). Listening in a pub with Hilary to a Rummidge pop band called Morte d'Arthur and speculating that the lead guitarist and weakest member of the group might be called Arthur, he muses, "In which case the group's name was a consummation devoutly to be wished" (CP, 204). Philip Swallow's less aggressive viewpoint is rendered with equal verve, as when we learn that one result of the "sudden eruption" of the sexual revolution has been that "his girl tutees suddenly began to dress like prostitutes, with skirts so short he was able to distinguish them, when their names escaped him, by the colour of their knickers" (CP, 26).

Temporary situations, as well as more sustained threads of narrative, also contribute to the novel's comic tone. These range from Morris's discovery, in the opening section, that he is the only male aboard a charter flight for women going to England for abortions to the extended Chaplinesque chase scene, typical of the sort of madcap dilemmas Lodge developed throughout *The British Museum Is Falling Down,* in which Zapp tries to elude, by going up and down in an elevator, a presumably deranged English colleague who he believes is bent on murdering him. This chase ties in with a larger pattern of misunderstanding that began when Morris discovered in the bathroom of the Swallow home a copy of a harsh review of one of his books—which he suspected Philip to have written but turns out to be the work of his pursuer, who is guiltily tracking him down to apologize. The hapless Philip's comic misadventures include the whole sequence of his innocent involvement with student defiance of the police and culminate with his being put in jail and enduring his cellmates' taunts:

> "That's a sharp pair of pants the Professor is wearing, Al."
> "Sure is, Lou."
> "I like a pair of pants that fits nice and snug around the ass, Al."
> "Me too, Lou." (CP, 189)

Some of the other discomforting incidents and situations show come-uppance that is more deserved. As Philip looks forward to being called "professor" (a more generic title in the United States than in Britain), to being complimented on his accent, and indeed "to being an object of interest simply by virtue of being British" (CP, 21), it is amusing that a young man named Charles Boon, whom Philip knew as a dissolute and rather disrespectful student back at Rummidge, turns up on the same plane to America as he (addressing him as "Mr. Swallow") and turns out to have become quite a media celebrity in Euphoria (as well as Melanie's boyfriend). And it seems a fitting conclusion to Philip's sexual interlude with Melanie—which, anticipating the Dudley Moore character in the Blake Edwards film *10* and Lodge's own Vic Wilcox in *Nice Work,* Philip regards much more romantically than she—that "[a]fterwards, in her sleep, tightening her arms round his neck, she whimpered, 'Daddy' " (CP, 103). This is an especially ironic twist, given the identity of her true daddy.

Zapp, too, seems to be getting what he deserves when, just after he imagines luring Désirée to live with him in Rummidge, his ego is doubly wounded by the discovery that she has been having an affair with Philip. Talking it over with Hilary at this point hardly provides consolation:

> "I know Désirée. She hates men. Especially weak-kneed men like your husband."
> "How do you know he's weak-kneed?" Hilary demanded, with some irritation.
> "I just know. Désirée is a ball-breaker. She eats men like your husband for breakfast."
> "Philip can be very gentle, and tender. Perhaps Désirée likes that for a change," Hilary said stiffly.
> "The bitch!" Morris exclaimed. . . . "The double-crossing bitch." (*CP*, 236)

Suddenly he seems to be losing out on all fronts, and he knows it.

In the desires and dilemmas besetting its central figures, *Changing Places* conforms to patterns that have come to be associated with the campus novel. Morris Zapp and Philip Swallow are related to types that have emerged in the proliferation of such fiction, especially in their respective combinations of sexual ambition and ambition for power. If, as Lodge has claimed, "a typology of campus fiction might be based on a consideration of the relative dominance of these two drives in the story" (*WO*, 170), so the characters in such novels might be arranged along a continuum having these two drives as its opposite poles. *Changing Places* conforms, of course, in other respects, such as its emphasis on academics' tendency to become excessively aroused by campus issues; the Rummidge academic who compares the mild form of student protest there (mild especially compared with what is going on at Euphoria State at the same time) to Dunkirk and the Blitz is a perfect example. Any precise placement of this novel in terms of the entire genre (or some abstract ideal) of campus fiction is, of course, a matter of definition. Morace praises *Changing Places* for not conforming to the campus novel tradition but, instead, negotiating among that tradition, postmodernism, realism, and perhaps others as well (Morace, 170). Steven Connor, on the other hand, sees the campus novel as an inherently looser type (one that allows, and even invites, self-violation) and would probably find Lodge's practices here perfectly orthodox.[11]

Certainly both Morace and Connor would agree that one of the novel's central thrusts is its satire of academicians and academic life in both Britain and the United States. The basic premise on which *Changing Places* rests permits a revealing perspective on the foibles of each academic culture through the relentlessly comparative method of the narrative. Lodge's observation that the looser British tenure system permits more eccentricity than the tighter American system (*WO*, 170) is borne out not only by the generally more buttoned-down manner of the Euphoric State faculty but by the fact that the novel pokes fun more at the extravagance of American life and manners generally (illustrated by Morris Zapp at Rummidge as much as by what Philip Swallow encounters and observes at Platoons) than at the peculiarities of individuals. The less efficient (and some would say more humane) style of British universities is illustrated in the comparison of Rummidge's vice chancellor ("a tall, powerfully built man who affected a manner of extreme languor and debility . . . and moved about with the caution of an elderly invalid" [*CP*, 220]), as well as his personal manner of soliciting Morris's advice regarding faculty promotions, with Chancellor Binde, his largely invisible counterpart at Euphoric State, who works his will mostly through terse memoranda and press releases. To be sure, Morris's success in securing Philip a promotion speaks to the force of personal influence and ulterior motives in the workings of both academic cultures, but significantly such influence works at Rummidge without the multitiered committee structure (or the more recent threat of litigation) accompanying it in most American institutions.

Like Lodge's other novels, *Changing Places* reflects attentiveness to social and historical detail. Thanks to the premise of academic exchange between two societies, the potential to inform here is especially rich. Because of Lodge's close and ongoing contact with the American academic community, *Changing Places* can familiarize British or American readers with what they do not know about each other's country, mainly through straightforward (if generally sporadic) narrative commentary, and it can defamiliarize what each takes for granted by showing it through the eyes of an observant foreigner. And all readers, regardless of nationality, may learn either from Lodge's singular perspective on the two societies and their respective academic cultures or from his portrayal of contemporary university life, with which they may feel out of touch. The novel's version of the Berkeley free speech movement, and in particular the 1969 People's Park episode, differs in tone and emphasis from the descriptions of journalists and historians and even from the 1969 account Lodge himself wrote for a Birmingham University publication shortly after he returned to England that year.[12]

The pleasures of *Changing Places* thus exceed the considerable amusement afforded by its comedy and satire. It informs on a number of fronts. It speaks explicitly to the dividedness of the campus novel's readership (both participants and nonparticipants in university life) in its portrayal of the struggle between academic and nonacademic values (Connor, 73). It represents the coalescence of issues and styles exhibited separately in Lodge's earlier fiction, the securing of a central style with which he could feel confident, and the standard against which his later novels would be measured.

Small World

"I write layered fiction," David Lodge has said, "so that it will make sense and give satisfaction even on the surface level, while there are other levels of implication and reference that are there to be discovered by those who have the interest or motivation to do so" (Haffenden, 160). It is not surprising that the context for these remarks was a discussion of *Small World*, since of all Lodge's novels it seems the most obviously "layered." Because *Small World* represents Lodge's most densely and variously plotted novel (and certainly the most challenging to characterize in a study such as this), it has afforded the richest opportunity for Robert Morace and others interested in applying various modes of poststructuralist reading to Lodge's work. It can be argued, too, that *Small World* affords the greatest insight into the pleasures both of reading and of writing the kind of fiction most associated with David Lodge.

As suggested earlier, *Changing Places* (subtitled "A Tale of Two Campuses") illustrates handily the central qualities of postwar university fiction. Lodge takes full advantage of the closed campus world and its attractions for readers, especially its purportedly distinct values, norms, and rituals, which, as Connor has noted, are "thick with intrigue" (especially, but by no means exclusively, sexual intrigue). Connor has commented also on how the "membrane of self-satisfaction" surrounding the university proves semipermeable, as outsiders constantly enter the university—some to stay as longtime students or faculty members, others to pass through fairly quickly—and as the institution and its members are forced to cope with society and politics on the outside (Connor, 69). All of these characteristics show up in the dealings of Philip Swallow and Morris Zapp with the larger communities of Plotinus and Rummidge and with student demands fueled in part by political forces outside the university. True to the central tendencies of campus fiction, Lodge centers his attention on students and teachers of English, which John Sutherland describes as "traditionally the quietest and most self-engrossed corner of the university"[13] and Connor relates to the anxiety surrounding the presentation of English literature to a modern (and now postmodern) world increasingly indifferent, if not hostile, to such a project (Connor, 72–74).

All such conventions, plus many others associated with campus fiction, come into play in *Small World,* partly through its explicit links with *Changing Places.* Swallow and Zapp reappear here (as do Hilary and Désirée), to command much more important roles than Lodge envisioned for them when he began writing *Small World* (Haffenden, 161). The stories of certain lesser figures from the earlier novel likewise are extended to 1979, when *Small World* takes place. The faculty-exchange scheme by which Philip, Morris, and their wives originally got together and the spouse-swapping in which they temporarily engaged 10 years earlier are alluded to, as are many other incidents from the earlier book, so that some readers may feel they are taking up where they left off at the end of *Changing Places.*

But in one crucial aspect this is a significantly different novel. It depicts not simply a later period in the lives of academic characters encountered earlier but a strikingly different academic culture. Here the local campus communities in which Swallow, Zapp, and their colleagues worked have been replaced by a single global campus that knows neither national nor linguistic boundaries. A worldwide marketplace of ideas has supplanted the various national ones as the site for agency and exchange. As Morris explains, "Scholars don't have to work in the same institution to interact, nowadays: they call each other up, or they meet at international conferences."[14] Or as he more bluntly puts it later, "The American Express card has replaced the library pass" (*SW,* 64). The premise of the two-way faculty exchange supporting *Changing Places* is thus enlarged exponentially, with seemingly endless possibilities for exchanges among countless scholars on campuses in every part of the world.

An important corollary to this globalization of academe, and a key component of the global campus as Lodge depicts it, concerns the incursion of postwar continental theory into Anglo-American literary study. Not until the 1970s did such theory come to be read widely in England and America or enter the general academic parlance, partly because English translations of many of the major texts (such as Michel Foucault's *Archeology of Knowledge,* Jacques Derrida's *Of Grammatology,* and several key essays by Roland Barthes) were not available until then and partly because what would prove the most influential commentaries on the new theories and theorists (Jonathan Culler's *Structuralist Poetics,*

1975, and Terry Eagleton's *Literary Theory*, 1983, to name just two) were yet to be written.

One measure of this shift to a new body of theory is provided by the two anthologies that Lodge edited. The first, *Twentieth-Century Literary Criticism: A Reader* (1972), includes methodological statements representing the New Criticism and related formalist approaches, literary history, the history of ideas, Marxist and other sociopolitical approaches, myth and archetypal criticism, the psychoanalytical approach, and what Lodge termed "prescriptive criticism—credos and manifestoes." In the foreword he described his collection as "an anthology of critical comment by the most distinguished critics of this century upon a good deal of the world's greatest literature, past and present."[15] Significantly, of the 50 included selections, only 9 were not written originally in English.

Later Lodge admitted this English-language bias and explained it in terms of the audience for which the anthology had been intended, mostly American and English college and university students.[16] But like *Small World*, his second anthology, *Modern Criticism and Theory* (1988)— which he termed both a sequel and a complement to the earlier one— reflects not so much a rewriting of the earlier critical map as a discarding of it. Here the majority of the figures and their writings are European rather than English or American. The list of categories has been broadened to include theoretical schools lately arrived on the Anglo-American scene (structuralism, poststructuralism, narratology, deconstruction, cultural history, reception theory, feminism). Even categorical labels held over from the earlier anthology (formalism, psychoanalysis, politics) accommodate a considerably broader range of concerns and issues. Perhaps most significant about this updating is that virtually none of the included writers is engaged in criticizing or even discussing prominent literary texts. Most, in fact, are concerned with scrutinizing, if not undermining, the assumptions behind the very idea of a literary high culture, or a literary work, or authorship, or reading and interpretation. Most pursue aims to which literature and literary study as reflected in Lodge's previous anthology are at most only tangentially related. The title of this newer anthology thus largely understates its foregrounding of theory and theorizing of a sort that has little to do with literary criticism in the earlier sense.

In his foreword to *Modern Criticism and Theory*, Lodge notes the "strains and stresses within the institutional structures that contain and maintain the academic study of literature" that have been brought on by recent theory and by the elevation of theory as a field of study.[17]

Although the "anxiety" Connor and others have imputed to English departments and the study of literature, especially as they have been portrayed in campus fiction, goes all the way back to the 1930s and the unease with which F. R. Leavis and his followers tried to advance the value of an English literary tradition in a society increasingly given to mass consumerism (Connor, 71–72), *Small World* shows how recent developments have stepped up that anxiety a considerable notch. By the late 1970s, Morris Zapp's ambition to exhaust the possibilities of commentary on Jane Austen by examining her work from "every conceivable angle, historical, biographical, rhetorical, mythical, Freudian, Jungian, existentialist, Marxist, structuralist, you name it" (*CP,* 44)—and thus to cover all of the categories from Lodge's earlier anthology—has given way to a sometimes open warfare in which the kind of pluralism Zapp proposed earlier has been rendered impossible by the relentless pursuit of the newer theoretical modes. In Lodge's portrait of the global campus, scholars mostly compartmentalize themselves into schools promoting the various "isms" of literary theory. They rarely search for common ground, and they tend to demonize those not of their persuasion.

As *Small World* begins, Morris has already abandoned his Austen project, which he now cites to illustrate the fallacies of the traditional criticism discredited by poststructuralism (and by his own most recent book, *Beyond Criticism*). "You see before you," he confesses to a conference audience, "a man who once believed in the possibility of interpretation" (*SW,* 24). He goes on to show the futility of his Austen scheme and of others like it by declaring that "[e]very decoding is another encoding" (*SW,* 25), so that the fixing of meaning for any statement is always just over the horizon. By Morris's deconstructionist logic, "Conversation is like playing tennis with a ball made of Krazy Putty that keeps coming back over the net in a different shape" (*SW,* 25), so much so that not even the listener's repeating back the exact words of a statement indicates an understanding of meaning "intended" by the speaker. Rather, the listener brings "a different experience of language, literature, and non-verbal reality to those words" (*SW,* 25)—that is, they become fundamentally "different" words when employed by another speaker. The apparently greater ease of fixing the meaning of a written text is illusory and, if anything, even more frustrating because it is more speculative ("not a to-and-fro-process," Morris explains, "but an endless, tantalizing leading on, a flirtation without consummation" [*SW,* 26]).

Other, lesser characters are identified specifically with other theoretical-critical stances. Their (and Morris's) competition for professional eminence in the form of a newly announced UNESCO Chair of Literary Criticism makes up a major area of the satire and comedy here. Part of the challenge of "layering" this novel and of setting up its comedy concerns the presentation of theorists and their theories so that both the academic insider and the reader unacquainted with literary theory can be amused. Lodge has written of his difficulties in writing the section, about 80 pages into the novel, that introduces a variety of figures representing different theoretical schools. Having focused up to that point on just a few characters (including Morris and Philip Swallow), he wanted to break out of such a leisurely, limited form and increase the scope and tempo of his book ("so that the idea of the global campus is actually being unfolded"). He aimed for a "sense of simultaneity" by introducing "a whole raft of minor characters from different countries, instead of having the main characters meet others in a picaresque fashion" (Haffenden, 163).

With the clarity and succinctness characteristic of his own critical writing (including his introductions to the various writers in the two critical anthologies), Lodge within 30 pages gives "language and context" (Haffenden, 163) to no fewer than 10 new persons whose stories will stretch to the end of the novel, even while continuing to narrate the doings of the Swallows and Morris Zapp. The newcomers include: (1) Fulvia Morgana, a wealthy and stylish Italian Marxist scholar; (2) Arthur Kingfisher, an elderly Viennese-American "whose life is a concise history of modern criticism . . . [and who is] doyen of the international community of literary theorists" (SW, 93–94), and one of the chief assessors for the UNESCO chair, who is accompanied by his beautiful young Korean mistress ("her life wholly dedicated to protecting the great man against the importunities of the academic world and soothing his despair at no longer being able to achieve an erection or an original thought" [SW, 94]); (3) Siegfried von Turpiz, a Berliner, a lover of fast cars, and a leading exponent of *rezeptionasthetik* (response theory), whose right hand is mysteriously hidden in a black glove he has never been known to remove, thus prompting all sorts of speculations; (4) Michel Tardieu, a leading narratologist at the Sorbonne, whose lover is a young man named Albert; (5) Rudyard Parkinson, Regius Professor of Belles-Lettres at All Saints' College, Oxford, an aging don lately given to writing mostly book reviews, whose hostility toward American scholars is especially directed at Morris Zapp (whom he scorns as "a brash, braggart American Jew, pathetically anxious to demonstrate his familiarity with the latest pretentious critical jargon" [SW, 100]); and (6) Roland

Frobisher, a successful English novelist (one of the Angry Young Men of the mid-1950s), who suffers writer's block and has written nothing for eight years. Robert Morace terms the chapter in which these and other characters appear for the first time a "narrative deluge," observing that "[t]he narrative intercutting is greater here than anywhere else in the novel, as is the reader's sense of narrative vertigo as Lodge yo-yo's back and forth between not only time zones but narrative zones as well" (Morace, 194).

Critics' speculations about the prototypes for the various portrayals in *Small World* include such prominent figures as Stanley Fish and George Steiner.[18] But even the reader unacquainted with such figures or their theoretical stances can readily grasp the types being portrayed and caricatured, as well as the comedy of wit and personality that ensues among them. The struggle over the UNESCO chair involves both the big names of literary criticism and the not-so-great. It shows the fawning and calculation with which would-be appointees seek Arthur Kingfisher's favor, as well as the old man's shrewdness in wielding his power—as in a telephone inquiry from von Turpitz disguised as a conference invitation (which Kingfisher deflects easily). And always the force of rumor persists, at conferences and in academic circles generally, so that, for example, Morris learns of the proposed chair only when he and Fulvia Morgana happen to be seated together flying from London to Milan.

Morris's subsequent quest for this ultimate professional prize is countered not as much by other superstar theorists or members of rival critical schools as by his archenemy Parkinson. The tool with which Parkinson seeks to defeat Zapp turns out to be Philip Swallow, whose elevation to serious candidacy for the UNESCO chair itself constitutes one of the comic-satiric gems of this novel. In *Changing Places* Lodge had fun noting that Philip's sole claim to professional distinction lay in his ability to examine undergraduates ("No one could award a delicate mark like B+/B+?+ with such confident aim, or justify it with such cogency and conviction" [*CP,* 17]). Now Philip again is cast as an academic lightweight with almost no solid accomplishments. His approach to literature lacks the rigor contemporary scholarship demands. He extols nothing more than a vague but enthusiastic love of literature and unapologetically invokes the unfashionable rubrics of great literature as the repository of great truths, of great writers as persons of genius and wisdom, of literary meaning as authorially intended, and of the critic's job as an obligation to "unlock the drawers, blow away the dust, and bring out the treasures into the light of day" (*SW,* 317).

Not that the Philip Swallow of this novel is precisely the same figure he was in *Changing Places*. "I built up his character a little," Lodge admitted (Haffenden, 164). Now older, Philip is also more confident—a development one colleague attributes to the affair with Désirée. Thanks largely to attrition, he has assumed the position of English chair (and professorial rank) at Rummidge. He has published a modest book on the early-nineteenth-century English essayist William Hazlitt (significantly titled *Hazlitt and the Amateur Reader* and said by Morris to be "totally brainless" [*SW*, 235]). And he has gotten on the British Council circuit, so that he often travels to distant lands to lecture on the love of literature or on Hazlitt (or on both).

Even so, he remains a monumental longshot for the kind of advancement the UNESCO chair represents. Of course, Parkinson first sees Philip as a way of promoting his own candidacy. Wanting some way to subvert Morris, he latches on to a review copy of Philip's book, which he receives long after its publication because the publisher forgot to send review copies out and belatedly found them on his firm's basement floor while having sex there with his secretary. Parkinson makes Philip and his book the center of a *TLS* essay titled "The English School of Criticism," which discredits contemporary theory. But the creature outstrips the creator in this instance, as a U.N. official misinterprets the motives behind the *TLS* article and leaks to the press that Philip Swallow is the leading contender for the UNESCO chair, to Philip's puzzlement and the other candidates' consternation.

Philip's rapid rise is but one of many opportunities this novel gave Lodge to satirize the global campus. International conference hoppers are shown as generally intent on everything but scholarly concerns—and mostly on the conviviality and riotous escape from ordinary existence afforded by fancy hotels, rich cuisine, heavy partying, and late sleeping, usually paid for by a university or granting agency. Not surprisingly, since they are freed temporarily from domestic constraints, the participants are hardly averse to sexual adventuring. As Lodge observes elsewhere, "It is precisely the *tension* between professional self-display and erotic opportunity, between the ambition to impress many and the desire to impress one, that, among other things, makes the conference such a fascinating human spectacle, and such rich material for fiction" (*WO*, 71). Thus in *Changing Places* he notes the intense irony of one person being sexually attracted to another of whose scholarship (s)he disapproves, as when an American at the Joyce Symposium in Zurich discovers only after spending the night with Fulvia Morgan that she is "the raving Marxist poststructuralist whose essay on the stream-of-consciousness novel as an instrument of bourgeois hegemony . . . he has rubbished in a review due to appear in the next issue of *Novel*" (*SW,* 238). An equally amusing moment occurs when, as the only creative writers at von Turpiz's response-theory conference, Roland Frobisher and Désirée Zapp (now also a best-selling novelist on the strength of one book, based on her marriage to Morris) end up in bed together, each fearing that the other will use their liaison as material for publication.

Désirée is not the only holdover character from *Changing Places* whose love life follows the trajectory suggested by the earlier novel. Morris's, predictably, seems to have come to a halt. As he explains to Hilary Swallow: "I gave up screwing around a long time ago. I came to the conclusion that sex is a sublimation of the work instinct" (*SW,* 59). Philip's involvement with women, on the other hand, has widened. Hilary admits that he has grown handsomer in middle age and notes the mutual attraction between him and pretty students, a phenomenon Morris ascribes to Philip's having become department chair ("They wet their pants at the thought of his power" [*SW,* 59]). Hilary knows of one sexual encounter with a student, and she suspects more. What she doesn't know, though—and what Philip reveals to Morris—is that a few years earlier he became briefly but intensely involved with a married woman named Joy whom he met on a trip for the British Council. Though technically it was but a one-night stand (he learned that Joy and her family were later killed in a plane crash), he continues to venerate her and their encounter and to believe that a relationship with her could have given him the "intensity of experience" and "desire undiluted by habit" that he craves and that he finds so lacking in his marriage (*SW,* 66, 77).

Romantic though Philip's longings for Joy seem, they are overshadowed in intensity and significance by the quest of another of Lodge's international scholars, a young Irish poet named Persse McGarrigle. Although it is inappropriate to speak of a main character in *Small World* or even of a discernible multiple protagonist—especially once Lodge lets loose the flood of the "new" characters—Persse comes closest, as his romantic quest represents an extreme against which the others are measured, as it frames the novel's other lines of action, and as Lodge uses Persse's point of view much more than any other.

To the surface allegory of Philip Swallow's quest for Joy, Lodge added a rich literary dimension by developing the story of Persse, whose beloved is named Angelica—the name of the woman praised in the famous romantic epic of the Italian Renaissance, *Orlando Furioso*. Ever since its first publication in 1532, *Orlando Furioso* has contributed to modern definitions of the romance mode and has served as a model and point of departure for the writing of romances, beginning with Edmund Spenser's *Fairie Queene* in the 1590s. Lodge's use of it here is but one of the more recent extensions of its place in the literature of romance and illustrates the deeply allusive agenda pursued in *Small World*.

Of course, literary reference is hardly absent from Lodge's earlier fiction. Some of the books related to the academic ambitions of Jonathan Browne in *Ginger, You're Barmy* have been noted, as have the forceful stylistic parodies in *The British Museum Is Falling Down*. And since the main character of that later novel, Adam Appleby, is the graduate student in English literature that Browne is only looking forward to becoming, his actions and ways of thinking are even more caught up in general literary matters and particular texts. More important, the structure of *The British Museum* depends heavily on parallels with Joyce's *Ulysses,* and a full response to its comedy requires recognition of this technique.

Given the allusive tendency of these earlier novels, in hindsight it seems almost inevitable that Lodge would gravitate toward an account of full-fledged academics, with numerous references to standard English writers. This, of course, is what happened with *Changing Places*—and not only in the descriptions of Philip Swallow's and Morris Zapp's careers. One especially telling scene in this regard finds Morris lecturing a tutorial group on how Jane Austen "invariably came down on the side of Eros against Agape—on the side, that is, of the private communion of lovers over against the public communion of social events and gatherings which invariably caused pain and distress" (*CP,* 215). Ironically, he is just then interrupted by a telephone call from Hilary, who invites him to spend the night with her, and by a colleague asking advice about Hilary's request to do master's-level work in the department.

Equally striking is Philip's lengthy reverie during the final stage of his long attempt to compose a letter telling Hilary of his decision to leave her. With increasing lyricism he catalogs the details of the passing campus scene at Euphoric State (especially the women students) and concludes that he himself is "part of a great historical process—a reversal of that cultural Gulf Stream which had in the past swept so many Americans to Europe in search of Experience" (*CP,* 194)—a process described in Whitmanesque fashion, with reference to James, Twain, Henry Miller, Gertrude Stein, and other American writers. We are told that "[Philip] understood American Literature for the first time in his life that afternoon, sitting in Pierre's on Cable Avenue as the river of Plotinus life flowed past, understood its prodigality and indecorum, its yea-saying heterogeneity" (*CP,* 195). Morace is probably right to claim that this outburst represents not so much a step forward as merely an alternative to the "British rhythms (and ideas)" that have dominated Philip in the past and will continue to influence his thought and behavior in the future. (Indeed, Morace argues, such "linguistic alternations" reflect the comic situation Lodge assigns Philip [Morace, 161]). Certainly Philip's thinking at this point illustrates Lodge's manner of integrating literary materials into *Changing Places.*

But such integration appears superficial beside what happens in *Small World,* which is the supreme instance of Lodge's "layering" practices and, according to one critic, a novel "filled to the brim with literary allusions and disquisitions on literary theory."[19] To be sure, *Small World* might be enjoyed simply as high comedy, since, as one reviewer noted, it provides "enough surface diversions to beguile readers who have never heard of Sir Thomas Malory or the Modern Language Association."[20] Persse McGarrigle is presented as inexperienced, both academically and sexually, and Lodge exploits fully the comic potential of his naiveté. When the novel opens, he has just finished his M.A. and is teaching at an obscure Irish university and attending his first professional conference. He has little sense of the protocol operating among the veteran academics he finds there. His initial meeting with the beautiful, intelligent Angelica Pabst—a doctoral candidate writing a thesis on romance (what else?)—is love at first sight. Unlike the older (and mostly married) men buzzing around Angelica, Persse is interested not in sex but in marriage with what he considers this most perfect of women ("What the blazes do all these old men want with you?" he asks her at one point [*SW,* 41]). When they are first alone together, he proposes marriage immediately, but she points out that nowadays people usually sleep together before they marry ("Or so I understand," she says coyly). But then, in a bit of Wildean role reversal, Persse replies: "It's against my principles. . . . But if you promised to marry eventually, I might stretch a point" (*SW,* 40). Later he may be saddened when Angelica gives him the slip or when he sees her with another man, but he is not deterred; never does he blame her or suspect that she may be less than what he believes her to be. Disappointment only spurs Persse ("a hopeless romantic," Angelica calls him) to further effort—from conference to conference, all over the world, in quest of his mysterious, elusive love (*SW,* 39).

This broadly comic plot comes in a literary package hard to ignore. Lodge prefaces his storytelling here with a prologue explicitly drawing on that of *The Canterbury Tales*. He begins with a modern rendering of Chaucer's opening lines and suggests that one contemporary parallel to the medieval pilgrimage is the modern academic conference, with its pleasure-seeking disguised as self-improvement. (Morris later reinforces this medieval strain by comparing international conference-goers to "the errant knights of old, wandering the ways of the world in search of adventure and glory," though noting that "[s]ome are more errant than others" [*SW*, 63, 64]). Our first glimpse of Persse finds him reciting to himself the opening lines of *The Wasteland*—lines that, while referring literally to the M.A. thesis that he has just completed (on Shakespeare and T. S. Eliot) and to the dreary site of the novel's opening conference (Rummidge in April), also introduce the problems of decay and renewal developed in Eliot's poem and connected to Persse's story and the others Lodge will be presenting. And after Angelica turns down his marriage proposal, they make a date for the next night to reenact "The Eve of St. Agnes" ("Be my Madeline, and let me be your Porphyro!" he insists [*SW*, 40]), to begin a Keatsian strain that continues throughout the novel.

The comedy of *Small World* is thus encased in the modes of romance and myth. Chaucer, Eliot, and Keats provide but a beginning for this wildly rich texture of allusion and cross-reference. These elements are integrated here in such a pervasive manner that the reader untrained in these matters—or uninterested—is forced at least to suspect that something funny (and not just in a comic sense) is happening with this novel. And such are Lodge's satirical and parodic skills that the reader wholly familiar with his allusions and references—although they are so profuse that such a reader seems but a theoretical construct—can derive amusement from the way Lodge deploys them. The very abundance of such materials—the overly determined dimension of allusion in the text—thus contributes to its impressively broad appeal and no doubt has helped make this most learned of Lodge's novels also his most popular.

Stock materials of romance, both traditional and modern, flood the narrative. Early on, Angelica points out to Persse how his name draws on the legends of Sir Percival and Parcifal. This latter reference, which includes the Wagner opera of the same name and the attendant grail legend, not only figures significantly in *The Wasteland* but illustrates the archetypal element that helps hold together the disparate story lines of *Small World*. Besides these sources, Lodge later added the Perseus-Andromada myth to enlarge Persse's quest for Angelica (Haffenden,

163), and connections with the American philosopher and semiologist Charles Sanders Peirce and with Persse O'Reilly from *Finnegans Wake* have also been noted (Morace, 202). The legend of the holy grail and the courtly love tradition are appropriated in a highly satirical fashion through the novel's various quests, including Philip's for Joy and that of the competing academics for the UNESCO chair. Lodge plays on Eliot in naming the novel's most venerable scholar, who no longer has anything to say to the scholarly world, after the aging Fisher King of Jessie L. Weston's *From Ritual to Romance* and in dwelling on Kingfisher's impotence and quest for coitus as his most pressing problem. This *Wasteland*-Weston issue of "dryness" and unproductivity is extended to the various writers of the novel—not just Frobisher in his eight-year dry spell or Désirée, blocked from beginning her second novel, but also the academics, from Morris and others who essentially recycle the same papers from conference to conference to an obscure Australian aspirant named Rodney Wainwright, who struggles throughout the novel (even up to the day of his conference paper's scheduled presentation) to get past writing his opening paragraph.

Such description as this only begins to suggest the complexity and variety of conventions employed here or the deftness with which they are presented. Indeed, it is the very congestion of such traditional romance elements within so many story lines that mitigates against the high seriousness of their sources, thus helping sustain the novel's essentially comic tone. Its stock romance figures include an oracular old lady (named Sybil, of course) who keeps turning up to deliver cryptic predictions—a convention Lodge lampoons with a story line concerning one of Philip Swallow's former colleagues who persists in seeking advice from a computer. A different sort of stock female is Fulvia Morgana, linked to Morgan le Fay in Malory's *Morte d'Arthur* and to a figure named Morgana in *Orlando Furioso* (both of them wily women). The seductive Fulvia lures Morris Zapp to her luxurious villa, where she tricks him with rich food and drink as well as with the promise of sex ("He felt desire stirring in him like dull roots after spring rain," we are told, in an appropriation of Eliot [*SW*, 136]). She also tricks him into getting undressed (and handcuffed) as part of a scheme she and her husband prearranged. The traveler in a strange land, invited to spend the night in luxury and tempted to enjoy his absent host's wife (like Philip's situation with Joy, also in Italy), the vague sense of peril accompanying the pursuit of such pleasures, the sudden return of the husband, and the revealed collusion against the traveler all recall legends and traditional romances. Lodge

then tacks on a comic sequel in which Morris, after eluding his two cap-
tors, is kidnapped by friends of Fulvia's husband seeking a hefty ransom
from Désirée, who enrages Morris by reluctantly offering a relatively
paltry sum for his release.

But it is in the profusion of coincidences that the novel most suggests
traditional romance and, not incidentally, recent metafiction. The world
here becomes small indeed, as we learn that the same student who had
sex with Philip and later tried to blackmail him for a passing grade is
now enrolled in a class Rodney Wainwright is teaching at his home university in Australia and, by the end of the novel, will be engaging him in
the same way. Or when Persse, seeking Angelica in Japan, just happens
to meet up with the translator of Roland Frobisher's novels, who has
been involved in a long series of comic miscommunications with the
novelist. Or when the Heathrow Airport check-in agent Cheryl Summerbee—whose command of seating assignments seems a spoof on
divine intervention in human affairs (as when she purposefully seats
Morris next to Fulvia)—is able to fetch from her counter a copy of *The
Fairie Queene* (recommended to her by Angelica herself), which Persse
needs for a clue in his romantic quest, and to recall for Persse Angelica's
destination on the single occasion when she saw her. Lodge has explained that despite the implausibility of this particular meeting and the
information it yields Persse, "[B]y this stage of the novel it was almost a
case of the more coincidence the merrier" (*AE* 152). Of course, surprising—and convenient—meetings like this extend to the novel's other
story lines, as in Philip's shock at suddenly finding Joy alive after all and
a widow, and eager to resume their love affair.

The outcome of Persse's quest for Angelica and the solution to her
identity push *Small World* beyond the level of imitation or revival of the
romance mode and into the realm of burlesque. Key elements of Lodge's
tour de force—Angelica's having been found as an infant, along with
her twin, in the toilet of a transatlantic airliner; Persse's tracking down
the twin sister, distinguished only by a birthmark shaped oppositely
from Angelica's; and his last-minute exposure of Sybil Maiden as the
twins' mother—suggest, in the pleasure they provide the reader, not
only the relative strength of such devices compared with strict adher-
ence to more realistic principles but at the same time the impossibility
of maintaining even the romance mode in its traditional form.

Lodge has said that the subtitle of his novel ("An Academic
Romance") means not only that it deals with academics but that it
draws on "a traditional rather than a contemporary notion of romance as

a genre" (*WO*, 73). Even so, *Small World* may be academic also in the sense of being irrelevant or purely theoretical; it may illustrate Alastair Fowler's idea of the tertiary or final phase in a genre's development, far removed from its primary phase and, indeed, critical of its original values.[21] However, the appeal of the Philip-Joy story—both the first part, from the past, which Philip narrates to Morris, and its resumption in the present, dependent as it is on the creaky mechanism of resurrecting Joy from her supposed death—suggests the potential of the romantic mode, when properly updated, to capture our attention even today, the updating here being the style of *Casablanca* and similar 1930s movies in which Lodge casts this particular story line.

When Persse at last finds Angelica, at the MLA meeting in New York, and after he has finally made love to her and again proposed marriage, she turns out to be the twin sister Lily, whose image he has seen in strip clubs, pornographic films, and escort service flyers. Even though he cannot tell one sister from the other, even though sex with Lily has been wonderful ("He had fed on honey-dew and drunk the milk of paradise. Nothing could be the same again" [*SW*, 325]), and even though Lily would now be truly his in a way the already engaged Angelica ("the archetypal pricktease," according to Lily) could never be (*SW*, 326), Persse is sick with disappointment.

"[Y]ou're not really in love with Angelica," Lily tells him. "You were in love with a dream" (*SW*, 326). But such is the lure of what Angelica has meant to him, and so much of himself has Persse invested in that dream that he must pursue it again in the shape of another idealized female. Rather than acknowledge the impossibility of attaining the imaginary, he prefers to substitute a new image for the old and to risk the likelihood of more pain and disappointment. Specifically, he goes off in search of Cheryl Summerbee, the airline clerk who has been so nice to him and who, saddened by Persse's indifference toward her, quit her job and is not to be found without at least another novel's worth of searching. Cheryl, herself an avid reader of romance (and a recent convert to the traditional variety, having thrown away her Boon and Mills collection), has been in love with Persse during much of the time that he was yearning for Angelica, who, in turn, has been engaged to another man all along. (We are not told how satisfied Angelica's fiancé is.)

Of course, behind such a potentially endless chain looms the poststructuralist theories of Derrida and others, and the whole notion of infinite deferral—of meaning, of love, of closure in any search for an absolute. Morris introduces this idea in the conference paper he presents early in the novel, delivered with his characteristic flair and designed, in part, to shock the sensibilities of his audience of British academics mostly trained in the Leavisite moralistic tradition. With a tacit nod to Barthes, he compares the lure of fixed meaning to the striptease, with its "promise of an ultimate revelation that is infinitely postponed" (*SW,* 26), and develops the parallel between the interpreter's desire and that of the striptease patron, for whom the removal of layers of clothing and underwear, and even the exposure of female genitalia, leads only to further mystery and desire. "The attempt to peer into the very core of a text, to possess once and for all its meaning, is vain—it is only ourselves that we find there, not the work itself," he declares (*SW,* 27). Mystery, desire, and reemergent dissatisfaction—the quests for love and truth, which are endlessly delayed—are seen as authentic to humans both as sexual beings and as users of language, while "the hermeneutic fallacy of a recuperable meaning" attached especially to traditional realism and its rubric of truth telling is said to be inauthentic ("all strip and no tease," according to Morris [*SW,* 26]).

Depending on the perspective one wants to take, then, either Morris's ideas here operate as a gloss on the narrative that will follow (indeed it has already begun, since Persse meets Angelica before Morris delivers his paper) or the remainder of the novel represents a working out, ultimately to the parody level, of Morris's poststructuralist thinking. Lodge's recovery of the romance mode—beginning with introductory epigraphs from Horace, Hawthorne, and Joyce—allows him not only to undercut the realism traditionally associated with the novel but also to show the limitations of the contemporary attack on that realism. Hawthorne's preface to *The House of the Seven Gables,* from which one of the epigraphs is taken, is a classic statement on the tension between romance and realism in the novel and speaks to the "latitude" appropriate to the romance mode—a latitude Lodge observes in *Small World* through various violations of the code of verisimilitude already noted, plus many others. Perhaps chief among these violations is insistent repetition and circularity—to which the epigraph from *Finnegans Wake* ("Hush! Caution! Echoland!") refers—as evidenced through repeated patterns among the various story lines (dissatisfaction, desire, quest, peril and test, momentary satisfaction, dissatisfaction) and within individual lines, as well as the numerous literary allusions throughout the text. Such insistent repetition—and the nature of the repeated elements—links this novel to the centuries-old romance tradition, as well as to the strain of poststructuralism Morris elucidates.

Conference papers frame the central developments in *Small World.* The links Morris suggests in his paper are echoed and made more explicit in another, which Angelica delivers almost at the novel's end at the MLA meeting in New York. Referring to Barthes's connection between narrative and sexuality, she contrasts the pleasure of epics and tragedies, which engage the reader's curiosity and desire and move "inexorably" to "an essentially *male* climax (a single, explosive discharge of accumulated tension" [*SW,* 322]), with that provided by romances, which are not structured in this way:

> " [Romance] has not only one climax but many; the pleasure of this text comes and comes and comes again. No sooner is one crisis in the fortunes of the hero averted than a new one presents itself; no sooner has one mystery been solved than another is raised; no sooner has one adventure been concluded than another begins. . . . The greatest and most characteristic romances are often unfinished—they end only with the author's exhaustion, as a woman's capacity for orgasm is limited only by her physical stamina. Romance is a multiple orgasm." (*SW,* 322–23)

This view of romance, as an affront to the more respectable genres, squares with the traditional complaints leveled against romances. Renaissance critics of Ariosto attacked *Orlando Furioso*'s indecency, its lack of unity, and its unabashed borrowing from other texts as scandals against the dominant notions of literary, social, and moral decorum.[22] Romance operates similarly in *Small World,* as an escape hatch from the constraints—formal, intellectual, and ethical—of realistic fiction. The comedy and satire of the novel reinforce, and indeed compound, the potential of the romance mode to satisfy the appetite of Lodge's postmodern readers for metafiction. While Robert Morace has argued persuasively that rather than a romance or a satire, we have here an instance of "dialogical convergence of the two" (Morace, 199), it is important to note how the salient features of the novel—and virtually all of its subversive elements—hark back to the romance tradition.

This relates to the views put forth in Patricia A. Parker's *Inescapable Romance: Studies in the Poetics of a Mode* (1989), to which, in his introductory note to *Small World,* Lodge acknowledged a special debt. Indeed, the labyrinthine proliferation of story lines, of quests, of doubling-backs, and of delaying tactics in Lodge's novel—not to mention the direct allusions to and borrowings from particular romance writers and writings—seems designed to confirm and perpetuate the values Parker ascribes to romance.

This appears especially true in relation to her conclusion that the romance mode is echoed in modern theories of linguistic errancy and narrative structure and that it provides "an emblem for the preapocalyptic, or threshold, nature of language itself."[23] Given the scandalous past of the romance, even the parodic level to which Lodge carries things here seems very much in keeping with that tradition. And while Lodge admittedly was reading "a lot of Bakhtin" (particularly Bakhtin's book on Rabelais) while writing *Small World* (Haffenden, 166), the slant the novel takes on Ariosto, Spenser, Milton, and Keats suggests his agreement with Parker. Whether one wants to describe *Small World* as "carnival" or "romance" seems immaterial, so nearly identical does it make the two concepts appear.

For all of the connections drawn between romance and poststructuralist theory, however, the latter hardly escapes Lodge's critique. The mere fact that the novel reveals how many ideas central to recent theory were prefigured in romances written centuries earlier undercuts poststructuralism's claims to originality and invests with renewed value certain texts from the same literary canon so disparaged by many advocates of the new theories. And perhaps most important, the novel questions the basic value to human well-being of such theorizing, particularly the deconstructionist variety.

Philip Swallow anticipates the more concerted attack on recent theory made later in the novel by asking, after Morris Zapp has delivered the "striptease" paper outlining his deconstructionist position, what is the point of discussing "some imperfect memory or subjective interpretation of what you said." Morris answers that in terms of arriving at "some certain truth" there is no point, and he appeals to his audience's professional experience: "Be honest, have you ever been to a lecture or seminar at the end of which you could have found two people present who could agree on the simplest précis of what had been said?" (*SW*, 28). Though momentarily outwitted, Philip nevertheless persists by questioning the value of their work generally as professional scholars. But this time Morris's response—that the "point" is "to uphold the institution of academic literary studies" by performing "a certain ritual" analogous to those practiced by "other groups of workers in the realm of discourse—lawyers, politicians, journalists" (*SW*, 28)—sounds more disingenuous than honest and clearly begs some crucial questions that Philip, despite his lack of rigor, at least recognizes as important.

Near the novel's end, Lodge uses Persse to reinforce Philip's line of questioning. In an MLA session entitled "The Function of Criticism," and after a number of speakers—Tardieu, von Turpitz, Fulvia, Morris, and even Philip—have forcefully presented their views, Persse stymies them all by asking simply, "What follows if everybody agrees with you?" (*SW,* 319). Morace calls Persse's unanswered (and perhaps unanswerable) question the "decrowning act" of the novel in its exposure of literary study as a carnivalesque game (Morace, 204). More existential in its import—and often cited in the same way as Persse's "decrowning" question—is Morris's paradoxical admission, brought on by his brush with death by kidnappers, that despite his disbelief (as a card-carrying deconstructionist) in the individual, the deferral of meaning cannot be infinite "as far as the individual is concerned." "[D]eath is the one concept you can't deconstruct," he explains. "Work back from there and you end up with the old idea of an autonomous self" (*SW,* 328). Many readers have connected these statements to the more somber sections of Lodge's earlier novel *Souls and Bodies.*[24] On a more domestic level, the same line of reasoning is repeated after Philip abandons his renewed affair with Joy and returns to his wife. Though Morris caustically comments that "Philip decided he was getting to the age when he needed a mother more than a mistress," Philip's own explanation is more wistful: "I failed in the role of romantic hero. I thought I wasn't too old for it, but I was" (*SW,* 316, 336). And in what is perhaps the novel's most telling concession to the quotidian, the haughty von Tirpitz's mysterious right glove is shown to have been hiding nothing more than a perfectly ordinary right hand.

In the opposition of the ever-questing Persse to the pragmatic Philip (or to Morris), of youthful energy to middle-age stock taking, and of romance to realism, Lodge describes the dilemma of living in a time when the struggle to reconcile such conflicting claims seems especially difficult. While unquestionably there is merit in Siegfried Mews's claim that *Small World* ultimately shows Lodge's "basically traditional orientation" (Mews, 726), the novel hardly settles into an easy acceptance of it. In the end Philip is too wistful and Persse too buoyant for that. One critic has likened the philosophical underpinning of *Small World* to that of Samuel Beckett's plays and novels, the crucial difference being that "Lodge's writing communicates great zest for life."[25] Certainly whatever understanding of contemporary life is dispensed in this "academic romance" depends on its cheerful expectation that the romance—as a mode of writing and existing—will persist in trying to transcend the constraints of the academic.

Nice Work

In 1987 David Lodge retired from teaching at the University of Birmingham and began to devote himself full-time to writing, a decision he later attributed to "a number of convergent reasons" (*AB*, 8). Shortly before this, Lodge had commented to an interviewer that as he got older he was finding it harder to juggle teaching and writing even under the half-time arrangement ("four months on, four months off") he had had at Birmingham for several years (Marecki, 303). In a 1985 *New York Times* interview connected with the publication of *Small World,* he had referred to the continuation of the debate, begun in *Changing Places,* between conservative humanism and poststructuralism (represented by Philip Swallow and Morris Zapp, respectively) and had described literary studies then as being "somewhat demoralized" because of their increasing specialization and reliance on "highly technical language." Noting the general absence from contemporary criticism of commanding figures comparable to Leavis or Lionel Trilling in the previous generation, he concluded: "Those working at the coal-face are unintelligible to the general public. Those who are intelligible often have nothing valuable to say."[26]

Lodge's next novel, *Nice Work,* appeared in 1988. That same year an Australian journal published Lodge's essay "A Kind of Business: The Academic Critic In America," a review of a book of interviews with several leading contemporary literary critics, most of them Americans. In reviewing the book, Lodge decried certain trends in American literary studies, notably the star system and the competitiveness attending it; the "arcane and jargon-ridden form of discourse" by which traditional humanism was being undermined in the most prestigious American universities;[27] the uselessness of recent theory for the teaching of literature; and the pretentiousness, inaccessibility (for all but the initiated few), and irrelevance to sociopolitical reality of even the most politicized strains of contemporary theory (essentially Marxism and the New Historicism). "There surely is a hidden link between the professionalism of the American academic world and the eagerness with which it has devoured, domesticated and developed European theory," he observed:

> The very difficulty and esotericism of theory make it all the more effective for purposes of professional identification, apprenticeship and assessment. It sorts out the men from the boys, or, to put it another way,

speeds the tribal process by which boys become young men and push out
the old men. Whereas the methods of traditional humanistic scholarship
have hardly altered since the nineteenth century, the rules of the theory
game are changing all the time, and you have to be fast as well as smart
to keep up. (*AB*, 181)

It seems difficult not to associate whatever campus fiction Lodge was
writing at this time with his own immediate career decisions and with
attitudes he expressed in this essay. Indeed, it is difficult to imagine his
writing such a novel as *Nice Work* without such attitudes close at hand.
Unquestionably they come through in the novel, though less emphati-
cally than in the essay. Significantly, almost all of the novel's action
occurs in England and none of it in the United States. In a crucial decision near the end, the heroine, an ambitious young lecturer in English
literature, chooses the uncertainties of provincial university teaching in
Margaret Thatcher's England over a fast-track career at a major institution in the United States—despite the lure of a considerably higher
salary, the likelihood of rapid advancement, and easy access to the kind
of research and publication support unobtainable in Britain. Unlike
Changing Places or *Small World,* this novel concentrates not on comparing
British and American academic styles or on the jet-setting international
scholarly community—subjects with a decidedly modern, even postmodern, focus—but on the more traditional concern with the gap
between major segments of British society. In this instance, the gap is
between the community of university teachers and students, the postwar growth of which is suggested by all of the novels David Lodge
wrote before this one, and the world of business and manufacturing outside the university, which encompasses most of British society. It is
hardly coincidental that in "A Kind of Business" Lodge cited E. M.
Forster's *Howards End* for having raised, 75 years earlier, the issue of how
in good conscience one can question a society's values while living off of
it ("[always] a problem for teachers of the humanities under bourgeois
capitalism," he noted [*AB*, 178]), while at the end of *Nice Work* he has a
student wearing a T-shirt with the famous *Howards End* epigram, "Only
connect."

The issue of societal connectedness is raised in *Nice Work* mainly
through its social comedy. Like most of the other Lodge novels discussed
thus far, *Nice Work* turns on a premise involving a change of situations.
Specifically, it turns on a "shadow scheme" designed to promote better
understanding between the academic and business worlds of Rummidge

(which, to refine further his earlier discrimination of fiction from fact, Lodge here describes as "an imaginary city . . . which occupies, for purposes of fiction, the space where Birmingham is to be found on maps of the so-called real world").[28] Robyn Penrose, a 30-something member of Rummidge University's English Department, is assigned to "shadow" Vic Wilcox, the middle-aged managing director of a local casting and engineering firm. They approach each other with all the biases appropriate to their respective ages, social backgrounds, and occupations. But despite Vic's misgivings about Robyn, he soon responds to her, as she is an interesting and attractive younger woman. Much of the novel's comedy revolves around the ways each negotiates a relationship by turns professional, friendly, romantic, and briefly, sexual.

Having completed her Ph.D. in English during the 1970s, Robyn has enthusiastically embraced the discipline's newer theories and methodologies—particularly feminism and semiotics—and has applied them in her teaching and in her scholarly work. In the spirit of seeking connections, or of exposing disconnections, Lodge appears to relish showing the inconsistencies between the proclamations of Robyn's professional life and her private behavior. Sometimes she is aware of such inconsistencies, as when, after praising *Jane Eyre* and *Wuthering Heights* to Vic as "classics" while she accompanies him on a business errand through Brontë country, she recoils at the realization that she has been pursuing "a suspiciously humanist train of thought" ("the very word *classic* was an instrument of bourgeois hegemony"). She quickly recovers her public, postmodern stance with the follow-up insistence "You have to deconstruct the texts to bring out the political and psychological contradictions inscribed in them" (*NW,* 141).

Usually, though, Robyn is not given to such self-correction; usually she doesn't even sense her inconsistency. After describing her dismissal of the concept of the self central to capitalism and realist fiction—her belief, instead, in a subject position arising out of the multiplicity of discourses forming the consciousness (the belief that " '*you are what you speak,*' or rather '*you are what speaks you*' ")—Lodge goes on to note that "in practice this doesn't seem to affect her behaviour very noticeably—she seems to have ordinary human feelings, ambitions, desires, to suffer anxieties, frustrations, fears, like anyone else in this imperfect world" (*NW,* 22). After remarking how the clothes Robyn chooses not only keep her body from being an object of sexual attention but disguise her "smallish breasts and widish hips," he adds coyly, "[T]hus are ideology and vanity equally satisfied" (28).[29] The egalitarianism of her public politics appears outweighed by her conservative upbringing when she judges her brother's girlfriend as "decidedly lower-class" or when she enjoys hearing her mother pronounce the same young woman "frightfully common" (*NW,* 124, 221). Relatedly, when Robyn backs off from an unqualified defense of one of Vic's Indian workers, we are told that "[a]s a piece of action in a Victorian novel she might have judged it harshly as a case of one bourgeois supporting another when the chips are down, but she had persuaded herself that it was for the greater good of the factory workers—not to save Wilcox's skin—that she had lied" (*NW,* 107). Whether Lodge or the reader is persuaded is questionable.

What the novel shows, among other things, is Robyn's coming to recognize, mostly through her exposure to Vic Wilcox and to the world of business and industry in which he must operate, some of the limitations of her earlier outlook. Both she and her boyfriend Charles, also an English literature lecturer, have long been aware "cognitively" that a life outside the universities exists, "but she knew nothing about it, nor did Charles, or her parents" (*NW,* 29). Such ignorance seems especially ironic in that Robyn's academic specialty is the industrial fiction of the 1850s (or "condition-of-England novels," as they are often called) written by Dickens, George Eliot, Elizabeth Gaskell, and Charlotte Brontë, among others. One of these, Gaskell's *North and South* (1855), is especially relevant to the story of Robyn and Vic, as it turns on the exposure of its young heroine to the problems of labor unrest in an industrial city and on her growing friendship with a factory owner there.

If, as many critics have suggested,[30] *Nice Work* represents a late-twentieth-century version of these earlier novels ("a wryly, self-conscious intertextual condition-of-England novel," according to one [Waugh, 34]), Robyn has as much to learn as most of Lodge's readers. Feminist critics and others may feel that in assigning her a more elaborate development than Vic (though he, too, has changed markedly by the end), the novel is unfair and is emphasizing her shortcomings more than his.[31] Indeed, Terry Eagleton sees this as part of Lodge's general refusal to take Robyn's socialist-feminist politics seriously.[32] It is true that even in areas in which she is the more knowing and confident—in matters of love and sex, for example, in which she dominates the repressed middle-aged man—Lodge seems unable to resist showing her in at least a somewhat satirical light.

But if he does favor Vic, the extended parallels with the Forster novel—such as Vic's last name, the identity of which with that of Henry Wilcox, the industrialist in *Howards End,* Lodge claims he realized only halfway through writing *Nice Work* (*AF,* 38)—become ironic, or at least complicated, since Forster seems to side with his own intellectual heroine (Margaret Schlegel) against the Wilcox of his novel. And to be fair to Lodge, much of Robyn Penrose's ignorance of the industrial world, as well as her subsequent shock, directly reflects his own experience as he found his way into that world, mostly through the guidance of the "several executives in industry" who showed him around factories and offices and "patiently answered my often naive questions" (*NW,* author's note). Because Lodge's own "awed and appalled reactions" to the first foundry he visited while researching the novel were "transferred" to Robyn (*PW,* 35), his portrayal of her should not be viewed as entirely unsympathetic. (Lodge has said that he originally invented the shadow scheme as an explanation to a businessman friend he wanted to follow around.)[33] If the novel comes off as more critical of the academic world than of business and industry, this is partly because Lodge has known and scrutinized that world much longer, and because a central thrust of the novel is to critique the academic world more strenuously than any of his earlier fiction did.

Given the connection between *Nice Work* and the essay "A Kind of Business," the novel might be seen as part of a more general reaction in the 1980s against the Americanization of British culture. Once again Lodge represents the American academic community through the figure of Morris Zapp, who, despite having become what Robyn terms "almost elderly" (*NW,* 236), is as flamboyant and amusing and as much an operator as ever. Though sensing that he has "rather opportunistically" converted himself from a Jane Austen specialist in the New Critical mode into "a kind of deconstructionist," once she meets him Robyn readily concedes that he is "well up in the literature" (*NW,* 232, 237). Though Morris's appearance in *Nice Work* is late and brief, Lodge assigns him a cameo role crucial to Robyn's development.

Throughout the novel, the realities of university funding in 1980s England make it seem virtually certain that her three-year contract as a temporary lecturer at Rummidge will not be renewed and that no position for her will open up elsewhere. But suddenly, at the beginning of what looks like her final term of teaching, Morris Zapp visits Philip and Hilary Swallow, en route to his annual European conference circuit. When he meets Robyn, they discuss her work and her bleak prospects, and he immediately encourages her to submit her almost-completed second book to the Euphoria University Press, for which he happens to be a reader. After returning to America and reading her manuscript, he telephones to praise her work and to say that he will be recommending publication. He also advises her on negotiating with the press ("Ask for double the advance they're offering") and informs her of an opening at Women's Studies at Euphoric State for which he thinks she should apply (*NW,* 257). "Your life would be one long round of conferences and visiting lectures," he assures her:

> "And Euphoric State has just put in a bid to be the home of a new Institute of Advanced Research on the West Coast. If that works out, we'll have all the fat cats from Yale and Johns Hopkins and Duke lining up to spend semesters with us."
> "Sounds exciting," said Robyn.
> "Yeah, you'll love it." (NW, 259)

The only reservations come from Philip Swallow, who since *Small World* has become dean of the arts faculty at Rummidge. When Robyn tells him of Morris's encouragement and especially the possible job at Euphoria State, Philip points out that this is an honor indeed, as Morris would support only someone he felt could succeed. However, he also speculates that Morris's ex-wife Désirée may be a rival candidate (Robyn knows that someone Morris wishes to defeat is a rival) and goes on to caution:

> "[Désirée] can fight dirty. You'd better know what you're letting yourself in for. American academic life is red in tooth and claw. Suppose you get the job—the struggle only begins. You've got to keep publishing to justify your appointment. When the time comes for your tenure review, half your colleagues will be trying to stab you in the back, and not speaking to the other half. Do you really fancy that?" (NW, 260)

Such a warning is related to Lodge's observation in "A Kind of Business" that "[t]he world of American academic criticism is a small, insulated one, but it mirrors the macro-society in being highly competitive. In both worlds it is possible to succeed spectacularly, because it is also possible to fail" ("AB," 176).

Despite having "succeed[ed] spectacularly" in such a system, Morris is allowed by Lodge to retain his basic likability. To his credit, he takes Robyn's problems seriously and goes out of his way to help her. However, the Zapp character continues in many ways to reinforce Lodge's comparison of top-ranking American critics to film or sports stars: "[T]hey attract fans, they improve their earnings by transferring or threatening to transfer their services to other employers, they maintain a high public visibility (by attendance at conferences etc.) and suffer a high degree of anxiety about their performance and popularity" ("AB," 176). The essential vulgarity of such a system and Morris's place in it come through when he boasts to Philip of his Euphoric State contract's stipulation that no one in the humanities is to be paid more than he. Or as he more bluntly puts it, "If they want to hire some hotshot from one of the Ivy League schools at an inflated salary, they have to pay me at least one thousand dollars more than he's getting" (NW, 237).

When Morris encourages Robyn to pursue the Euphoric State position, Lodge momentarily provides her (and the reader) with an escape from the dilemma confronting her. However, he quickly blunts its appeal. Rather than challenging Philip Swallow's grim description of academic life in America, he has Robyn respond, "I have no choice. . . . There's no future for me in this country" (NW, 260). Although her financial need to work is soon removed when she receives a large inheritance from an uncle in Australia, she gives the bulk of it to Vic Wilcox for a new business venture and determines to pursue the American job instead of an easy retirement. However, personal work ethics and self-respect, rather than any keen desire to become an academic in America, seem to inspire this decision. In a culminating act of transparent authorial manipulation, the Lodge-Swallow position is made to triumph when, on the last page, Philip discovers the possibility of an extension at Rummidge for Robyn, which she accepts, with all of its risk, over the high-paying tenure track job at Euphoric State.

The precariousness of Robyn's employment situation, which Lodge never permits to disappear entirely, dramatizes the crisis atmosphere pervading British universities under the Thatcher governments of the 1980s. Lodge's three academic satires describe the relatively rapid arrival and departure of the heyday of university education in Britain. "I spend all my time on committees arguing about how to respond to the cuts," Philip Swallow complains in Nice Work, and the final pages find him qualifying Robyn's good fortune by insisting, "I can't guarantee anything" (NW, 233, 276). Again a note from "A Kind of Business" seems relevant, for there Lodge describes the combination during the first Thatcher government of drastically reduced university funding and increasingly stringent conditions for academic appointment, tenure, and promotion. Robyn's plight—and especially the sense of constraint marking even the "happy ending" Lodge concocts for her—bears out his observation that "British academics have had the worst of both worlds, finding it possible to fail, but not, in any significant sense, to succeed" ("AB," 177).

However little Robyn may realize it, this vulnerability to cold market forces and to principles of accountancy puts her and her fellow academics in the same category as Vic Wilcox and his factory workers. Vic senses this immediately when, during the second stage of the shadow scheme (after Robyn has shadowed him for several weeks), he sits in on a meeting of the Rummidge English Department at which syllabus reform is being considered. He cuts through a rather directionless discussion of staff reductions, increased teaching loads, and curricular design by pointing out that "rationalization" (in a business sense) is what really is being discussed: "Cutting costs, improving efficiency. Maintaining throughput with a smaller workforce. It's the same in industry" (*NW,* 252). While making no specific suggestions, he prompts department members to acknowledge the confusion endemic to most academic planning. Interestingly, he opposes a scheme of entrepreneurship by academic departments sponsored by the administration, observing that it runs counter to the protection of inefficiency and incompetence afforded by the tenure system. "It's not that I don't believe in the market, I do," he tells them. "But you people don't belong in it. You'd be playing at capitalism. Stick to what you're good at" (*NW,* 255).

Vic knows about these things because he has had to deal with them ever since he entered the workforce. The implication here, that most of the business world knows more about the academic world than vice versa, is hardly shocking, given the shelter that tenure and other practices largely peculiar to academe provide most of its longtime members. Lodge's view parallels C. P. Snow's in *The Two Cultures* (1959), that scientists probably know more about the humanities than humanists know about science. Vic reminds us of many of the problems of the university system, if not their solutions. He suggests that universities cannot expand indefinitely to provide positions for promising young people while tenure for older faculty prevails. "[I]f they can't be shifted, there'll never be room for you, no matter how much better than them you may be at the job," he tells Robyn (*NW,* 77). ("Who pays?" he persists in asking during their many debates throughout the novel.)

Eventually his position softens, at least to the extent that rather than being "more struck by [Robyn's] colleagues' security than by her own vulnerability" (*NW,* 76), as he is initially, he comes to attend to the larger implications of her dilemma. He comes to value the kind of work Robyn does and to see evidence everywhere of concepts to which she has introduced him. He comes to appreciate literature as never before ("I've read more in the last few weeks than in all the years since I left school" [NW, 256]), to the point even of liking to memorize and recite Tennyson—remarkable developments in one with a polytechnic engineering background and the hard-nosed scorn for the arts which he exhibits initially.

Robyn, in turn, revises her estimate not only of Vic but of people like him and of the great majority of the population, which universities largely ignore. Even at the beginning she senses Vic's intelligence and honesty—it rather unnerves her that repeatedly he holds his own in arguments with her over education and labor issues. By the end—after he has attended her tutorials, begun to read considerably, participated in discussions, and even taken her on in an interpretive dispute—she concedes that "Charles was wrong to say that we shouldn't teach theory to students who haven't read anything. It's a false opposition" (NW, 256). Instead, she develops a Ruskinian vision of workers such as those she has observed at Vic's factory filling up universities like Rummidge in their time off. "We have an Open Day once a year," she tells Vic:

> "Every day ought to be an open day. The campus is like a graveyard at weekends, and in the vacations. It ought to be swarming with local people doing part-time courses—using the Library, using the laboratories, going to lectures, going to concerts, using the Sports Centre—everything. . . . We ought to get rid of the security men and the barriers at the gates and let the people in." (NW, 170)

In this spirit she encourages Vic's wife to enroll in an Open University course and advises his daughter on university admission. Even her decision about the Euphoric State position is informed ultimately by her desire to help close the gap between the traditional students she is accustomed to teaching and the rest of the population. "Physically contiguous, they inhabit separate worlds," she reflects as she opts for an uncertain future at Rummidge (NW, 276).

But despite the attractiveness of her newly acquired vision, it seems largely futile. The novel shows the social divisions Robyn wishes healed being exacerbated every day by government policies and by a bottom-line mentality increasingly marking all strata of society. Ironically, her employment fortunes turn out to be rather the reverse of Vic's: as she finally gains at least a tenuous hold on a job, Vic loses his. What defeats him—what he is up against from the beginning in his managing director's position—is a combination of cheaper foreign competition, corporate impatience with the modest profits his management is beginning to produce, and the greed and backstabbing of colleagues he has trusted. While in the end Vic remains optimistic about his personal prospects—as he and his family agree, not unhappily, to live on less; as he regains his commonsense outlook, which was disturbed temporarily by his infatuation with Robyn; and as he proceeds into a new business venture—clearly his earlier faith in the structures of corporate industry has been shaken.

Both he and Robyn, as well as the institutions they have been serving, are dominated by forces they can hardly fathom, much less influence. The Americanization of British culture by worldly-wise theorists and their attacks on literary tradition are given a large, ominous dimension in *Nice Work,* where a postindustrial and globalized economy makes Robyn's humanist concern for societal connectedness appear as irrelevant and obsolete as the old factory machinery Vic scrambles to replace. The threat to both of their worlds is represented by Robyn's younger brother Basil, a London banker who epitomizes the new plutocracy that futures capitalism has created. When Basil visits Robyn at her house, we are told that "[e]verything about him and his girlfriend signified money, from their pastel-pale, luxuriously thick sheepskin coats that seemed to fill the threshold when {Robyn} opened the front door, to the red C-registration BMW parked at the kerb" (*NW,* 124). Gradually Robyn's boyfriend Charles is drawn into the world of finance, first by curiosity, then by his attraction to Basil's girlfriend, and finally by total conversion to a banking career. Lodge wryly has Charles explain to Robyn that business is not about buying and selling real commodities. Rather, he says, "It's all on paper, or computer screens. It's abstract. It has its own rather seductive jargon. . . . It's like literary theory" (*NW,* 153). Or as he says of his career shift, "I regard myself as simply exchanging one semiotic system for another" (*NW,* 225).

Freed from the values attaching to both industrial and artistic production and from all sense of moral or social obligation, such a viewpoint attacks the very basis for whatever confrontation or rapprochement occurs in *Nice Work.* Commenting on Lodge's portrayal of this new order, Patricia Waugh observes, "Here neither the academic text nor the machine part is an end-product of the work process, for all transactions and commodities exist only in the realm of pure signification":

> As knowledge itself becomes the most powerful if least stable commodity, the modern and tangibly productive worlds of Robyn and Vic are

shown indeed to be shadows of each other; two sides of a modern political economy which is itself now paradigmatically under threat. . . . An
academic theoretical critique which claims to have wiped out character
(and authors, too) is shown to be dangerously complicit with the dehu-
manizing drift of a monetarist economics which promises to be even
more brutal than what it supplants. (Waugh, 35)

This aspect of *Nice Work* no doubt contributes to a sense of the novel
as "more sober and realistic" than Lodge's earlier academic satires" (and
as a "hymn of praise to the signified" (*PW*, 34).[34] Of course, the main
features of Lodge's central style remain. As in his earlier novels, droll
commentary and witty comparisons punctuate the narrative, and
snappy one-liners often mark the dialogue. Lodge continues to expose in
masterfully ironic fashion the illusions of romantic love—in this
instance, Vic's for Robyn. The mirroring techniques of the other novels
become central here, as do comically embarrassing situations. Whatever
the validity of the charge that Lodge treats Robyn unfairly, it is note-
worthy that Lodge found narrating half of this novel from a young
woman's point of view an "interesting and rather refreshing experiment" and that making her "an avowed feminist" kept him from ignor-
ing his own sexist writing practices as easily as he had done previously.[35]
His descriptions of factories and machinery reflect the same care and
attention to telling detail as do those of the airport or air travel in *Small
World*.

While that earlier novel is obviously thick with literary parallels and
allusions, the comparable practice in *Nice Work* often consists more of
what Mary Jo Salter terms its "deceptively thin surface." Noting, for
example, that a misspelling of Robyn Penrose's first name in an official
letter causes Vic to be amusingly surprised when his "shadow" turns out
to be a female, Salter shows how the name of Lodge's heroine (over
which he labored, to strike the right note of androgyny [*AF*, 38]) recalls
the title character of Charlotte Brontë's industrial novel (*Shirley*, 1849),
Shirley having been a man's name in nineteenth-century England.
Lodge even carries the parallel one step further by naming Vic Wilcox's
secretary Shirley. In many ways the opposite of Brontë's Shirley, Lodge's
turns out to be having an affair with one of the colleagues plotting Vic's
downfall. According to Salter, this illustrates how Lodge typically "twists
parallels into contradictions."[36]

Despite its more realistic manner, *Nice Work* retains many of the
metafictional properties developed more extensively in *Changing Places*

and *Small World,* though at least one critic dismisses them as nothing more than "twitches of self-reflexivity" occasionally troubling the "[otherwise] comic composure of the novel" (Connor, 79). The narrative sometimes reflects on itself, as in Lodge's manner of first shifting its viewpoint from Vic to Robyn: "And there, for the time being, let us leave Vic Wilcox, while we travel back an hour or two in time, a few miles in space, to meet a very different character. A character who, rather awkwardly for me, doesn't herself believe in the concept of character" (*NW,* 21). On the very next page he reiterates his intention, despite Robyn's unbelief, to treat her as a character. Such touches, as well as the patently implausible complex of reversals marking the ending (which Connor calls "magically contrived" [Connor, 79]), mesh well with the extended allusion to the industrial novels of the 1850s, an allusion reinforced by the epigraphs from *Hard Times, Shirley,* Eliot's *Felix Holt,* Gaskell's *North and South,* and other works from that genre that introduce the various chapters of *Nice Work.*

But because part of the aim here is to produce a novel comparable, in its way and in its time, to what those earlier writers produced, such metafictional gestures seem belated; they reflect a postmodern reaction against the Jamesian realism to which the nineteenth-century industrial novel was but a forerunner. While effective in their way, they necessarily seem more self-conscious here than in the novels of the 1850s. What *Nice Work* does share with the earlier novels, though, and what sets it apart from the two other academic satires is its determined focus on the problems of society. Though comic elements persist throughout *Nice Work*—mainly in the personal relationship between Vic and Robyn but also in such details as the hilarious misunderstandings arising from Philip Swallow's deafness—its manner and tone generally do not encourage the degree of comic digressiveness found in *Changing Places* or *Small World.*

As noted earlier, the retrospective glow of visits to America that seems to have inspired *Changing Places* and the still-exuberant comic distance marking *Small World* had, by the mid-1980s, given way for Lodge to a more serious perspective. Perhaps Steven Connor is right to critique the parallels Lodge invokes with a novel like *North and South* and to accuse him of "anti-realistic hedging" throughout *Nice Work,* especially in its resolution (Connor, 75–76, 79). If so, Connor's related contention that this novel questions the very act of reading and the place of novels generally in contemporary society—his assertion that, like Vic and Robyn, *Nice Work* is uncertain of its own power or position in a postindustrial world controlled by finance capitalism (Connor, 82)—is most significant. Seen in this way, *Nice Work* suggests that hard times have struck not only industry or the university, or even literary criticism, but literacy itself and the uses of language as traditionally defined. While the tone of *Nice Work* is lighter than that of "A Kind of Business," its implications may be just as ominous.

Chapter Three
Literary Theory and Criticism

In a 1970 essay titled "Crosscurrents in Modern English Criticism," David Lodge described three main kinds of literary critics (and corresponding kinds of criticism) that came into prominence during the modern period. The first is the academic, who writes mainly for fellow academics and who regards literature as a body of knowledge and the study of it as a "discipline." Second is the creative writer, whose criticism is an offshoot of his own creative writing and who is therefore "less disinterested than the academic, more concerned to work out in the practice of criticism the aesthetic principles of his own art."[1] Finally comes what Lodge terms the "freelance" critic, who, despite his academic training or whatever success as a creative writer he may have enjoyed, devotes himself mainly to articles and reviews in magazines read by a broader audience than that addressed by either the first or second kind of critic. Lodge further observed that where, despite occasional overlapping, these categories had previously remained more or less secure, in the 1960s a greater "fluidity" developed, so much so that for the first time in history there were a number of critics combining all three roles.

Clearly Lodge's own critical writings have come out of this more fluid situation. In terms of variety of topics and outlets—and perhaps sheer bulk—he may have made his mark mostly as a freelancer, publishing hundreds of reviews and occasional pieces from the late 1950s onward, before becoming an academic or publishing his first novel. This kind of criticism no doubt shaded over into the second variety, especially as he gradually came to be known best as a novelist; a connection between the kinds of fiction he was writing and the kinds he favored would be difficult to avoid. But in terms of a targeted audience, he may have achieved his most sustained reputation—though a necessarily limited one—with the dozens of scholarly essays concerning literary theory and related matters that he wrote between the early 1960s and the late 1980s. These essays are mostly contained in five books published during that period: *Language of Fiction* (1966), *The Novelist at the Crossroads* (1971), *The Modes of Modern Writing* (1977), *Working with Structuralism* (1981), and *After Bakhtin* (1990). Two of these (*Language of Fiction* and

The Modes of Modern Writing) are book-length monographs in which Lodge argues for and applies a language-based theory of fiction. The other three are collections of essays, most previously published, concerning the implications and applications of Lodge's thinking about fiction or related literary and professional issues.

The period since Lodge came to his work as a reviewer and critic has, of course, seen enormous changes in theoretical commitments and critical modes within the academic community, changes that bear at least some relation to the kind of fiction (and to a less discernible extent, poetry and drama) being written, and to the general public's consideration of literature and literary matters. (Whether these developments have been salutary is, of course, a topic of considerable debate both inside and outside academe.) The theoretical legacy into which the young David Lodge came when he began his undergraduate English studies in the early 1950s was, broadly speaking, that of the so-called New Criticism. Tied to some of Coleridge's writings about poetry a century earlier and to Matthew Arnold's distinction between science and poetry, this extremely influential way of approaching literary texts emerged in England shortly after World War I, mostly through the work of I. A. Richards and William Empson, and then passed to the American literary community in the 1930s through essays by a number of writers and critics, especially John Crowe Ransom, Allen Tate, and Cleanth Brooks. In the United States, the force of the New Criticism as a way of teaching literature grew dramatically with the two textbooks Brooks coedited with the poet-novelist Robert Penn Warren, *Understanding Poetry* (1938) and *Understanding Fiction* (1943), which continued to be adopted by university teachers and reprinted as late as the 1960s.

With a nod to Coleridge's pronouncements on organic form in his *Biographia Literaria,* the New Critics stressed the inseparability of form and content in the literary work and insisted that the distinctive nature of its language—to which they attached such labels as *emotive, ambiguous,* and *paradoxical*—set it apart from other writings, particularly those concerned with factual or scientific description and demonstration. Theirs was an essentially intrinsic approach to literature that employed close textual analysis and, as Lodge himself would often note, privileged poetry above all other literary writing, including fiction. Powerful in themselves, the New Critics were aided by other influential critics who proved broadly sympathetic without becoming full-fledged practitioners of their techniques—notably by T. S. Eliot, in his downplaying the importance of the poet's personality; by F. R. Leavis, in the attentiveness

to textual detail of his own criticism; and by both Eliot and Leavis, in
the moral and cultural high seriousness they attached to the critical
enterprise. And as detractors would frequently point out, the New Critics were also aided, particularly in America, by a Cold War climate conducive to so apolitical an approach to art, literature, and education as
theirs appeared to be.

Some of the contemporary critics David Lodge mentioned most in his
early theoretical and critical writings, usually with praise, perhaps suggest his orientation at that time. These include Mark Schorer, Dorothy
Van Ghent, John Holloway, W. H. Harvey, Barbara Hardy, Wayne
Booth, W. K. Wimsatt, and Ian Watt. Schorer, Van Ghent, and Holloway published essays and books in the 1940s and early 1950s, applying to established English and American novels the same frequent cita-
tion and close reading of particular passages, and the same insistence on
the importance of verbal details that the major New Critics had given to
poems. Later Lodge would acknowledge the influence ("direct and indirect") of Schorer's 1948 essay, "Technique as Discovery," on his own
thinking and would note how "with good reason" it was one of the most
frequently reprinted of all modern critical essays.[2] Similarly, Lodge
would praise Van Ghent's *English Novel: Form and Function* (1953) as a
"dazzling and perpetually challenging achievement in explicatory novel-
criticism" and Holloway's *Victorian Sage* (1953) for showing how an
examination in long prose works might go "beyond the limits of stylistic
description" (*LF,* x).

Somewhat later, and further illustrating the potential of broadly New
Critical techniques for uncovering the art of the novel, Harvey, Hardy,
and Booth would win Lodge's praise: Harvey and Hardy for their
"attention to language" (*LF,* 30), and Booth for his concern with a theory that would accommodate all kinds of literature, particularly the
"whole body of prose fiction."[3] While admiring the entirety of Wimsatt's collection, *The Verbal Icon* (1953), Lodge was especially impressed
by the two essays that Wimsatt had coauthored with Monroe Beardsley
("The Intentional Fallacy" and "The Affective Fallacy"), presumably for
their affinity with Eliot's notions about poetic (and critical) impersonality (*LF,* xi). And while repeatedly expressing admiration for Ian Watt's
classic study *The Rise of the Novel* (1957), he would single out for inclusion in his critical anthology Watt's 1961 article "The First Paragraph of
The Ambassadors: An Explication" (Lodge called it "a model of close
analysis applied to narrative prose" [*LF,* xi]). In the same vein, Lodge
championed a renewal of interest in Vernon Lee's *Handling of Words and*

Other Studies in Literary Psychology (1923) as a pioneering attempt in the
close analysis of prose fiction.[4]

In Search of Satisfactory Fiction Theory

"I have always been a formalist critic," Lodge has written (*MM*, xi), and
indeed his critical writing is sprinkled with other similar declarations.
Accordingly, in his long search for a theory appropriate and adequate to
fiction—a search that is perhaps the most prominent ongoing strand in
the many articles and critical books he has written—and even in the
many shifts of direction and interest taken in that search, he has consistently exhibited more a refinement than any overturning of his early
allegiance to a critical mode that can broadly be termed formalist.

Certainly this allegiance is in evidence throughout *Language of Fiction*.
What Lodge argued for there was the need for a theory of fiction that
recognizes that novels, even the most unselfconsciously realistic ones,
are as much verbal constructs as those lyric poems on which the New
Criticism lavished so much explication of verbal pattern and texture.
The premise operating for Lodge here, and one often stated, is that *all*
literary texts differ from nonliterary ones in their ultimate separation
from any life prior to them or otherwise existing apart from them. Criticism of the novel in terms of its correspondence to "life" or "reality" does
not, therefore, constitute authentic literary criticism, which must exam
ine the internal structuring of the piece, and for Lodge this means a
structuring of words. The susceptibility of novels to critiques of their
"truthfulness" to reality stems, he argues, from early novelists' need to
"disguise the fact that a novel is discontinuous with real life" (by affect-
ing an illusory similarity to the nonliterary genres of history and journalism (*LF*, 42). This is a need that novelists writing more or less in the
realistic tradition (including, Lodge notes, James Joyce) have never been
able to shake off entirely but that most poets, as well as novelists working in a radical, more "poetically" self-conscious manner, do not feel.
Though "[t]he novelist moves cautiously from the real to the fictional
world, and takes pains to conceal the movement" (*LF*, 42), the final
product is fictional, and the pains of concealment involve verbal techniques and strategies as deserving of critical respect and scrutiny as
those of poets. The failure of critics to recognize the true nature of the
art of fiction accounts, Lodge suggests, for the considerably greater
muddle in the theory and criticism of fiction than that in the study of
poetry since the emergence of the New Criticism.

According to Lodge, the novelist's art had been shortchanged by traditional arguments privileging poetry and relegating fiction to an almost nonliterary (or even subliterary) status, arguments based on the nonessential distinction drawn between prose and poetry. Among such traditional arguments are the claims that poetry differs categorically from all prose (including fiction) by being connotative, emotive, and nonreferential; that poetry is less translatable than fiction (so that the "exact words" of a novel are less important); and that bad writing is more tolerable in fiction than in verse. Lodge answers all of these claims, and several others, by demonstrating, through analysis of specific texts and passages, that while such claims for poetry may in some instances point to tendencies, the relevant distinctions are not absolute. Rather, he contends, all literary writing—whether verse or prose—falls along a spectrum, so that differences are matters of degree and most novels exhibit qualities presumed to be "poetic." In the terms of the New Criticism, works of fiction have the potential to be as "ironic" as poems, the order of words constructed by the novelist is every bit as significant as that constructed by the poet, and fiction is no less unparaphrasable than poetry. (At one point he wryly observes that the New Critics' close analysis of poems is itself only a "disguised form of paraphrase" [*LF,* 35]).

All of this was meant to support the conclusion that an appropriate critical methodology for fiction, no less than that for poetry, must concern the way a writer uses and arranges words in terms of his or her sense of "aesthetic logic" (*LF,* 64). While offering the term *stylistics* for what he is seeking, Lodge finds the claims of linguists and stylisticians for a "science of style" inadequate in accounting for the literary use of language and argues for a method of "textural" (rather than wholestructure) analysis of novels that would stress repeated verbal elements and patterns—a method to be illustrated by the several essays of practical analysis making up the remainder of *Language of Fiction.* Mostly dealing with traditional novels (such as *Mansfield Park* and *Jane Eyre*) rather than with more modern (and therefore more obviously "poetic") fiction, these essays are intended to show the wide applicability of the proposed method.

But the value of these illustrative essays—indeed, their very relevance to the main theoretical argument advanced in *Language of Fiction*—is something on which reviewers could not agree. Some judged the critical essays superior to the book's theoretical sections, whereas others found them inferior.[5] Laurence Lerner, who found most of them "illuminating" and even "excellent," nevertheless contended that "only in the most general sense" do Lodge's salient discussion of the novels really concern their language. "[V]erbal analysis leads him on to discussion of setting and moral attitudes," Lerner noted, "so that he can engage with previous debates on these novels with very little sense of his offering a different approach from the other critics."[6]

This response relates to comments by Malcolm Bradbury, who felt that Lodge had not gone far enough in developing a formalism appropriate to fiction. It would be better, Bradbury argued, to explore the issue of "the structure of a novel," which Lodge had introduced but abandoned. "Lodge uses the word, inevitably enough, since he wants to talk about principles of organization which give us a sense of broader shapes and designs than those gained only by principles of verbal repetition," Bradbury pointed out.[7] Invoking neo-Aristotelianism as a possibility for Lodge yet understanding Lodge's hesitancy to discuss "plot" too extensively (lest such discussion "encourage the desire to regard it as something which transcends or is otherwise separable from language" [Bradbury 1967, 132]), Bradbury ultimately argued that what Lodge needed—and perhaps what he wanted, whether or not he realized it— was an intermediate position between that presented in *Language of Fiction* and that presented by R. S. Crane and other neo-Aristotelians.

For Bradbury, Lodge dismissed Crane too readily. However, he appreciated Lodge's sense of the "danger" in some neo-Aristotelian arguments to regard "the achievement of plot as prior to the articulation of it" (Bradbury 1967, 134). Even so, Bradbury insisted, there are certain things a writer decides before he begins to write. Lodge was no doubt right in claiming that "[c]onfusion about the novelist's art is likely to persist as long as we think of his use of language (or style) as a skill that can be distinguished from, and on occasion weighed against, his ability to create characters and actions" (*LF,* 76). But Lodge's own talk of "literary structure," "aesthetic logic," and "appropriateness" of language points to some type of parts-whole (or material-form) relationship between words and what they are used to describe or develop in a literary text, and ultimately to something not unlike the "unifying principle" idea invoked by the neo-Aristotelians.

As for what a writer may formulate prior to articulation in an actual novel (or even a poem of any considerable length), Lodge's own practice in this regard may be instructive. He has described the process by which he plans a novel in the following way:

I start a notebook on the book I think I am going to write, with brief
synopses of the plot as I see it. Then I begin the novel with a very vague
sense of where it's all going, and at various stages when I think I must
make a decision about the plot-direction I will write another synopsis. So
I accumulate about six or seven synopses which are different, and the
book itself is actually different from the last synopsis. (Haffenden, 162)

Such a process seems not fundamentally different from that envisioned by Crane, Bradbury, and others. In the neo-Aristotelian view,
"plot" and "diction" refer to tightly related, simultaneously emerging
aspects of the literary text and to corresponding skills that would be
employed simultaneously in writing it. What Lodge starts out with (his
preliminary "synopses") are not inflexible formulas but hypothetical
sketches, presumably formulated in words mostly different from those
of the emerging text. Out of such preliminary synopses comes a rough
"plot" according to which, in the neo-Aristotelian scheme, the writer
would set out to compose the novel. They thus represent the first stage
of "plotting" the novel, with the formulating and discarding of subsequent synopses constituting later stages. Intuitive or more consciously
rational changes of mind along the way—and literary history offers evidence of such mind changing in the writing of many novels—reflect the
writer's gradual discovery of a unifying principle and represent part of
the "aesthetic logic" to which Lodge refers, as do decisions about which
specific words to use and in what order. All of this satisfies Lodge's insistence that the writer creates what she or he describes, or—in the spirit
of the Mark Schorer essay that Lodge so admired—that technique is discovery.

Whether one wants to label Lodge or his discussion in *Language of
Fiction* "neo-Aristotelian" is rather beside the point. Clearly there is an
affinity, which Lodge recognized in describing the neo-Aristotelians'
"intelligent conservatism which is concerned to accommodate *all* the
relevant literature in its categories, instead of selecting the kind of literature which will serve to support a fashionable theory."[8] And certainly
the same "Aristotelian virtues" Lodge ascribed to Crane and his followers—"lucidity, logic, and scrupulous attention to evidence"[9]—are exhibited throughout *Language of Fiction*. The argument there develops in an
orderly, systematic manner, and critical jargon is carefully avoided in
favor of ordinary language. In his theoretical discussion Lodge tried to
be fair to critics whose approaches he was questioning, and he seemed
especially aware of the limitations of *all* critical analysis, his own in-

cluded. His insistence on the primacy of language in fiction and in the criticism of fiction anticipated his interest in structuralism and particularly in Jakobson and Barthes.

Certainly the same qualities of style and personality informing *Language of Fiction*—which might be seen as the first (or purely "formalist") stage of his search for a critical theory appropriate to fiction—marked as well the next stage, represented by *The Modes of Modern Writing*, published in 1977. In between had come the several essays collected in *The Novelist at the Crossroads* (1971), some of them further illustrating the methodology advocated in *Language of Fiction* and others concerned with more distant literary topics. However, one of them ("Towards a Poetics of Fiction: An Approach through Language") responded to Malcolm Bradbury's similarly titled "Towards a Poetics of Fiction: An Approach through Structure," appearing the fall 1967 issue of *Novel*. Bradbury had continued the same call for a theory of fictional structure more inclusive than "verbal modes of unity" and had cited Lodge's "recent excellent book" as nevertheless illustrative of an excessively word-centered approach to fiction.[10] In response Lodge reiterated his insistence on language as the "all-inclusive element" in every aspect and every "mental act" in the creation of a novel ("however far one projects back" [*NC*, 56]). Even so, he did modify slightly the seeming strictness of his earlier stance by allowing that all "good criticism"—using whatever approach—is a response to language "whether or not there is any explicit reference to language in the way of quotation and analysis" (*NC*, 63).

The newly emergent types of fiction Lodge discusses in the title essay of *The Novelist at the Crossroads*—such as the "fabulation" Robert Scholes and others celebrated during the early 1970s, as well as various new generic mixes—were challenging the established concept of the novel. Clearly these required accommodation in any theory purporting to cover all novels, something Lodge had been insisting on as a requirement for such a theory. Even as he acknowledged these new types as interesting challenges to the novelistic tradition, he felt compelled to suggest that "[o]bsequies over the novel" might be "premature" (*NC*, 34). This uneasiness over the novel in the wake of new modes of writing, as well as a defensiveness about realism evident in a number of his essays written about this time, related to the "problem of how to account aesthetically for the realistic novel," which he later confessed feeling unable to solve (*MMW*, x). New works of the 1960s like Truman Capote's *In Cold Blood* (1965) and Norman Mailer's *Armies of the Night* (1968)—"nonfiction novels" that, as Lodge noted, "straddled" the boundaries between history, journalism, and fiction (*NC*, 10)—raised questions about the relationship between fiction and "reality" that Bradbury felt Lodge's language-based theory failed to consider satisfactorily.

These and other problems found, at least for Lodge, a solution through his crucial encounter with structuralism, the excitement of which has already been noted. This encounter led him to write his most tightly constructed and most influential critical book, *The Modes of Modern Writing: Metaphor, Metonymy, and the Typology of Modern Literature.* While this might be seen as the "structuralist" phase in his development as a theorist, Lodge himself admitted that even his discussion of Jakobson's theory was less a summary than "a speculative expansion of it, a personal exploration of the hints, possibilities and gaps" in Jakobson's "fascinating, cryptic, endlessly suggestive" paper entitled "The Metaphoric and Metonymic Poles" (*MM*, xiii).

The Modes of Modern Writing offered, first, a rehearsal of the principal problems connected with adequately defining literature, then a development of a definition stemming from Jakobson's distinction between metaphor and metonymy, and finally an examination of that definition's implications for reading a range of twentieth-century writings in English. According to Lodge, the most fundamental problem existing definitions pose is that they tend to be either rhetorical or mimetic: they define literature in terms of either its language or its fictionality, its form or its content, its pleasure-giving capacity or its relationship to reality. Although these categories had seemed irreconcilable, Lodge insisted on their reconcilability, as he found each by itself inadequate. Invoking Barthes, Todorov, and others associated with structuralism, he suggested that literary discourse is "either self-evidently fictional or may be read as such" (*MM*, 6). But even so, the dependence of "literariness" on modes of reading is "only a half truth." "Writing requires reading for its completion," he conceded, "but also teaches the kind of reading it requires" (*MM*, 9). This dialectical relationship between reading and writing, and the differing effects of literary and nonliterary readings, is explored in terms of texts displaying varying degrees of "literary" foregrounding (ranging from a newspaper article to a poem and including some conventionally realistic writing).

The kind of theory called for at the conclusion of part 1 of *The Modes of Modern Writing* differs markedly from what Lodge had called for 10 years earlier, at a similar point in *Language of Fiction*. Here he considered two kinds of writing from the twentieth century: the modernist variety (such as that of Joyce, Woolf, and Lawrence) and that more tied to the practices of traditional realism (that of Wells, Orwell, and Greene, for example). He compared the range and sophistication of the structuralists with the relatively "limited apparatus" of the New Critics. But while finding the structuralists' insistence on the primacy of language "exhilarating," he decried their polemic against realism. Though claiming that a synthesis of European rationalism and Anglo-American empiricism could be found only in "linguistic form," he insisted that such a synthesis be "catholic": "[I]t must account for and be responsive to the kind of writing normally approached via content via the concept of imitation, as well as to the kind of writing usually approached via form via the concept of autonomy" (*MM*, 71).

Such synthesis could come, Lodge argued, through Jakobson's metaphor-metonymy distinction. Lodge's application is, indeed, a "speculative expansion" and a most intriguing one. It moves through the basic differences between the two terms as outlined by rhetoricians as well as through Jakobson's more extreme emphasis, whereby metaphor refers to the selection axis of language (substitution, based on similarity or virtual synonymy) and metonymy to the combination axis (deletion, or what Lodge termed "condensations of contextures" [*MM*, 76], based on association, such as having a part represent the whole). Lodge then reviews the corresponding types of disorder and deficiency in aphasiacs cited by Jakobson to validate the fundamental nature of his distinction (i.e., the type of disorder and deficiency concerned with selection or substitution, and that concerned with combination or contexture). Lodge schematized Jakobson by describing the metaphoric and metonymic poles, the metaphoric being related to such ideas as paradigm, drama, montage, dream symbolism, poetry, lyric, and romanticism-symbolism, and the metonymic to their opposites (syntagm, film, close-up, dream condensation-displacement, prose, epic, and realism).

Like so many other of Lodge's critical writings, *The Modes of Modern Writing* exhibits his penchant for problem solving, or at least a tendency to cast his views in a problem-solution mode. This is particularly true of the fairly lengthy section scrutinizing Jakobson's concept of "the poetic function of language." Specifically, Lodge expressed puzzlement over Jakobson's seeming inability—or unwillingness—to deal with the metonymic mode of writing despite his ready ability to identify it and indeed his tendency sometimes to ignore the metonymic mode altogether, as in his well-known claim that the poetic function "projects the principle of equivalence from the axis of selection into the axis of combination." (At this point it might be helpful to inject Graham Hough's suggestion that Jakobson's idea of the "metonymic" be thought of as "sequential—the axis of language along which a sentence is constructed, a story is told, an object described, or an argument carried on,"[11] or Lodge's later substitution of "similarity" and "continuity" for metaphor and metonymy [AB, 6].) Given the binary nature of Jakobson's theory, Lodge asked, shouldn't there be greater equity for metonymy (or "sequence," or "continuity")? He understood why poetry is easier to talk about in a linguistically based poetics, since the poet is "constantly diverted" by the arbitrary demands of prosodic patterning from combining items in the natural, logical, or temporal order pursued by the prose writer (MM, 89). But, he insisted, a "comprehensive poetics" ought to tell us why we do not feel less confident in labeling Middlemarch as literature than we do In Memoriam (MM, 92).

To deal with this problem, Lodge first moved out of the conventionally literary to compare an encyclopedia entry and a newspaper description of the same subject, the former being shown to rely more on metonymic structure. Next he examined the celebrated "literary" openings of Bleak House and Passage to India, showing how the Dickens becomes more metaphorical than the Forster. These examples led him to observe that "any prose narrative, however metaphorical, is more metonymically organized than a lyric poem" and also that the metaphorical mode tends to dispel questions concerning a text's "realism" (MM, 103, 105–7). While ultimately every literary text has metaphorical status, Lodge saw it as more "secretly sustained" in some (e.g., most novels) than in others. Metaphorical substitution is much more constrained in metonymic texts, and much more sensitive to context, than in metaphorical texts, and it tends to take the form more of simile than of outright metaphor. (Several detailed illustrations show how simile better satisfies the empirical and realistic needs of the metonymic text than does metaphor.) As for verse, where modern poets radically disrupted the combination axis on which metonymy operates, Wordsworth, for example, tried to push poetry back toward the metonymic pole. As a result, according to Lodge, Wordsworth's poetic technique, like that of metonymic texts generally (and like prose fiction under the New Criticism), has suffered from a lack of rigorous analysis.

The Modes of Modern Writing had its origins in a previously published essay titled "The Language of Modernist Fiction: Metaphor and Metonymy,"[12] which documented and discussed the tendency of the experimental modernists to depend on metaphor in their fiction and of their more traditional contemporaries to employ metonymy. While, as

Lodge admitted, parts of this essay were "embedded" in *The Modes of Modern Writing* (*MM,* xiv), the scope of his book-length investigation was much more ambitious and the range of writers and texts consulted much more extensive. Thus the third principal part of the book—which considers matters of literary history, through a range of writers and texts, in terms of the issues and distinctions developed in the earlier parts—begins with a thoughtful discussion of James Joyce (one of several that Lodge has written through the years) and concludes with a look at postmodernist fiction (Beckett, Barthelme, Vonnegut, Barth, and others). This sustained application of theory results in many interesting observations, as when Lodge notes the "cover of plausibility" under which *Ulysses* operates ("realistic fiction equipped with psychological hi-fi," he terms it [139]) or when he examines Gertrude Stein's work as both radically metonymic and radically metaphorical. The reliance on metonymic and synecdochic devices by young British poets and novelists of the 1930s is usefully linked to the "documentary" effects their writings produce. And the observation that in Philip Larkin's most characteristic poems "the metaphors are foregrounded against a predominantly metonymic background, which is in turn foregrounded against the background of the (metaphoric) poetic tradition" captures succinctly the stylistic complexity of that uncomplicated-appearing poet and has continued to be regarded as significant commentary ever since its first publication (*MM,* 217).[13]

Language of Fiction had been generally well received. Most reviewers had good things to say about its theoretical proposals, its methodology, and its textual analyses, and more than one commended what Tony Tanner termed the "international inclusiveness" of Lodge's discussion.[14] *The Modes of Modern Writing* likewise fared well with most of its readers and critics. Again Lodge was praised for bringing together disparate literary traditions, in this instance the Russian formalism represented by Jakobson and the New Critical tradition of I. A. Richards.[15] One reviewer noted the "mutually beneficial trade agreement" (rather than "wholesale defection") involved in Lodge's encounter with French structuralism, as well as the "uncluttered and unskewed sense of literary history" evidenced in his analyses of writers and texts.[16] Another commented on the persuasiveness of his use of the developed typology to enrich our reading experience ("We should read fiction more closely and systematically for having read this book").[17] When Lodge's next critical book appeared in the early 1980s, *The Modes of Modern Writing* was still being cited as a model of "critical tact" and praised for its "sure-footed lucidity, the crispness of its exposition."[18]

In his preface to *Working with Structuralism* (1981), Lodge wrote of the "state of crisis" that had befallen literary criticism, principally the increasing gap between academic criticism and ordinary book reviewing as well as the parallel gap within the universities between teaching and research—"the same individual giving bland, old-fashioned tutorials on *Middlemarch* in the morning, and in the afternoon reducing it to something resembling algebra, or a treatise on phenomenology badly translated from the French, for the edification of a small peer group."[19] Some years later, he would complain more sharply of the "barrier of noncomprehension between academic and non-academic discussion of literature" (*AB,* 7). In each instance he noted his own complex situation, as a participant in both the academic and nonacademic literary communities, as both professor-scholar and novelist-reviewer. By the late 1980s he was finding this "bridging posture" increasingly untenable.

What Lodge had banked on earlier to help bridge the gap was the analytical apparatus he had developed from Jakobson and the structuralists. Most of the essays in *Working with Structuralism* represent extensions (or applications) of the manner of classifying and analyzing literature texts described and illustrated in *The Modes of Modern Writing* and were intended to popularize such practices beyond a narrow academic circle. But what he came later to hope would reconnect university teaching, academic criticism, book reviewing, and novel writing—for himself, as well as for a sizable public—were the insights of Mikhail Bakhtin, with whose work he became familiar as translation made it available in the 1980s. Roughly half of the essays that would make up *After Bakhtin* (1990) carried the force of Lodge's fruitful encounter with Bakhtin's ideas and represented his last attempts to pull together increasingly disparate interest groups.

For all of their useful insights into structuralist theory, as well as their persuasiveness on the applicability of the analytical tools structuralism affords, both *The Modes of Modern Writing* and *Working with Structuralism* appear limited beside what Lodge accomplishes in *After Bakhtin.* As he describes and uses them, the basic Bakhtinian opposition of monologism and dialogism, as well as the concept of the carnivalesque, seems more accessible and more flexible than Jakobson's metaphor-metonymy pairing. Because Bakhtin, too, was primarily interested in prose fiction, the concepts and distinctions—and indeed, his overall theory—are inherently more novelistic and satisfy Lodge's intentions better than those of Jakobson, whose greater attention to metaphor paralleled that of the New Critics to poetry. And if Bakhtin's work was largely unheralded—

in fact, largely unknown in the West—until after his death, Lodge nevertheless credits the belatedly discovered Bakhtin with having contributed to contemporary theory "a timely reaffirmation of the writer's creative and communicative power" in contrast with structuralism and poststructuralism's downplaying of the writer (*AB*, 7).

Unlike almost all of the theories Lodge had previously encountered, Bakhtin's helped him answer the question of the value of novels—and thus to understand why it was acceptable, even commendable, that he preferred writing fiction to all other literary modes: "It explained to me why, as a novelist, I have been drawn to pastiche, parody and travesty—often of the very kind of discourse I produce in my capacity as an academic critic" (*AB*, 7). Bakhtin caused him, too, to rethink some of the assumptions marking his earlier search for an adequate fiction theory. The realization that "narrative is a kind of language in itself that transcends the boundaries of natural languages" led him to recant his earlier tendency "to reduce all questions of meaning to questions of specific verbal usage" (*AB*, 75). Rather than the defensive posture he took on behalf of classic fiction, Lodge learned from Bakhtin some significant ways in which the novel is superior to the "canonized genres" of poetry and drama. He realized that instead of seeking out those portions of a novel exhibiting fiction's peculiar advantage over lyric poetry—dialogism (or polyphony or heteroglossia, to use Bakhtin's other terms)—ironically he too often had tended to play the New Critical, poetry centered game by seeking and citing passages more given to a single voice and monologism (*AB*, 76). In a spirit similar to that of Wayne Booth's introduction to the English translation of Bakhtin's *Problems of Dostoyevsky's Poetics* (an introduction that Lodge cites), he says that knowing Bakhtin's work earlier, even knowing key passages from Bakhtin, might have saved him from some "theoretical cul-de-sacs" in his thinking about fiction (*AB*, 7).

Most of the essays in *After Bakhtin* reflect this same sense of excited discovery. Despite having been prepared over a number of years and published separately, they constitute a remarkably unified body of writing. In more than one Lodge offers a characteristically lucid exposition of the salient features and concepts of Bakhtin's thinking. In "The Novel Now—Theories and Practices," originally a paper delivered in 1987 at a Brown University conference marking the 20th anniversary of *Novel*, the journal he helped found, he reviews complications that had arisen during the preceding 30 years in the relationship between writers and critics, complications due largely to the various theoretical upheavls among academics. He notes how the novelist has always been caught between wanting to be universal and wanting to be empirically specific and how uncomfortable it is to be hounded by autobiographical readings of one's own novels—thus the attractiveness of the thinking of Barthes, Paul de Man, and others in combating a "reductively empiricist reading" of fiction (*AB*, 16). In a move characteristic of his determination to join disparate communities, Lodge then cites Bakhtin for transcending both the humanist and poststructuralist viewpoints and for offering a "linguistics of the parole" broad enough to accommodate both and to accommodate the conflicting impulses tugging at the novelist (*AB*, 21).

In another essay ("Mimesis and Diegesis in Modern Fiction"), he invokes Bakhtin's typology of literary discourse to formulate the differences between classic realism, modernist fiction, and the postmodern variety. The classic novel is said to be characterized by a "balanced and harmonized combination" of direct speech of the author and "represented speech" (the second of Bakhtin's categories, which includes not only the quoted words of characters [Plato's "mimesis"] but also their reported thoughts and feelings). Modernist fiction involved the increasing suppression or displacement of diegesis. Using Bakhtin's third category, "doubly-oriented speech," Lodge examines passages from *Ulysses* as examples of "pseudodiegesis" ("mimesis not of a character's speech but of [another] discourse" [*AB*, 36]). But according to Lodge, because modernism could not abolish the author entirely, postmodernism has restored it by foregrounding diegesis against a mimetic background, so that "the stream of consciousness has turned into a stream of narration" (*AB*, 44). He pinpoints the value of metafictional self-consciousness for a practicing novelist like him as being "a way of continuing to exploit the resources of realism while acknowledging their conventionality" (*AB*, 43).

Other applications of Bakhtin proved equally useful for Lodge. In "*Middlemarch* and the Idea of the Classic Realist Text," he uses Bakhtin to help explain his sense that earlier novels were not necessarily as transparent as modernist and poststructuralist critics have supposed. He suggests that the old mimesis-diegesis distinction is not as clear cut as is often thought, so that rather than displaying a controlling authorial omniscience, the diegesis of *Middlemarch* is often "contaminated" by mimesis. George Eliot was aware of the indeterminacies of her writing, he argues: its discourse is never entirely unambiguous but rather, like all language, "inexhaustible" (*AB*, 50). An even more striking reading of a

standard novel emerges in "Lawrence, Dostoyevsky, Bakhtin," in which
Lodge appropriates the ideas of "dialogism" and "polyphony" to explain
many features of *Women in Love*—such as its erratic movement, the con-
tingency of its plotting, its fluid handling of point of view, and its radical
shifts in narrative style—that make it singular and strange even among
Lawrence's novels. Lodge's intelligence as a reader and the power of
Bakhtin's theory of the novel reinforce each other here, as at several
other points in this book. And Lodge refuses to be simply the blind
admirer; in the title essay, for instance, he reflects on the confusion
caused by Bakhtin's enigmatic references to monologic discourse.

   With the essays of *After Bakhtin* Lodge clearly entered a "poststructuralist" phase in his quest for a satisfactory theory of fiction, though it
was a phase obviously antithetical to much of the thinking to which that
label is usually applied. Both the antithesis and the usefulness that
Lodge found in Bakhtin for formulating it are exemplified in the final
sentences of the title essay: "Barthes says: because the author does not
coincide with the language of the text, he does not exist. Bakhtin says, it
is precisely because he does not so coincide that we must posit his existence" (*AB*, 99). This, in turn, connects with another essay in the collection, "Milan Kundera and the Idea of the Author in Modern Criticism,"
in which Lodge notes that Kundera's fiction, even though it exhibits no
secure authorial position, seems the work of a distinctive, self-conscious
author. He goes on not only to link with humanism and capitalism the
idea of the author that Barthes and Foucault sought to discredit but to
connect collective, anonymous authorship with "eras when slavery and
serfdom were deemed ethically acceptable." Further, he insists:

> Copyright is only one of many "rights"—freedom of speech, freedom of
> movement, freedom of religious worship—which the bourgeois ideology
> of liberal humanism has claimed for the individual human being. Only
> those who take such freedoms for granted in their daily lives could per-
> haps contemplate with satisfaction the obsolescence of the idea which
> sustains and justifies them. (*AB*, 157)

Having referred to the loss of citizenship that Milan Kundera suffered
on the publication of *The Book of Laughter and Forgetting,* Lodge observes,
"That a government should be stung into taking such revenge on an
individual author is perhaps a good reason for wanting to defend the
idea of authorship" (*AB*, 158).

   Such aggressive defense of the closely related concepts of individual-
ity and authorship against poststructuralist attack ties in with concerns

that date back to Lodge's entry into academic writing. Throughout his academic career he had been attracted to the promise of a more objective, more rigorous brand of literary analysis and criticism that formalism and structuralism held out—more objective and rigorous than that of the New Critical or Leavisite approaches or than the subjective interpretive and critical modes they had sought to supplant. He had been willing to entertain more complex views of authorship than the various twentieth-century offshoots of romanticism had engendered (such as the idea of the "implied author" that Wayne Booth put forth in the early 1960s) and to allow for the contributions to writing made by the force of community and by shared codes. But Lodge was never willing to relinquish entirely the idea of the individual author as the intending composer of the text. His persisting belief in authorship, of course, tied in with his ongoing defense of classic realism (thus his joy in discovering a forceful ally in Bakhtin) and with his championing of certain largely realistic authors and novels emerging in recent decades. Not surprisingly, it ties, too, to Lodge's repeated insistence that the political viewpoint of realism is liberalism and to his own self-identification as a liberal.

Manifestations

Lodge has reviewed for a variety of publications, mostly mainstream British outlets, such as the *Spectator,* the *Encounter,* the *New Statesman,* and the *TLS* early on, and the *London Review of Books,* the *Sunday Times,* and the *Independent* later. He regularly contributed pieces to the Catholic biweekly the *Tablet* until the early 1980s, when he began reviewing occasionally for the *New York Times Book Review* and the *New York Review of Books.* Whether Lodge's academic writings, particularly those concerned with literary theory, have influenced his book reviewing—or whether they could, since his first published reviews came before his first academic articles—is perhaps questionable. And of course, the reviews might have influenced his academic writings. Nevertheless, there are significant links between the two bodies of his work.

For one thing, Lodge's hundreds of reviews of literary works—mostly novels—have tended from the beginning to reflect this same respect for authorship and for the idea of the author. When a single novel has been in question, such respect has often taken the form of an extended introductory account of the reviewed writer's previous work, with the aim of fitting the text under consideration into some sort of framework suggested by that earlier work, or of measuring it against the author's other writings. Of course, such a practice is hardly unusual in book reviewing; it is a convention, which illustrates the increasing gap between contemporary academic writing about literature and writing for a more general readership. But it seems unusually developed in Lodge's hands and somehow more central to his purposes as a reviewer than to those of many others. Thus his 1980 critique of John Barth's *Letters* begins with a lengthy description of *The Sot-Weed Factor* and *Giles Goat-Boy,* to suggest that the cleverness of *Letters* is more strained than that of the two earlier books.[20] Such disparate works as Milan Kundera's *Unbearable Lightness of Being,* Jeanette Winterson's *Passion,* and Robertson Davies' *Lyre of Orpheus* are approached in the same manner, to expose the relative shortcomings of the latest novel.[21] Each of these reviews, as well as many others, develops gradually into an essay at least as much about the novelist as about the novel, and usually with the effect of defining the author's characteristic excellences despite the shortcomings of the book being reviewed. Of course, with a fully established writer of the stature of E. M. Forster or even Kingsley Amis, such framing is hardly necessary, though the question of how *Maurice* or Amis's *Old Devils* fits into its author's work as a whole is at least implicitly asked (and answered) in Lodge's critique.[22]

Lodge's theoretical commitments are manifested more openly in the critical collections he has edited. As noted earlier in connection with *Small World,* these two collections reflect the considerable change the study of literature underwent in the late 1960s and the 1970s. But they also show changes in Lodge's interests and commitments, changes that informed the direction his theoretical and critical writings took. In both volumes Lodge included, besides the basic chronological ordering of the selections, an arrangement according to critical school or approach. Under this alternative arrangement each collection presents one grouping similar to that in the other, labeled in *Twentieth-Century Literary Criticism* (1972) "Formal Criticism—Structural and Rhetorical Analysis—'New Criticism'—Literary Techniques and Conventions" (or what M. H. Abrams, who is also included here, might call "work-centered" or "objective" criticism), and in *Modern Criticism and Theory* (1988) "Formalist, structuralist and post-structuralist poetics, linguistics and narratology." As suggested earlier—and as this change in labeling confirms—the contents of the two collections mark a shift away from writing in English and from more practical criticism and analysis toward more broadly theoretical writings by Europeans.

In addition (and directly related to Lodge's own theoretical investigations), of the 50 critics included in the 1972 collection, 31 were, by Lodge's account, sufficiently concerned with a single literary mode (poetry, prose fiction, or drama) to be so designated. But of these 31, fewer than half deal with fiction. In the 1988 collection, on the other hand, all of those theorists concerned with any mode in particular (essentially only Bakhtin, Todorov, and Barthes) discuss fiction exclusively, which suggests the heightened attention given fiction in the English-speaking world since the 1960s, Lodge's own preoccupation with new fiction theory, and the belated recognition of relevant continental contributions in this area. Interestingly, Roland Barthes appears in both collections (the only figure to do so). However, his essay in the earlier collection ("Criticism as Language") is clearly a product of his earlier, structuralist period—indeed, it is the only piece in that collection reflective of structuralism—while the two Barthes essays included in the later collection ("The Death of the Author" and "Textual Analysis: Poe's 'Valdemar' ") reflect decidedly poststructuralist leanings.

Because so many of Lodge's novels concern university teachers or students—most of whom are, in fact, writers and literature specialists—that literary theory should turn up openly in his fiction is hardly remarkable. Of course, it can be reflected in particular techniques, such as the narrative doubling in *Ginger, You're Barmy,* which, according to Robert Morace, anticipates Lodge's later interest in Gerard Genette's structuralist theory of narrative grammars (Morace, 117), or the carnivalesque atmosphere in which Lodge bathes the International James Joyce Symposium in part 4 of *Small World,* suggestive of his fascination with Bakhtin in the early 1980s. That Jonathan Browne in *Ginger, You're Barmy* is boning up on Empson's *Seven Types of Ambiguity* as he contemplates graduate study in English after his release from the army reminds us of the time when the Empson was a set text for practical criticism in universities and its methodology provided an established way of analyzing literature—a way further confirmed by the research Adam Appleby is conducting in *The British Museum Is Falling Down* as well as by the various literary discussions that punctuate that novel. These two novels belong to that period in Lodge's career when he was still working off the New Critical and Leavisite models in his quest for a satisfactory fiction theory.

The stages of this quest are most evident in the three academic satires, which correspond roughly to the shift among Lodge's three principal critical books. In *Changing Places,* as in *Language of Fiction,* the orientation of everyone—even the trendy Morris Zapp—is still basically New Critical and humanist. *Small World,* like *The Modes of Modern Writing* (and like *Modern Criticism and Theory),* moves into structuralist and poststructuralist concerns and debates. And the affinity, pointed out earlier, between *Nice Work* and the essay "A Kind of Business," extends to many of the other pieces in *After Bakhtin* in their critique of the extremes of poststructuralism—as well as to the "elegiac ring" (*AB,* 8) that Lodge sees marking the spin-offs from this final period of his career as a university teacher, of which *Nice Work* itself surely counts as one. Seen in retrospect, those parts of *Nice Work* that show Robyn Penrose teaching—or Vic Wilcox demonstrating what he has learned from her—take on this elegiac tone, as they speak to what Lodge was leaving behind. Were there not some abiding affection for teaching, for the university, and for formal literary study—and perhaps even a small measure of regret as he felt compelled to abandon them "for a number of converging reasons"—the satire of *Nice Work* might have been harsher.

Chapter Four

Novels about Catholics and Catholicism

On the basis of his novels, and despite the many subjects they deal with, it might be argued that ever since David Lodge started writing fiction, as a teenager, his most sustained concern has been religion, particularly Catholicism as practiced in England during the latter half of the twentieth century. Dennis Jackson has noted how Lodge became "vitally interested" in Catholicism at St. Joseph's Academy, his London grammar school (Jackson, 471). The majority of his novels have centered on issues of religious belief and observance, with no fewer than half stressing the Roman Catholic identity of their central characters. Most of Lodge's American readers would probably be surprised to know this. They, like most of his other readers outside Britain, first became aware of him through his satires on academe; probably for them his reputation has rested more or less exclusively on those three novels. And except for *How Far Can You Go?* (1980)—retitled *Souls and Bodies* for the American market—all of Lodge's fiction dealing extensively with Catholicism predated the first academic satire, *Changing Places,* with which he himself has equated his first real success as a writer.

Interestingly, even as Lodge has persisted in asserting that his novels are principally "about" academics and Catholics,[1] he has kept the two categories mostly separate in his writing. Religion seemingly has no place in the fictional world of this academic satirist. But for the briefly mentioned fact that Morris Zapp is a Jew or Fulvia Morgana a Catholic—which seem more sociological than religious designations— no religious labels attach to the characters of these novels. We learn nothing about the religious backgrounds, beliefs, or practices of any of them. While it seems plausible, for example, that in *Nice Work,* the most English of the three academic satires, Vic Wilcox and Robyn Penrose might share a Church of England upbringing—as, for that matter, might Philip Swallow and many of the other Rummidge academics, as well as some of Vic's business associates—we are not told whether they do, and it seems not to matter. Religion enters not at all into their deliberations over personal or professional problems. Their modes of living and thinking are wholly secular.

Of course, in the English-speaking world of the late twentieth century, and especially in England itself—where Christian observance often seems to have disappeared—a neglect of religion and religious issues in fiction feels wholly acceptable and perfectly in line with most contemporary literary practice. But because this is in marked contrast with what we find in most of David Lodge's earlier novels, right up to the 1980s, it suggests an important shift of emphasis as he has altered the focus and broadened the appeal of his writing. What now seems notable about those first novels—and what presumably still seemed acceptable in the decades during which they were written—is the assumption that religion must occupy if not the center, at least some fairly significant place in narrative and characterization.

Consider the two novels discussed in chapter 1. The casting of Jonathan Browne as the main figure in the punitive comedy *Ginger, You're Barmy* depends on the contrast provided by Mike Brady, who increasingly, even to the very end of the novel, helps define Browne's weaknesses. Lodge has recounted how it was not enough to cast one as an idealist and the other as a pragmatist; to this split he added the explicitly religious opposition between the Catholic and "agnostic" outlooks. Given the heavily British context of the novel, Browne's outlook understandably could be taken to be that of a lapsed Protestant (perhaps an Anglican), especially by readers unacquainted with the Catholic Lodge's admission that Brady-Browne represented a split within himself. And as a further foil to Jonathan Browne, Lodge augmented the Irish Catholic (and red-haired revolutionary) Mike Brady with Percy Higgins, whose family, not incidentally, were not only Catholics but "Old Catholics" (those who had kept their faith unwaveringly through the penal era) and whose innocence—an anomaly among the rough army recruits—had been nurtured by a seminary education preparing him for the priesthood.

Once Percy's hopelessness in camp and the likelihood of his being bullied become apparent, both Brady and Browne are acutely sensitive to religion as an issue, if not a barrier, between them. The resulting tension surfaces immediately after Percy's death on the firing range. Although Mike has helped Jonathan understand the nature of Percy's upbringing and the minority position of his people even among English Catholics, Jonathan resents Browne's arrogant way of explaining what suicide would have meant to Percy. "Why did Catholics always assume

that their theology was beyond anyone else's comprehension," he wonders (*GB,* 99). But when Jonathan counters that how Percy's death is
interpreted by the living can hardly affect Percy himself in his present
state, it is Mike's turn to be indignant: "The trouble with you Agnostics
is that you regard theology as a kind of cold mathematical science like
economics. It's not like that at all" (*GB,* 100). Although their discussion
calms down, and though nothing so starkly theological appears anywhere else in the novel, it resonates throughout the ensuing differences
in outlook and behavior between Brady and Browne and even into the
"comic" resolution featuring them.

Like Percy Higgins but to a much lesser degree, Timothy Young, in
Out of the Shelter, is an innocent. And as with Percy, it is clearly a Catholic
upbringing that marks Timothy's initial response to the new situation in
which he finds himself. Catholicism provides the terms both of his caution and of his entry into a more sophisticated, adult outlook during his
time in Germany. It sets him apart from the others he meets there, especially from Don Kowalski, who insists, "I am not a Christian. I'm not
anything" (*OS,* 159), but also from his sister, whom a disillusioning love
affair and a generally liberated lifestyle overseas have caused to stray
from the Catholic observances of her youth. The epilogue depicts Timothy many years later, happily married, in pursuit of a promising career,
and still a practicing Catholic. Although he seems to have married a
Protestant, he assures his sister Kate that religion is "no problem"
between him and his wife. "Sheila doesn't mind the kids being brought
up as Catholics," he says. "I don't mind her planning when to have them"
(*OS,* 268). Having Timothy enter into a "mixed" marriage reflects not
only Lodge's own family background—his mother was a Catholic, his
father a "non-Catholic" (as, according to Lodge, "one said in those same
circles implying there was no positive form of faith outside the One True
Church" [*WO,* 2])—but also that after World War II over half the marriages in England involving Catholics were "mixed."[2] During Timothy
and Kate's epilogue discussion, she remarks that she herself has "gone
back" to the Church. "Mind you, it's all changed," she notes. "More like
the Protestants, now, wouldn't you say? It's funny, I miss the Latin
mass, though I used to find it boring" (*OS,* 268). Her reference to
changes in the Church, like Timothy's to his presumably Protestant
wife's family planning scheme, acknowledges the reality of how English
Catholics increasingly had been living, a reality Lodge would explore
more extensively in *The British Museum Is Falling Down* and *Souls and
Bodies.*

In terms of when they were written, *Ginger, You're Barmy* and *Out of the Shelter* straddle the divide created by the Second Vatican Council. But because the bulk of the action in *Out of the Shelter* is set well before Vatican II and because young Timothy (like young David Lodge) was clearly a product of that earlier time, the epilogue seems much more up to date sociologically than the rest of the novel. Timothy and his parents observed their religion rather scrupulously: "Sunday was mainly devoted to Church. They usually went to the ten o'clock Mass on Sunday mornings, unless they were going to Communion. In which case they went to the eight-thirty, because of the fast. Sometimes they went to Benediction in the afternoon" (*OS*, 42).

While David Lodge experienced the same wartime dislocation as Timothy, and while his postwar home's location was similar, geographically and socially, to Timothy's ("a drab nineteenth-century London suburb, mainly lower-middle-class and working-class in social composition" [*WO*, 2]), religion seems not to have been so vital a force in his upbringing. Though he remembers many things about his Catholic childhood, including early attendance at Mass, what appears to have impressed him most about it was its atypicality:

> My mother was a dutiful but undemonstrative daughter of the Church. I was given a Catholic schooling, but the atmosphere of the home was not distinctively Catholic. . . . [T]here was little of the regular and complex social interaction with parish clergy and laity that is a feature of the typical large devout Catholic family. I had no brothers or sisters to reinforce the Catholic cultural code, and my friends in the same street happened not to be Catholic. The result was that as a child I always felt something of an outsider in the Church. . . . I never, for instance, learned to serve at Mass, as did most of my Catholic peers. (*WO*, 29–30)

The context of these remarks was a 1976 essay titled "Memories of a Catholic Childhood," first published in the *Tablet,* the Catholic biweekly magazine founded in the 1840s. That Lodge contributed dozens of pieces to the *Tablet* (for a period of over 20 years, starting in the early 1960s) as well to other Catholic publications suggests his long-standing concern with broadly Catholic issues and his ongoing identification with an English Catholic community.

Of course, much about his upbringing as he recalls it did resemble that of Timothy Young. And how atypical it was, especially by the time he was recalling it, is at least somewhat questionable. The distinct subculture that Catholics had constituted in England up to the 1940s, as

well as their corollary sense of exclusivity, had begun to disintegrate
rapidly after the war, aided by such developments as the wartime evacu-
ation of civilians from urban areas largely inhabited by Catholics, the
1944 Education Act's strengthening of Catholic secondary education
and related weakening of local parish control, and the general change in
outlook fostered by the postwar welfare state.[3] This greater sense of
belonging to an inclusive British culture was helped, too, by an increase
in the number of Catholics from three million in 1940 to over five million in the early 1970s, especially in proportion to the Protestants.[4] Even
so, as late as 1967 it appeared that while Anglicans and other Protestants were growing increasingly lax in their religious observance,
Catholic attendance at Mass was continuing undiminished.[5] If being
Catholic no longer meant being wholly distinct from the rest of society,
it had not ceased to have considerable meaning for its adherents.

How all of this played out has fascinated David Lodge. His early
sense of being an "outsider" in the Church may explain his affinity not
only for James Joyce but for writers who had converted to Catholicism
(Greene, Waugh, Spark, and others). Yet Lodge has noted how, unlike
Joyce, he left school to attend a wholly secular local university—which
he has amusingly called "the original 'godless university,' founded by
Jeremy Bentham, whose wizened, mummified corpse is seated in a glass
case under the College dome, as if mocking commentary on the Christian doctrine of the resurrection of the body"—and how being Catholic
at University College, London, was no disadvantage by the 1950s but
rather enabled one "to strike a rather interesting, almost exotic pose
before one's peers" (WO, 60). But despite the departure from the past
undeniably represented by the postwar integration of Catholics into
British society, an even more striking sense of change and upheaval
would confront English Catholics as Vatican II approached. Vatican II
and key spin-offs from it would segment the history of English Catholicism as nothing else in this century. It would also segment David
Lodge's writings on religion.

The Picturegoers

Lodge's first published novel was completed a good while before it
appeared in print. Like the book Jon Browne is writing in *Ginger, You're
Barmy, The Picturegoers* was written mostly while Lodge was in the army
(1955–1957); he finished it soon after returning to civilian life. Though
he eventually found a publisher, his return to the university and the

need to complete what turned out to be a lengthy M.A. thesis—over 700 pages ("monstrously long," according to Lodge [*PW,* 71])—kept him from revising his novel immediately and delayed its publication until 1960 (Haffenden, 149). Lodge has called *The Picturegoers* "a very imma- ture piece of work" (Bergonzi 1970, 111). Though strictly speaking it was not his first novel—an earlier one, titled *The Devil, The World, and the Flesh,* written when he was about 18, had failed to find a publisher— its "immaturity" probably relates to that earlier effort, at least to the extent that one or two episodes and incidents from *The Devil, The World, and the Flesh* were retained in *The Picturegoers* (Bergonzi 1970, 108).

To be sure, *The Picturegoers* exhibits many of the excesses often associ- ated with youthful writing. Sometimes there is too much authorial com- mentary and analysis, as in the three pages of what Henry James surely would call "telling" (as opposed to "showing") in which Lodge presents his principal male character's meditation on his religious character.[6] Not even the skillfully deployed indirect discourse with which Lodge attempts to vary and dramatize Mark Underwood's thought processes can save those pages from tedium, in contrast to the more exciting cor- responding section of *Portrait of an Artist as a Young Man.* A few of the scenes showing Mark with his girlfriend Clare Mallory or with her younger sister Patricia likewise seem excessively prolonged. Images and comparisons here often feel forced and even misplaced, as when we are told, when Patricia is leaving the movie theater, that "[d]epression and worry seeped under the exit door, and trickled down the aisle to meet her," or when an equally depressed young man elsewhere in the theater is said to have "left his heart on the floor with [an] empty ice-cream car- ton" (*P,* 70, 141). Entire scenes can seem excessive, more authorial exer- cises than integral or necessary parts of an unfolding story—such as the meeting between two charwomen at the theater (*P,* 183–85), which feels more like an opportunity for Lodge to show his considerable skills at dialogue (and dialect) than a functional part of the novel. Such criti- cisms relate to Dennis Jackson's complaints about the novel's extrane- ous elements, excess of characters, and insufficiency of dramatic inter- play between some of them and about the disconnectedness of its second half (Jackson, 471). Perhaps they relate also to Morace's contention that the novel is marred by "melodramatic excess" (Morace, 110).

But despite such problems, *The Picturegoers* is of considerable interest even 40 years after it was written and a valuable reflection on a certain slice of British life and society in the 1950s. Certainly its 1960 reviewers appreciated it, one of them complimenting Lodge's "alternation of dic-

tion, tone, and rhythm" and declaring the entire effort "quite funny."[7]
Many years later Bernard Bergonzi, who had read *The Picturegoers* when
it first appeared and had felt an "overpowering sense of recognition" of
his own lower-middle-class Catholic upbringing, continued to find it
"vigorous in its writing and successfully complex in its organization."[8]
Dennis Jackson has seen in many passages Lodge's promising future as
comic novelist and prose stylist (Jackson, 471), and Robert Morace has
praised the novel's "reach" and its "carnivalized forms," the number and
extent of which, he suggests, may connect *The Picturegoers* more to
Ulysses than to *Dubliners* or *Portrait of the Artist* (Morace, 112–13). Probably the most elaborate and sustained positive response to this novel,
though, has come from Park Honan, who rather early saw in Lodge's
deployment of multiple viewpoints a celebration of the novelistic
medium as essentially cinematic (Honan 1972, 167–72). For this reason, as recently as 1990 he pronounced *The Picturegoers* one of Lodge's
three finest novels.[9]

The specifics of Honan's case for *The Picturegoers* relate to Lodge's
sense, which he would express in *The Novelist at the Crossroads,* that traditional realism had run its course as a source of inspiration for writers and
entertainment for readers, coupled with a skepticism regarding the
wholesale abandonment of realistic devices by many contemporary writers, especially in America. According to Honan, *The Picturegoers* represented a way out of the dilemma facing novelists—in the linguistic
"finesse" with which it treats ordinary experience, the manner in which
"the novelist's own camera . . . is set behind the characters' eyes," and
the unobtrusiveness of Lodge's method ("[almost] perfect cinematism
. . . the novelist is not linguistically on view at all" [Honan 1972, 167,
171). This was a method Lodge would pursue further, though less successfully, in *Ginger, You're Barmy* and *Out of the Shelter.*

The importance of movies and moviegoing in this novel is undeni-
able. Its title points to the single activity uniting all of its many characters and to its most prominent setting. It is divided into three major sections, each related to a particular Saturday at the movies (in autumn,
spring, and early summer, respectively) and to the concerns and behaviors of various characters that flow toward and away from picturegoing
at these particular times. Besides Mark, Clare, and Patricia, we are presented with the rest of the Mallory family—in particular Clare and
Patricia's parents and their younger brother Patrick—with whom Mark
is renting a room. The novel's cast also includes Father Kipling, the
Mallorys' parish priest in Brickley, the lower-middle-class area of South

London where they live (its name and atmosphere inspired by the Brockley area of London where Lodge grew up); Mr. Berkeley, the middle-aged manager of the local cinema; and Len and Bridget, a young couple engaged to be married. These and several others, all of whom are followed throughout the novel, constitute Lodge's picturegoers.

But going to the movies is more than a uniting activity among fictional persons here, and the Palladium theater is more than the "structural peg" Jackson terms it (Jackson, 471). The various characters provide Lodge with hypothetical examples—case studies, in a sense—for an extended examination of the place of film in British society, its relationship to more traditional cultural centers, and its position among other forms of popular entertainment, an examination significantly written and set when the burst of mass consumerism that had increasingly characterized the 1930s, but was temporarily interrupted by the war, had been resumed and was being modified by postwar innovations. Such an examination was partly inspired by Richard Hoggart's *Uses of Literacy,* which appeared while Lodge was writing *The Picturegoers* (P, xi).

By implication—and as Honan would have it, by the very techniques employed in its presentation—the novel's discussion of the impact and meaning of film concerns the novel's place in society as well, particularly as a young writer like Lodge might be seeking to reconcile the traditions inscribed in the canonized fiction of the past with the more popular trends of the present. If, as Honan suggests, Mark Underwood is a "rather restless media student" (Honan 1972, 167), his restlessness relates in part to the fact that, like David Lodge in the early 1950s, he is also an undergraduate English literature major and an aspiring novelist.

The narrative records differing responses to particular films. Reactions to a steamy main feature of adulterous love titled *When the Cat's Away* (starring a Hollywood goddess with an equally satirical name, Amber Lush) range from young Patrick's bored indifference and preference for detective films to Father Kipling's shocked indignation and include Len and Bridget's disregard for whatever serves as backdrop to the rare couple of hours they can be together, Mrs. Mallory's mild disapproval of something she considers unfit for her children, Mr. Mallory's enthusiasm for the voluptuous Amber Lush, and Patricia's preoccupations with personal problems.

The priest shares with Patrick an innocence as to what will happen in *While the Cat's Away.* This is Father Kipling's first visit to the Palladium, prompted partly by curiosity as to what has been attracting so many of his parishioners and partly by the mistaken notion that *Song of Bernadette* will be shown on this particular evening. His amusing discovery of his mistake provides Lodge with an opportunity to defamiliarize film conventions:

> The scene melted into a picture of a really execrable hat—a kind of inverted lampshade decorated with seaweed. This time Father Kipling laughed with the rest of the audience. Very cleverly the picture was lowered to take in the wearer's face—an angry, rather hard-faced woman. She was having a furious argument with the man seen earlier, now dressed in a light-coloured suit. Suddenly it flashed upon Father Kipling that this was happening in the past. He felt quite pleased with his perspicacity, and wondered if everyone else around him had understood. (*P,* 63)

Once the priest realizes he has come on the wrong night, Lodge cannot resist a bit more fun:

> There was no reason why he should continue any longer to witness this unsavoury performance. Now, for instance, she seemed about to undress—well really! Good gracious, she *was* undressing! But this was disgraceful. Why one could almost see her. . . . He could swear he could see her. . . .
> Behind his spectacles, Father Kipling strained his eyes to see if he could see her. (*P,* 67–68)

The second part of the novel looks in on these same figures six months later, when the Palladium is featuring a foreign feature titled *The Bicycle Thieves.* This time the responses are less varied, as most patrons are either bored or puzzled by what they see. For Mr. Mallory it seems a "worthy, well-made film" but depressing and definitely "[n]ot his idea of a Saturday night's entertainment" [*P,* 129]). His daughter Clare appreciates it even less, despite Mark Underwood's enthusiastic analysis of its technique and meaning. Indeed, her feelings for Mark have progressed so that she can hardly concentrate on what he is saying: "There was nothing of interest to her in the present conversation except as a means of promoting their intimacy and retaining his arm around her waist" (*P,* 144).

Mark's didactic account of *The Bicycle Thieves* links with his response earlier to *When the Cat's Away,* which he regarded as formulaic and predictable, and with his analysis of audiences and their needs and tastes. Honan maintains that Mark experiences a "McLuhanite epiphany" concerning the picturegoers ("Like fish in a glass tank, their stupid, gaping faces were pressed to the window on a world they could never hope to

achieve") when he realizes that they are finding "a substitute for religion
. . . a more satisfactory conception of paradise than the sexless and
colourless Christian promise—the questionable rapture of being one
among billions of court-flatterers" (*P,* 58). The point, according to
Honan, is that "the content of the film-message—though it does matter—matters less than the experience of a medium of such intimacy that
'superlife' becomes, for the movie-goer, a personal possession" (Honan
1972, 168).

Such considerations of the movies as a powerful substitute for religion
coincide with Father Kipling's worries along the same lines and mesh
with yet another character's concerns about broader shifts in popular
entertainment. Like the priest, Berkeley the theater manager worries
that his institution is failing, but unlike Father Kipling he sees the
church and the theater not so much as competitors as fellow victims in
the face of larger forces they cannot control. He knew the Palladium in
better days, before the war, when it was called the Brickley Empire ("the
grandest music-hall south of the River, and the first stop on the suburban circuit for the big names of the West End"), and he has watched its
decline in the face of "TV, entertainment tax and the contempt of the
young" [*P,* 10]). Now, as dwindling attendance threatens its survival
even as a cinema, he seeks out films that will draw large crowds. Eager
to appeal to the latest fashion determined by the free-spending younger
generation, he nevertheless despairs that "never before did it change so
rapidly, never before were the older generation so pathetically afraid of
being left behind" (*P,* 129).

In its immediate appeal to young people, popular music represents
particularly threatening competition. Lodge has often described its
peculiar hold on the emotions, most notably in *Nice Work,* where Vic
Wilcox feeds his romantic longings on the recordings of female pop
vocalists. Here we see the same appeal at work in the vulnerability of
Doreen Higgins, an usherette at the Palladium, to a crooner named Laurie Landsdowne. Through Doreen, Lodge satirizes the star-worshipping
sensibility of young women of a certain age and class, which, besides the
"photographic gallery" of movie actors decorating her bedroom, finds
expression here through items ordered from the Laurie Landsdowne Fan
Club. Doreen rushes home from work to unwrap the latest, a pair of
panties with Landsdowne's fingerprints on them, which she immediately tries on and models in her mirror: "She turned and peered over her
shoulder. Like the finger-bones of some amorous skeleton Laurie Landsdowne's printed hands gently clasped each swelling buttock" (*P,* 91). As

she dances before the mirror, she hums "Love is a Many-Splendoured Thing," her favorite of his recordings, which she heard just that night between features at the Palladium.

The force of such popular music and the romantic images it evokes far exceeds that of films, even one like *When the Cat's Away*. Indeed, Doreen notices only the plush apartment provided the Amber Lush character, particularly its bathroom ("hot water galore and a thing for showers if you wanted one. Everything warm and clean" [*P,* 73–74]); the film's relationships and action have no interest for her. The romantic ballad, rendered by the passionate singing and lush orchestral background of the recording, overcomes the tawdriness of her present circumstances and remains more fixed in her mind because it is less tied to concrete specifics and more open to a free-ranging imagination than anything film can provide. The song allows, and probably encourages, her to become Berkeley's mistress and to accept his seedy office as the place where they must conduct their affair.

The survival of the Palladium and Berkeley's employment thus hinge on winning members of Doreen's generation away from other, more tempting forms of entertainment. By the end of the novel he seems to have found at least a temporary solution with the film *Rock around the Clock* and its virtually plotless appropriation of a new type of music. The youngsters in the audience respond enthusiastically to what they see and hear. They dance in the aisles of the Palladium while the movie is still running, and they continue to dance in the foyer and even in the streets outside when it is over. They seem happier and more likely to return than any audience Berkeley has seen in years.

The most dramatic indication of this new type of film's appeal is the transformation of Harry, a lonely teddy boy who in the depth of his anger and insecurity, and in the violence of his imaginings, resembles the young gangster Pinkie in Graham Greene's *Brighton Rock*. While the similarities between these two characters may relate to the fact that Lodge was reading Greene for his thesis on Catholic novelists while writing *The Picturegoers* (Bergonzi 1970, 31), he puts Harry on a redemptive track that differs greatly from Pinkie's. Earlier Harry stalks Bridget and even roughs her up one night after Len leaves her at a bus stop. Movies hardly pacify Harry, as he feels compelled to slash a theater seat with his switchblade while watching the Amber Lush film. Now, however, he gets caught up in the happy frenzy of *Rock around the Clock*. After being persuaded by a girl near him to join in the dancing, an activity he has only scorned in the past, he ends up walking her home and kissing her good night. "It seemed to Harry that he had never been so tired," we are told. "Or so happy" (*P,* 232). Where religion serves as a source of strength for Greene's Pinkie and might help redeem him, we are asked to believe that rock music does it for Harry, confirming both Berkeley's and Father Kipling's sense of the tremendous force of popular entertainment. But the unreliability of the youthful patronage on which Berkeley has become dependent is shown when Harry agrees to meet the girl the next week not at the Palladium but at a dance hall (named, ironically, the Empire).

For all of its interest and intricacy, though, the novel's examination of film and popular culture is hardly its center. If part of the problem with *The Picturegoers* is that it contains too many elements competing for the reader's attention, at least Mark Underwood and Clare Mallory's relationship eventually becomes more prominent than the others, and it is marked at every turn with questions of religious belief and conduct. Mark is the first of the long line of characters Lodge places in a strange setting. While hardly as exotic or exciting as postwar Germany or Berkeley in the 1960s, his situation in the Mallory home contrasts sharply with what he has known before. An only child from a prosperous upper-middle-class suburb, he is fascinated by the dynamic of this large family in their busy, boisterous, and sometimes cramped household. Though technically a Catholic, having been baptized in the Church, Mark experienced little religion at home and has for some time considered himself a nonbeliever. Now he finds himself in a house full of religious objects and living with people for whom attendance at Mass and other church-related activities are a significant part of everyday life. Even as he notes the clutter of their house ("where the icons of Christianity jostled incongruously the symbols of pagan cults") or their indifference to news or the arts, he recognizes the "superficial sophistication" of his critical stance and succumbs to the easy warmth of the family circle extended to him—a development modeled partly on Lodge's own feelings when he visited the large family of his fiancée in the mid-1950s (*P,* 44, 48, xiv).

Mark's fascination with the Mallorys soon centers on Clare. Like him, she is a recent arrival, having returned home after two years in a convent. Immediately attracted by her beauty, which habitual restraint in makeup and dress cannot hide, he is curious about her break with the convent and about her attitude toward religion. The delicacy of his position as a family boarder and of her convent-refugee status somewhat constrains his pursuit of her, but they soon begin going out together, mostly to the movies. For her part Clare is struck by Mark as an attractive man of roughly her age and an outsider with some worldly experience, having already completed National Service and a year in the university. Once she learns of his literary interests and begins to notice the cynicism in his approach to religion, he becomes a challenge, and she determines to win him back to the Church. Before long she has persuaded him to attend Mass with her and to contemplate religion as never before.

Mark and Clare succeed in pursuing each other—he to the point that Clare comes to desire a more physical relationship with him and ultimately wants to marry him, she to the point that Mark intensifies his religious observance and even participates in a Catholic student procession. Midway through the novel, he shocks her by refusing to respond much to her passionate encouragement to touch her breast—an ironic twist of an earlier incident in which he tentatively tried to do so but received no encouragement. And in the third and final section he shocks her even more by telling her that he wants to seek a religious vocation and join the Dominican Order. Her angry response registers bewilderment as to what has been going on between them and how they could have so misunderstood each other. "Now I'm like you, you're like I used to be," she tells him. "It's like a see-saw: one side goes up, one side goes down. That's me gone down I suppose. I suppose we were once dead level, but I don't especially remember it" (P, 202). She finds some immediate solace in befriending the newly married Len and Bridget after Father Kipling has introduced them to her—one of Lodge's awkward attempts to connect the disparate story lines of the novel—and in Mark's revealing that he has been turned down for his novitiate for the time being. But his departure from the Mallorys and his return to his parents' home, to clarify his still-cloudy notions of Catholicism and to contemplate further his vocational needs, conclude the novel and underscore its essentially religious foundation.

Because *The Picturegoers* is generally serious in tone, the considerable comic potential of Mark and Clare's role reversal is limited to irony. The only truly comic element of their story, which compounds its irony while reinforcing its seriousness, comes with Clare's hapless cousin Damien O'Brien. A repressed ex-seminarian, the young Irishman reflects the worst aspects of religious life and points to dangers that the older, more mature Mark presumably would consider in weighing his future. In his longing for Clare and his spying on her with Mark, Damien resembles both the Satan of *Paradise Lost* and the frustrated monastic in Browning's "Soliloquy of a Spanish Cloister." Bergonzi sees in Damien "the malign vitality of a Dickensian caricature."[10] Because he combines physical repulsiveness with a general lack of social grace, readers might view him with some sympathy were he also given a measure of self-awareness. But Lodge apparently preferred to keep us emotionally distant from Damien and to direct Damien's mistaken notions about the relationship between Mark and Claire, as well as his hilarious fantasies of heroic intervention, toward an ironic effect. In this the young novelist succeeded wonderfully and showed the talent for comedy that would become much more apparent in his later fiction.

Terry Eagleton has derided the idea of David Lodge as a Catholic novelist, claiming that his work reflects a "necessary marginalization" of the rigorous Thomistic tradition, with its socially radical potential, in favor of the "commonsensical world of English middle-class humanism." For Eagleton the persona emerging from Lodge's fiction is "too hopelessly balanced and conventionally-minded" to entertain a creed of such rigor, which must then remain "a disconnected set of doctrines which for some private reason he happens to hold" (Eagleton, 97).

If we must tie the idea of "Catholic writer" to Eagleton's definition and if, relatedly, we must see the world as structured only politically (the latter a point on which Lodge has openly challenged Eagleton),[11] it is difficult to disagree with him. Interestingly, among Lodge's novels about Catholics and Catholicism, Eagleton mentions only *How Far Can You Go?* (*Souls and Bodies*), which he quickly dismisses as "ethical and sociological rather than theological in its focus" (Eagleton, 94). While he probably would not be satisfied with *The Picturegoers* either, he would at least see there a principal character ultimately unwilling to compromise between the easy domesticity offered him and the demanding religious outlook that comes to have an increasing hold on him—even if at least one critic (as well as the priest in the novel advising him) views Mark Underwood's return to Catholicism as "suspiciously self-indulgent."[12] Eagleton might even see, in Mark's increasingly religious orientation, the idea of some people being intended by God for a particular destiny, which has been said to link this novel with Graham Greene's *End of the Affair* (Bergonzi 1992, 70).

Of course, the process by which Mark struggles religiously occurs mostly offstage; it is more alluded to than shown or described. This is partly why the novel's ending, which concludes his relationship with Clare but not his religious quest, seems appropriate. The priest's judgment of Mark's view of Catholicism as "up the creek" connects with our sense that Mark has idealized the Mallory family (the narrative's shifting viewpoint allows us to know them better than he) and perhaps with Lodge's later admission that *The Picturegoers* is "somewhat sentimentally indulgent" in its portrayal of a Catholic environment (*P,* 201; Bergonzi 1970, 111).

Even so, we are given a fairly concrete sense of what Mark goes through. We see him moving from a derisive attitude toward the Mass and other mysteries of the Church to a more respectful desire to understand and, in the end, a considerably greater degree of appreciation and comprehension. Watching the religious routines of the Mallory household reawakens long-forgotten memories of his own brief encounter with Catholicism as a child, including the schoolboy's momentary fear of mortal sin and hell. Like many of Graham Greene's lapsed Catholics, Mark resents religion's tenuous claim on him as well as any suggestion that he might return to the Church.

Nevertheless, after being encouraged by Clare to attend Mass, he finds it at first merely interesting ("considered as liturgical drama" [*P,* 59]) but later, compelling. Within a few months he is attending more to questions of religion than to his studies, his writing, or even Clare. He meditates on the surprising meanness of Catholicism as actually practiced by typical believers in their cluttered little churches—"ugly, crude, bourgeois," he terms it all—yet marvels that in such circumstances and among such people the sacred is sought and found. Repeating the line from Browning with which he earlier scorned the Mass and its participants, he now concludes that "in their presence God was made and eaten all day long, and for that reason those people could never be quite like other people, and that was Catholicism" (*P,* 173). He studies religion, he discusses it with Clare, he searches for signs of a momentous change in himself, he keeps a diary of this search, and ultimately he comes to understand the appeal of life under a religious rule.

The British Museum Is Falling Down

Whether any of these themes or the prominence given them in *The Picturegoers* qualifies Lodge as a Catholic novelist in Eagleton's terms is doubtful. But certainly the story of Mark Underwood, as well as that of Clare Mallory, is at key points deeply spiritual and concerned with fundamental theological issues. In that respect it differs from most everything in *The British Museum Is Falling Down*.

Probably the only section in this, Lodge's third published novel, that compares to Mark's or Clare's soul-searching comes when, in a Joycean stream of consciousness, Barbara Appleby considers the larger, mysterious implications of human sexuality:

> [T]here's always a snag perhaps that's the root of the matter there's something about sex perhaps it's original sin I don't know but we'll never get it neatly tied up you think you've got it under control in one place it pops up in another either it's comic or tragic nobody's immune.[13]

Such thinking connects with Lodge's view, reported by Bernard Bergonzi from their 1992 interview, that religion is the "perennial symbolic and speculative mode in which we articulate the contradictions and anxieties which are ineradicably part of the human condition" and with which we seek a compensating "feeling of transcendence" (Bergonzi 1992, 72). Like Barbara Appleby, Lodge has little faith ultimately in the power of materialistic humanism to get or set things straight. This is why he has her engage in this authentic if brief bit of theological observation.

But her thinking along these lines is not only brief but belated; Lodge delays introducing it until the novel's epilogue. Moreover, it is embedded within a considerably longer soliloquy imitating Molly Bloom's in the final section of Joyce's *Ulysses* and illustrating the parodic nature of much of Lodge's novel. Neither the specific style nor the content of Barbara's soliloquy is typical of *The British Museum Is Falling Down*, and though significant, neither she nor what she thinks is nearly as central as her husband, Adam, and his activities. But despite even Adam's centrality, the biblical and mythical resonance of his name is undermined and put to ironic use through a narrative basically toned and structured as comedy and full of the kind of absurd situations that have become a staple of Lodge's central style.

Adam's story is replete with absurdities, starting with his recollection of having been so proficient at who-can-pee-highest at his school's outside lavatory that he wetted the biretta of the parish priest on the other side of the wall (chap. 1). In the final chapter, a young woman determined to seduce him is horrified to find him wearing Barbara's underwear, because none of his own got dry from the wash that morning:

> Virginia gave a little shriek of glee and threw herself upon him. He felt her fingers undoing his belt, and his trousers slowly receding. He struggled to retain them, but, on a sudden inspiration, desisted. "Oh," said

Virginia. She got up and stepped back. "Oh," she said again. She
snatched up a dressing-gown and held it in front of her. "What are you
wearing those for?" (BM, 157)

The hilarity of this discovery is prepared by a scene much earlier in
the day, when Adam first resists Barbara's suggestion that he wear her
panties out of expediency ("To hell with that! What d'you take me for—
a—transvestite?"), and then angrily responds to their precocious daughter's curiosity about transvestites (" 'Ask your mother,' Adam snarled"
[BM, 23]). Finally, having relented and summoned enough nerve to try
on a pair, he endures the watchful little girl's comment "Mummy says a
transvestite is a poor man who likes wearing ladies' clothes because he's
silly in the head" (BM, 25). Lodge keeps the absurdity of the underwear
dilemma alive by having Adam suffer a fit of absentmindedness in a
British Museum men's room: "He had been fumbling unsuccessfully in
his groin for some moments, and was beginning to suspect that he had
been drugged and castrated at some earlier point in the day, when he
remembered that he was wearing Barbara's pants. Hastily adjusting his
dress, he retired to the privacy of a closet" (BM, 87).

Adam's problem with underwear constitutes but one of many devices
that establish and sustain an absurdist cast to character and action here.
And even if the epilogue brings things back to at least a quasi-realistic
level, it too is complicit in this absurdism. More than most novels—and
certainly more than any other that Lodge has written—*The British
Museum Is Falling Down* explicitly concerns its own prolongation. The
shortest of his novels, it obviously needs to get somewhere, but not too
fast. As postmodern narrative, by its very form it raises narratological
issues.

Its absurdist devices seem to prolong as well. These include a jingle
contest ("I always choose a Brownlong chair . . .") for which Adam in
half-serious fashion sporadically imagines humorous entries ("For laying
girls with long brown hair," "Because I wrote my thesis there," "The
answer to a bottom's prayer" [BM, 24, 53, 160]), as well as a related
but less extended funny bit confined to sherry party conversation, in
which the names dropped obviously distort those of real writers (Kingsley Anus, C. P. Slow, Mormon Nailer, etc.). In fact, the scene of the
sherry party, attended by members of the English department in which
Adam is writing a thesis, contains many seemingly gratuitous nonsensi-
cal elements, amusing in themselves but scarcely advancing developments set in motion earlier. There is literary wordplay here (e.g., "[I]s it

called *The Bow and the Lyre* or *The Beau and the Liar. . . ?*" [36]), there is
funny speculation on a puzzle in Henry James, and there is a general
satire of academic manners. The scene, of course, belongs to the novel's
larger pattern of poking fun at the literary academy, as does Adam's vulnerability to any distraction from getting down to work, which operates
literally as a prolonging device. (The failure of his friend Camel even to
begin writing his thesis, after many years of preliminary work, points to
another tendency of academicians, especially in the humanities, which is
amusing at least to outsiders.)

Morace and others have suggested that such elements of seeming
nonsense—Adam's response to the jingle contest, for example—hang
together better thematically, as a protest against literary (and other)
authority, than might be immediately apparent.[14] Certainly these elements counter the realistic reading of the novel some have offered (for
example, Jackson, 373–74, and Burden, 141). At the center of such
reading, of course, is the figure of Adam Appleby himself—25 years old,
husband of Barbara and father of their three children, third-year graduate student in English literature, and not incidentally, a Catholic obedi-
ent to the Church's strictures on birth control. Though Adam ordinarily
worries a great deal about finishing his thesis and finding employment,
on the particular day we see him his anxiety level is increased by another
worry, the possibility that Barbara may be pregnant, as her period is
three days overdue and she is feeling strange that morning. The day's
ensuing comedy combines these and other motives for his behavior.

Lodge's admitted model for *The British Museum* was James Joyce's
Ulysses. While from the beginning he intended the novel's action to be
limited to one day's duration, not until he approached writing its conclusion did he realize the need for a shift from Adam's viewpoint to Barbara's. But this had to be done deftly and credibly; it had to be legitimized. The reader's acceptance of so radical and sudden a shift would
depend on recognition of a well-respected prototype. Lodge remembers
asking himself, "In what famous modern novel did the character of a
wife, up to the penultimate chapter an object in her husband's thoughts
and perceptions, become in the last chapter the subjective consciousness
of the narrative, and give her own wry, down-to-earth, feminine perspective on him and their relationship?" The realization of *Ulysses* as
such a model—and indeed, as the previously unrecognized basis for
much that he had already written—Lodge terms "one of those moments
of happy inspiration that make the labour of composing literary fictions
worthwhile" (*BM,* xix). And his last-minute recollection that Molly

Bloom starts her period in the Penelope section of *Ulysses* confirmed con-
clusively the workability of what he would be doing with the wifely
character in his own novel.

Barbara's soliloquy ("a rather cheeky *hommage* to Molly Bloom's,"
Lodge has called it) is full of parallels to Joyce (*AF,* 102). Not only does
it move into an interior monologue of unpunctuated run-on sentences,
and not only does Barbara too acknowledge the beginning of her period,
but Molly's famous "Yes" to the prospect of renewed sex with her husband is paralleled by the "perhaps" that Barbara says a dozen times during her soliloquy before making it her last word (and the novel's). Like
Molly, she recalls with intensity her earlier love life with her husband
before they married, particularly the day in the south of France when
Adam proposed to her—an analog to the scene of Leopold Bloom's
proposing to Molly under a Moorish arch. And even if Lodge is parody-
ing Joyce here—even if "perhaps" is a spoof on "yes"—the flood of Barbara's memories and emotions represents as much an optimistic and joy-
ous conclusion to this novel as does Molly's to *Ulysses.*

Lodge rested the effectiveness of his epilogue, and to some extent the
entire novel, on readers' recognizing the tie-in with Joyce. Indeed, once
readers make this connection and begin to reflect on previous chapters,
they can devise a list, not unlike that offered by Dennis Jackson (*AF,*
473–74), of many parallels running throughout the novel. We accom-
pany Adam to the places he ordinarily goes on a workday—mainly the
British Museum, as repository of the materials he needs for his research,
and its celebrated Reading Room, where he intends to accomplish his
day's work. We see him in conversation with cronies and other acquain-
tances, many of whom keep popping up as the day progresses. As Jackson notes, Adam, like Bloom, becomes increasingly disoriented and his
perceptions become "increasingly phantasmagoric" (Jackson, 473).
Adam, too, thinks constantly of his home and wife and entertains fantasies that are comically deflated. But if, also like Bloom, Adam suffers
because of his religion, his exasperation at the Church's birth-control
restrictions and at the convoluted and unreliable methods they entail are
much more amusing than the difficulties of the quietly dignified Jew
passing among anti-Semitic Dubliners and are a prime example of what
one critic calls the novel's mockery of Joyce's higher style with a "much
more basic domestic mood" (Burden, 142). Most of Adam's fantasies are
in response to the problems of sex in his marriage caused by the Church,
as when he mentally composes an article describing Roman Catholicism
for an imaginary encyclopedia many centuries in the future, which con-

cerns almost entirely the Church's fixation on birth control and mentions only incidentally such "other doctrines" as a belief in a divine
redeemer and a life after death.

Not unreasonably, Lodge expected his various takeoffs on Joyce—or
at the very least the broad strokes of the Barbara Appleby soliloquy—to
be recognized by knowing readers. But he also included imitations of
other writers that he expected readers to pick up on. In fact, judging
from his account of the novel's composition, in interviews and in the
introduction to the second edition, literary parody represented as much
a beginning point for *The British Museum Is Falling Down* (what Henry
James might call its "germ"), and an intended cause of amusement, as
the novel's treatment of Roman Catholicism, the debate over birth control, academic satire, or anything else that might seem its center. If
competing centers of interest in *The Picturegoers* had constituted a problem, the stylistic parodies had to mesh with other elements to make this
novel effective.

Of course, Lodge was not unaware of the risk involved in using parody and pastiche extensively. He knew that a reader unable to recognize
such references might be puzzled or even put off entirely by the novel.
"My aim," he has recalled, "was to make the narrative and its frequent
shifts of style fully intelligible and satisfying to such a reader, while
offering the more literary reader the extra entertainment of spotting the
parodies" (*BM*, xix)—an early instance of the practice of "layering" that
would mark many of the later novels. Thus he was disappointed when
readers he assumed would know better—in particular, many reviewers
who otherwise liked the novel—failed to notice or comment on the parodies. Having been unable to persuade his British publisher to highlight
them with a jacket blurb, he was more successful with the American
publisher of the novel, and he credited this for the parodies being more
recognized by American readers (*BM*, xx). Presumably one of the intentions behind his discussion of this technique in the introduction to the
1981 second edition of *The British Museum* was to safeguard against the
readerly nonrecognition that had plagued its initial reception.

Lodge wanted readers to notice his renderings not only of Joyce but
also of Hemingway, James, and several others. The Hemingway comes
when Adam first visits the home of the seductive young Virginia Rot-
tingdean and her mother, who has contacted him about some unpub-
lished letters of her uncle's, a deceased minor author. His trip there from
the British Museum is described in short sentences consisting mostly of
monosyllables organized into simple coordinate clauses, not unlike the

style of "In Another Country" and of many other Hemingway stories and novels.

At the house Adam encounters several rough-looking men drinking beer in the basement, where bull-fighting posters decorate the walls. The ensuing dialogue extends the Hemingway mode:

> "You are *aficionado?*" the hairy man said.
> "I beg your pardon?"
> "You follow the bulls?"
> "I've never been to a bull-fight."
> "Who is he?" one of the men at the table said. The thumb was missing from his left hand.
> "Who are you?" the hairy man said to Adam.
> "He's from the cafe," the third man said. This man's left hand was in a sling.
> "There must be some mistake," Adam said. (*BM,* 109)

The effectiveness of this otherwise tedious conversation, which continues for several pages and yields little that is germane to Adam's story, depends on our recognizing it as an exaggeration of the Hemingway style but banal and totally devoid of the intense feeling that Hemingway could convey with it. (Relatedly, the "mystery" of the mysterious tough guys with the missing fingers, revealed only after several chapters, turns out to be nothing more than the fact that they are butchers.)

A similar awareness and appreciation is required for the scene a few pages later between Adam and Virginia's mother, which, in its convoluted, slow-measured syntax and overstated, incremental dramatic tension, seems quite the opposite of Hemingway and more like *The Spoils of Poynton, The Beast in the Jungle,* or the other narratives written in the later manner of Henry James. "Her eyes followed his, and they communed in silence," we are told. "It took on quite a character of its own in the end, this silence, shaped by the consciousness they both had of the manifold things they, all understandingly, were *not* saying" (*BM,* 118). Such statements and the tortuous conversation near which they are placed reveal not only an excess of the Jamesian scenic method but its misapplication, since rather than any of the grave moral issues James raised while employing this method, what is involved here is nothing more than Adam's wish for a research topic, however trivial, that will land him a degree and a job effortlessly and speedily and the mother's wish either to find a husband for her randy daughter or to squeeze Adam for cash.

In similar fashion Lodge invokes Kafka, Conrad, Woolf, Lawrence, Snow, Greene, and Frederick Rolfe (Baron Corvo [1860–1913], author of *Hadrian the Seventh,* 1904)—the last two being writers with whose styles he had become particularly familiar while preparing his M.A. thesis, "The Catholic Novel Since the Oxford Movement: Its Literary Form and Religious Content." It is understandable that Lodge's increased interest in the question of fictional style while doing this research, particularly as he moved through the modern period,[15] would lead to the kind of work making up *Language of Fiction.* And even in the relatively undeveloped state of the poetics of fiction when he was writing *The British Museum,* the elements of Hemingway's style and that of others recalled in the novel were sufficiently familiar already to have been successfully parodied. But the effectiveness of his parodies in *The British Museum* is undercut by the "layering" technique on which he insisted. He admitted as much a few years later when he said that for the novel to be understandable and enjoyable for unknowing readers, he had kept the parodies "fairly well hidden," which in turn had made it more unlikely that even informed readers would notice them (Bergonzi 1970, 111).

The logic behind Lodge's parodic method relates to characterization. His plan for the novel involved the naturalization of such technical shifts by making Adam Appleby prone to daydreams and fantasies triggered by worry over Barbara's pregnancy (*BM,* xvi). Accordingly, the frustrations Adam encounters during the day call to mind particular writers and their characteristic styles. The episode in which staff members at the British Museum tell him he can't renew his Reading Room ticket because it's out of date (so that technically he has no card to renew) is amusingly described in the manner of Kafka, just as his negotiations for the letters of Egbert Merrymarsh (with which Lodge is satirizing the G. K. Chesterton–Hillaire Belloc school of Catholic belletrists with whom his graduate work had familiarized him) are presented in the Jamesian mode already noted. These and the other imitations reflect Adam's having been so immersed in literary texts that they have taken over his way of perceiving experience. In this he relates to the many other Lodge characters who confuse fiction with reality (such as Persse McGarrigle, who "relies on literary knowledge to cope with carnal knowledge").[16] And as Lodge later noted, "The basic irony of Adam Appleby's plight is that the only element in his life that seems authentically his, and not 'written' by some other novelist, is the very source of his anxiety" (*BM*, xvi), namely his plight as a Catholic husband anxious about his wife's condition.

Given this rationale, the unrecognizability of the parodies for so many readers constitutes a serious problem. Aside from Barbara's Joycean soliloquy, which is the most immediately recognizable parody yet the one that probably carries the most appropriate significance even without such recognition—in other words, the instance in which "layering" is most successful—for most readers none of them, not even the Hemingway or the Kafka imitation, is likely to seem much more than a bothersome distraction, a puzzling change from the stylistically more straightforward parts of the novel. Aside from the questionability of expecting readers even back in the 1960s to spot a Baron Corvo spoof, because these are all distortions, without recognition they can yield the pleasure of neither the original nor the parody—again the Joycean soliloquy being the exception. Nor would a jacket blurb—or even footnotes—necessarily provide adequate guidance. Nothing short of the full rationale that Lodge included in his introduction to the second edition would suffice to induce the appropriate appreciation and pleasure.

Of course, both the parodic method and Lodge's rationale for it link to the circumstances under which the novel was written, to related issues of literary theory raised throughout the novel, and to certain ideas developed in *Language of Fiction,* published the year following *The British Museum.* Lodge has pointed to the connection between the two books, noting how the issue of fiction's relationship to reality constitutes a principal concern of each. Adam Appleby's sense that his life is being written by the novelists he reads relates to concerns Lodge himself was having after completing two novels that he could as readily relate to literary sources as to personal experience or anything else outside of literature, and after having been involved in close study of particular writers in preparing both his M.A. thesis and *Language of Fiction.* He has suggested that using parody in *The British Museum Is Falling Down* was his way of coping with his own "anxiety of influence" at the time (*BM*, xvi). The formalist insistence in *Language of Fiction* on the ultimate divorce between the fictional world and any reality outside that may have inspired it—on the accountability of the novel only to the intrinsic terms on which it is constructed rather than to some standard of mimetic accuracy or truthfulness—finds an amusing twist in *The British Museum* when Adam observes that "[l]iterature is mostly about having sex and not having children. Life is the other way around" (*BM*, 63).

But however interesting, and however important to the novel, issues of literary theory seem overshadowed by the topics of birth control and the Catholic Church. Not that they are entirely disconnected here from literary theory, but what is bothering Adam most of the time we encounter him, and what inspires his most amusingly frustrated responses, is his dilemma as a healthy sexual being seemingly doomed to repeated parenthood and the attendant worry about parenthood through his obedience to a religious authority whose position on birth control seems arbitrary and even inhumane. His day is punctuated by anxious telephone calls to Barbara to check on her condition, which keep him on an emotional roller coaster.

Taunting him in his frustration is the spectacle of non-Catholics who apparently enjoy sex without fear of the parenthood penalty. When one of them boastfully attributes a limp to attempting various positions from the *Kama Sutra* with his wife, Adam is amazed: "You mean you're so sated with conventional sex. . . . Pardon me while my imagination boggles" (*BM,* 64). His and Barbara's thinking reveals how the notion of the so-called safe period inspires such anxiety among Catholic couples that pent-up frustration and overexcitement prevent their having much pleasure even when it is safest to enjoy sex. In this light, their non-Catholic landlady's ignorantly blaming "naughty" Mr. Appleby (whom she subjects to "the kind of half-fascinated, half-fearful appraisal usually reserved for prize bulls") for Barbara's last pregnancy and her recommending birth control clinics to Barbara carry an especially painful irony (*BM,* 28).

For someone in such a situation, the possibility that the recently convened Second Vatican Council might lead to a relaxation of Church doctrine is especially tantalizing. At one point Adam glances at a newspaper article about the Vatican II debate over reexamining the Church's teaching in this area and the pope's noncommittal stance and immediately imagines himself the first married pope, ordering married Catholics to be instructed in all birth-control techniques.

Relatedly, Barbara thinks of the unfairness of the Church policy allowing Catholic women who marry non-Catholics to use contraceptives under certain conditions:

> He has to sign a promise, but if he goes back on it and insists the priest will tell you to submit for the sake of saving the marriage. It's the lesser evil, they say, but it only applies if the Catholic partner's a woman.

That's typical—as if they never dreamed a woman might want to insist.
Perhaps they wouldn't have when they made the rule. The Vatican's
always about a hundred years out of date. (*BM,* 170)

Indeed, Lodge uses her remarkable soliloquy to survey from the Catholic
woman's perspective a variety of issues related to childbirth and birth
control: the riskiness of the so-called rhythm or safe method ("neither
rhythmical or safe," Lodge observes elsewhere—"so unreliable that
many couples wondered if it hadn't been approved only because it
wasn't safe" [*SB,* 73, 117]); disagreements between the prewar and
postwar generations of Catholic women over contraception; the myth of
the large family; and the likelihood of the Church's changing its attitudes.

But such seriousness is unusual in *The British Museum Is Falling Down.*
Lodge has noted how his commitment to a basically comic novel likewise committed him to an ultimately less than serious critique of the
Church and its doctrines. More typical, therefore, are Adam's encounters with the madcap priests Fathers Finbar and Wildfire, who illustrate
in different ways how little many clergy understand the implications of
Church policies on the everyday lives of contemporary Catholics, particularly policies concerning sexuality, or his forestalling an increasingly
insistent (and bewildered) Virginia with the same distracting precau-
tions that he and Barbara are obliged to observe routinely:

> "I'm trying to determine whether this is a safe time for relations," he
> explained.
> "Not very romantic," Virginia seemed indistinctly to say.
> "Sex isn't," he snapped back. He plucked the thermometer out and
> examined it. "97.6," he announced and wrote the figure down. . . .
> "Now, if you'll just go on taking your temperature every night and
> drop me a line when it rises sharply for three consecutive days, we'll see
> what we can do." He gave her a bland smile. (*BM,* 156)

In its ending, *The British Museum Is Falling Down* confirms the basic
conservatism at the root of traditional comedy. As Lodge has noted, the
novel's conflicts and misunderstandings are resolved "without fundamentally disturbing the system which provoked them" (*BM,* xiv),
including a windfall job for Adam provided by a fat American (a precur-
sor to Morris Zapp). For all of the Applebys' discomfort, and especially
for all of Adam's frustrated complaining about the Church and its doctrines, such concerns are swept aside in favor of a resolution upholding

their marriage and, by implication, the religious institution sanctioning it. Because in its final spirit of reconciliation *The British Museum* resembles *Small World,* Lodge's way of upholding bourgeois marriage has not gone uncriticized.[17] Of course, the priority given generic consistency here is not without its pleasures and rewards (its bribes, hostile critics might claim) for the reader. Through the tour de force of Barbara's soliloquy, parody and layering finally work together to defer the issue of how she and Adam, or others like them, can possibly bear muddling through even one more day.

Souls and Bodies

In his introduction to the 1981 edition of *The British Museum*, Lodge commented on how the writing had come more rapidly than for any of his previous novels, owing to his confidence in its subject's originality and immediate interest for readers, including non-Catholics. But he also recalled that speed of composition in this instance had been motivated in part by the possibility that the Catholic Church's action on the question of birth control might cut short its shelf life as a "live issue" for fiction. "I need not have worried," he ruefully noted (*BM,* xii), as the Church did not even attempt to settle the matter until 1968, more than three years after he had completed *The British Museum.* By that time, of course, he had also finished a much different novel, *Out of the Shelter.* And because new Lodge novels were appearing regularly at intervals of four or five years from the mid-1960s to the late 1980s, these recollections would postdate one other quite different novel as well, *Souls and Bodies.*[18] While *Souls and Bodies* may stand as "a kind of sequel, or companion piece" to *The British Museum* (Morace, 172), Lodge's recollections clearly reflect the attitudes and the historical situation more of the later book than of the earlier.

Although most of the reviewers of Lodge's third novel about Catholics and Catholicism were enthusiastic, a few criticized its style and somewhat unusual form. One noted the seemingly "willful ploddingness of [his] redbrick prose," while others complained of the frequency and abruptness of format shifts and authorial intrusions in the novel.[19] Nevertheless, it received the Whitbread Award for 1984, and these same critics acknowledged its profundity and truthfulness. These strains were picked up two years later by American reviewers, one of whom found *Souls and Bodies* "frequently funny, but quietly searing."[20] And as reviewing gave way to scholarly commentary and analysis, the novel received

even more vindication, with Dennis Jackson seeing in it more evidence
of Lodge's "firmer control" than in his earlier fiction (Jackson, 480),
Robert Morace pronouncing it Lodge's "strongest and most compelling
work" to date (and accusing Paul Theroux of having approached it from
the inappropriately narrow standards of realistic and historical fiction in
his hostile *New York Times* review several years earlier [Morace, 172,
176]), and Gerald Parsons finding it "more than merely Catholic in its
relevance and paradigmatic status" even a dozen years after its publication.[21]

   Souls and Bodies is indeed a striking piece of writing, more impressive
in many ways than any of Lodge's other novels. Its modest length belies
its structural complexity, depth of feeling, and scope of reference; the
results here of Lodge's joining the resources of traditional realism with
those of metafictional experimentation are quietly impressive. This
novel is singularly related to a number of his other works, both earlier
and later. It advances much more seriously and thoroughly the examination of Catholics and Catholicism in postwar British society initiated in
The Picturegoers and continued in *The British Museum Is Falling Down,*
particularly as it focuses on both the immediate consequences and the
ultimate implications of the debate over the Church's stand on birth
control. The mode of eschatological questioning only begun in the epilogue of *Out of the Shelter*—in which the older Timothy Young confronts
what the theologian Paul Tillich called "the riddle of inequality" in
terms of his own personal luck amid the unmerited misfortunes of so
many others—informs virtually all of the several story lines in *Souls and
Bodies.* Such was the force of this eschatological emphasis that it would
resonate in Lodge's next novel, *Small World,* through Morris Zapp and
Philip Swallow's acknowledgment of the undeferability of aging and
death. The decision to cast much of the final chapter of *Souls and Bodies*
as a film script connects with the last chapter of the novel Lodge had
published just before it, *Changing Places,* though his use of this form here
creates a considerably greater complexity of effect and meaning
(Morace, 189–90).

   Much had happened both inside and outside the Catholic Church in
the 15 years since Lodge had written *The British Museum Is Falling Down.*
By the time he again took up Catholicism as a central subject for his fiction, Pope John XXIII and his successor, Paul VI, had died. Despite
some significant reforms, notably the vernacularization of the Mass and
liturgy, the energy, optimism, and spirit of *aggiornamento* surrounding
the Second Vatican Council had given way first to official indecisiveness

and then to the dispiriting 1968 papal encyclical (*Humanae Vitae*), which effectively took the issue of birth control off the table of official discussion. The rebelliousness and ensuing suspicion of the Church hierarchy among practicing Catholics that the disappointments of Vatican II set off is suggested in the last pages of *Souls and Bodies,* where Lodge injects himself into the narrative to comment on the Polish cardinal who has just been elected pope. After ticking off the many strengths and wide popularity of John Paul II, he adds that the pope is "theologically conservative" and notes contemporary Catholicism's curious dilemma, in which "[a] changing Church acclaims a Pope who evidently thinks change has gone far enough" (*SB,* 244). (Many years later he would call John Paul II a "charismatic authoritarian.")[22]

What Lodge proposed to do in *Souls and Bodies* was to describe and appraise how the English Catholic community, in response partly to developments in the Church but also to changes in the larger society, had itself changed during the quarter century immediately prior to John Paul II's election. Having found in *The British Museum* a way of "releasing personal exasperation over the whole birth control issue at the time," he prepared for *Souls and Bodies* by considering the extraordinary changes the Church had undergone just in his lifetime ("a subject nobody had dealt with—even Catholics of my own generation"), by reading a good deal of theology and by thinking about the Church in a way he hadn't before.[23] Not surprisingly, the resulting description and appraisal of such change represent many voices and attitudes, some of them direct opposites; more than any of Lodge's other novels except perhaps *Small World,* this one epitomizes dialogism and rewards a Bakhtinian reading. And though Lodge could insist that the circumstances of Adam and Barbara Appleby's life never corresponded very closely to his own (*BM,* xii), in *Souls and Bodies* the correspondences seem intentionally established to permit him (or at least a narrative persona very close to him in temperament and situation) to step in and out of the narrative at will.

The formal premise of *Souls and Bodies* concerns a group of young Catholic students who begin the novel as members of a New Testament study group conducted by a young priest near the University of London. Lodge has recalled how, to do justice to the complexity of change with which the novel would deal, he sought "some kind of structure which would follow the fortunes of a number of different Catholics, who would start off believing in the same thing but whose ways would gradually diverge and differ" (Walsh, 4). We first see them in early 1952, the same

year David Lodge himself was a first-year student at London (and when
Timothy Young in *Out of the Shelter* might have been expected to begin
his university studies). After graduation, some of them will stay in contact with each other for the balance of the novel, others will renew
lapsed contacts, many will attend the wedding several years later of the
only two members who marry each other, and most will participate in a
1975 Pascal Festival, the setting for the final chapter. Structurally,
Church-related issues and activities function here much as literary theory and academic conferences do in *Small World*.

   As he traces the subsequent lives of these first-year students—and in
the cases of those who marry, of their spouses as well—through young
adulthood and into middle age, Lodge is careful to note dates and corresponding events in politics and popular culture, though Morace has
interestingly pointed out how this seeming precision is undercut by various blurring techniques (Morace, 173–75). By definition, all members
of the student group come from broadly middle-class backgrounds. All
are benefiting from the 1944 Education Act, which gave the mass of
English Catholics access to higher education for the first time, and all
are involved in the formation of what will become "something like an
educated [Catholic] laity" in England (*WO*, 34). If *Out of the Shelter* was
Lodge's way of looking back on an especially significant episode in his
personal development, *Souls and Bodies* looks back, though more imper-
sonally, on the unique generation of English Catholics to which he
belonged.

   Despite all that they have in common, and despite Lodge's fears that
readers might not keep straight so many characters belonging to a
"homogeneous social group" (Haffenden, 152)—nine students plus the
priest, who is not much older—they are surprisingly distinguishable
even at the onset and certainly in the varying directions the stories
assigned them take. (After introducing them, Lodge even includes a
tongue-in-cheek roll call of their names.) They include five male students, four females, and the priest. The women are differentiated mostly
by physical appearance and religious feelings—ranging from the most
attractive, Angela, who is also one of the most pious, to the plainest,
Ruth, who enters a convent after graduation. The male students are
sorted out more by their sexual attitudes, although, as Lodge notes, all
are virgins and "sexually innocent to a degree that they will scarcely be
able to credit when looking back on their youth in years to come" (*SB*,
12). Of course, he gives the reader plenty of information on the women's
sexual attitudes and practices (such as who masturbates and who

doesn't) and hardly excludes from his survey young Father Brierley, whose favorite group member just happens to be the sexiest of the young women and who, after years of doubt and conflict with Church authorities, will leave the priesthood and marry.

To develop 10 largely separate story lines in a medium-size work of fiction—against a backdrop of 25 years of religious, political, and social history and in at least a partly nonlinear fashion—posed a formidable challenge for David Lodge, forcing him to become, in Morace's words, "even busier than the linear God of Genesis" (Morace, 173). Such busyness, as well as the modest length of the novel, reflects Lodge's determination to avoid a "big saga" in which every character is fully realized and to write instead what he has described as "a very fast-moving novel, to give a sense of speeding up the process of change, to make it visible" (Walsh, 4). Chiefly contributing to this effect is what Lodge would later term the novel's "oscillating movement" between extremely realistic writing and authorial interventions that break into the illusion of reality promoted by such writing (Walsh, 4): "I was looking for something vaguely Brechtian . . . so that the reader would be shocked back into thinking about [the psychological illusion] intellectually as well as emotionally" (Haffenden, 154).

The most dramatic instance of this technique comes in the treatment given the story of Angela and Dennis, the group member she eventually marries. Of course, Lodge "breaks frame" (his term, borrowed from the sociologist Erving Goffman, to denote the violation of an established narrative mode) even before the Angela-Dennis story begins, when he apologizes to the reader for having to enlarge the novel's cast beyond the 10 characters already introduced, claiming it would be "too neat" to have them pair off with each other (*SB*, 14). Because it would be equally implausible if no marriage emerged from within this group of marriageable young persons, bound as they are by a shared religion (and indeed, according to one critic, "fiercely aware of their specifically Catholic identity" [Parsons, 182]), Dennis and Angela themselves represent more a device to promote an illusory verisimilitude than any "real" couple.

Even so, the novel proceeds to plunge us back into their story and to involve us emotionally as we follow them through their remaining university years and the time up to their marriage—including Dennis's National Service and the start of his civilian career, their relatively long engagement and Angela's reluctance to get married (of which Dennis is unaware), their wedding (one of the more sustained episodes of the novel, owing partly to its functionality in reuniting members of the

original group), and their honeymoon (which, despite their having
waited longer than their married classmates to have sex, is said to have
been "no freer from awkwardness and disappointment" than those of
the others [*SB,* 72]).

Dennis and Angela's subsequent struggles with the rhythm method
of family planning and the not-unrelated births of their first three children in fairly rapid succession are mentioned in connection with the
similar experiences of the novel's other couples. Not until after the birth
of their fourth child, in late 1966, does the narrative again focus very
much on them, and even then only indirectly. The occasion is the baptism of their baby daughter Nicole, to which they have invited Edward,
a member of the original group who has become a physician. By this
time Dennis has become sufficiently successful in his career to be
unbothered by the expense of children, and he and Angela have moved
into a comfortable new home in a fashionable housing development.

Lodge frames the visit of Edward and his family first by noting how,
contrary to the expectations of Catholics eager—even desperate—to use
the newly developed birth-control pill, Pope John Paul had once again
refused to make a pronouncement on contraception, thus upholding the
status quo for the time being. Then Lodge shifts to a fairly detailed
account of the disastrous mud slide in the small Welsh mining community of Aberfan at about the same time that year, which on a Friday
morning unexpectedly engulfed several houses and a school, killing 150
children and their teachers. The baptism and Edward's visit take place
on the Sunday afterward, while the Aberfan disaster is still very much in
the news and on people's minds. Edward and his family follow it on
their car radio as they drive to Dennis and Angela's house, and it is an
immediate topic of discussion when they arrive ("Ghastly, isn't it?" Dennis comments [*SB,* 110]). But then, after moving through Dennis's "private euphoria" over his new house and new baby while he shows Edward
around, the narrative shifts to the physician's thoughts as he first
observes the child. After confiding in his wife that he fears the child has
Downs' Syndrome, and "feeling like an assassin with a loaded gun in his
pocket" (*SB,* 112), he reveals his suspicions to Dennis.

The revelation itself is passed over quickly, and we are not told precisely what Edward says to Dennis or how Dennis responds. The intellectual process encouraged in the reader (as opposed to the immediate
emotional response triggered by the episode) is grounded earlier in
Edward's story, when he was troubled by the high incidence of non-
hereditary abnormalities in babies born to Catholic patients whom he

has counseled in the rhythm method, and by relevant research suggesting the greater chance of such abnormalities occurring when the egg is fertilized near the end of its life span (a situation more likely among couples, such as those observing the rhythm method, who restrict sex to the postovulatory, or "safe," period). The link between such misfortunes as Dennis and Angela's and the Church's rulings on birth control, and the critique of the Church's seeming indifference to the suffering caused by such rulings, is reinforced subsequently by the moving portrayal of Dennis's agonizing over what happened with Nicole—a portrayal informed by Lodge's own experience after a Downs' Syndrome baby was born to him and his wife (Haffenden, 153).

While the account of the Aberfan disaster clearly relates to baby Nicole in terms of the unexpectedness and inexplicability of most human misfortune—Dennis goes through a "Why me?" stage and Father Brierley, inspired by Aberfam, preaches on this topic—its significance becomes even greater through a further turning of the narrative screws. Again Lodge employs a strategy of indirection before offering a full exposition, in this instance using a later gathering of reform-minded Catholics attended by several of the original student group. When some do not understand a vague reference to a more recent misfortune suffered by Dennis and Angela, the narrator, who at the end of the novel will identify himself as an additional group member, feels compelled to explain to them (and to his "gentle reader") that two years after Nicole's birth Dennis and Angela's daughter Anne was knocked down and killed by a van outside their house. "I have avoided a direct presentation of this incident because frankly I find it too painful to contemplate," he explains:

> Of course, Dennis and Angela and Anne are fictional characters, they cannot bleed or weep, but they stand here for all the real people to whom such disasters happen with no apparent reason or justice. One does not kill off characters lightly, I assure you, even ones like Anne, evoked solely for that purpose. (*SB*, 125)

Like many of the other self-reflexive intrusions on the narrative, this Brechtian comment undercuts the verisimilitude that Lodge has managed so effectively to promote. It forces the reader to think beyond the momentary drama of the Dennis-Angela story, which will soon be superseded by other dramas in this multiplotted narrative, and to consider why a writer would "kill off characters" or create characters just to be killed off and by extension to wonder why so many have been "evoked" here anyway. Where a multiplicity of story lines in some of his other novels, notably *Small World,* helps create and maintain a necessary comic distance, here Lodge appropriates the techniques of serious realism to create figures that—though put in place quickly, mostly through the assembly-line introductory sketches of the opening pages, and without the elaborate strategies of characterization associated with traditional realism—nevertheless command emotional concern. But the rapid shifting of viewpoint and narrative focus among the various story lines combines with the many moments of broader commentary or authorial self-reflexiveness to push *Souls and Bodies* to the periphery of conventional mimesis and often to make it feel more like an essay than a novel even as its novelistic apparatus is kept in view.

The jolt of the narrator's intrusion on Dennis and Angela's second misfortune is naturalized and rendered appropriately functional by the many instances of authorial self-reflection that precede it, as when Lodge lets us in on the symbolic significance of the physical traits he is assigning to various characters and of their names, and even discusses his uncertainty in naming one of them. Though he has spoken of how such instances reveal the "provisional nature of writing" (Haffenden, 156), in fact they contribute to our sense of an author very much in control and to the self-assured tone of the commentaries on historical and religious matters distributed throughout the novel. Lodge has explained how he was led to rely on a "dominant, intrusive" authorial voice out of a need to communicate a lot of information in a short novel, especially to non-Catholic readers (Haffenden, 155).

For example, the basic metaphysic to which Catholics assented in the 1950s is described in a witty three-page essay inserted among the introductions of the individual students. In it the quest for salvation in the Catholic scheme is compared to Snakes and Ladders, purgatory to "a kind of penitential transit camp," and prayers for the deceased to "food parcels for refugees" (*SB,* 7). In the same vein, suggestive of both the author's familiarity with and distance from the worldview he is describing—and illustrating what one critic terms the "Voltarean irony" with which familiar Catholic doctrines are discussed in *Souls and Bodies*[24]— indulgences become "spiritual voucher[s]," and a plenary indulgence is termed "a kind of jackpot" (*SB,* 7, 8). Contrary to the supposition that young believers might be mindful of their own afterlives, the narrator observes that actually they look forward mostly to earthly life itself, with life after death being merely a sort of "retirement" calling for insurance: "Religion is their insurance—the Catholic Church offering the very best, the most comprehensive cover—and weekday mass is by way of being an extra premium, enhancing the value of the policy" (16–17).

In a fashion no less authoritative we are reminded of public events occurring while the various characters stake out their adult lives: developments in the arts and literature (such as the Angry Young Men, the *Chatterley* trial, and the publication of successive Graham Greene novels), in politics (the Suez crisis, the Profumo scandal, Vietnam), and of course in the Church. And just as this sort of panoramic view of public life is developed, so a nonlinear, spatial perspective on the lives of individual characters is encouraged, as the narrative often rushes us temporarily into their futures. Morace sees Lodge creating for readers a sense of time "at once specific and yet vague and confused, an ambiguous present, a pathless narrative wood" not unlike what E. L. Doctorow produced in *Ragtime* (Morace, 174). Our amusement at the slowly progressing physical contact between the awkward Dennis and the reluctantly yielding Angela in the years before the 1960s sexual revolution, or at the shyness of one of their classmates in requesting a room with a double bed during his honeymoon in 1958, is countered by hints that Dennis will have much more to worry him in coming years and that Violet, the most neurotic of the student group, will suffer many breakdowns.

Such prophetic interruptions seem intended to complicate the conventional suspense attending particular characters and their stories and to suggest larger patterns and more ultimate concerns that persons caught up in the relatively trivial issues of their daily lives tend to ignore. In the novel's opening scene, which finds the group of students along with some elderly worshippers at early mass celebrated by Father Brierley, the young people's indifference to the old people among them—their lack of curiosity about "whether a lifetime's practice of the Catholic faith and the regular reception of its sacraments has in any way mitigated the terrors [or] has . . . made the imminent parting of the spirit and its fleshly garments any less dreaded" (*SB*, 16)—points to future developments that will force each of them to wonder about such things. And later, referring to the "irresistible momentum" of the hedonistic spirit that has been set off among Catholics in their belated celebration of the sexual revolution, Lodge predicts all sorts of further reforms and insists, "Let copulation thrive, by all means." But, he adds, "[t]he good news about sexual satisfaction has little to offer those who are crippled, chronically sick, mad, ugly, impotent—or old, which all of us will be in due course" (*SB*, 121). Sex thus becomes emblematic of all activities and pursuits distracting us from the ultimate issues surrounding our existence.

The stark tone adopted in the caveat about sexual satisfaction is only one of many employed in the narrative and commentary. This variety of tones and voices relates to the multiplicity of attitudes and feelings latent even within the original group of students, which is compounded exponentially as they break out of their small circle and move into careers and new relationships, as the secular society in which they become increasing involved experiences profound developments and dislocations, especially in the 1960s, and as Catholicism itself takes a dramatically different shape. The postwar integration of Catholics into more mainstream English society meant that they would become increasingly vulnerable to outside forces and influences and that fiction representing the lives of English Catholics would increasingly need to examine the pluralist identities and allegiances taken on by believers. It is in this context that *Souls and Bodies* shows the rise of mixed marriages, as several from the original student group marry non-Catholics and as their converted spouses bring previously acquired social and moral attitudes into a Catholic community already becoming increasingly heterogeneous in its outlook.

Of course, the members of the original group themselves provide the most dramatic instances of change. They reflect Lodge's conception of his novel as a "historical project" requiring many characters to illustrate all the varieties of change he had witnessed (Haffenden, 154). The 1975 Paschal Festival in the final chapter—or more precisely, the aftermath of the festival and of the controversial film made of it by one group member's husband—operates as the end piece for the novel's frame and offers an updated inventory of the 10 original characters that mirrors the one at the beginning. Between the first chapter, titled "How It Was," and the last, "How It Is," come others with such titles as "How They Lost Their Virginities," "How Things Began to Change," "How They Lost the Fear of Hell," and "How They Broke Out, Away, Down, Up, Through, Etc.," titles indicative of Lodge's determination to move beyond the relatively narrow and static confines of *The British Museum Is Falling Down*.

While the controversy over birth control and the Church's intransigence on that matter is the source for much of the turmoil here, it seems only a symptom of a more significant dialectic between the Catholic community, as a collective and as individuals, and the modern world in general. To be sure, the issue of contraception touches the lives of all the novel's married couples and drives much of the divisiveness shown to exist within the Church. Certainly it troubles Father Brierley as he attempts to minister to his congregations through the years. But even in his story, as in all the others, it is tied to larger issues. The caustic suggestion at one point that the Catholic Church's concern with "the precise conditions under which a man was permitted to introduce his penis and ejaculate his semen into the vagina of his lawfully wedded wife, a question on which Jesus Christ himself had left no recorded opinion" (*SB*, 115), might be absurdly intrusive raises at least the additional questions of how an ancient religious institution can possibly be relevant in modern times and on what basis (and by whom) its jurisdiction is to be determined. (Not incidentally, this leads into a sketch of a contemporary secular society in which the ready availability of effective contraception has, according to the narrator, "turned Protestantism into a parody of itself" [*SB*, 115]).

Such issues are raised nowhere more sharply than through the story of Ruth after she becomes a nun, as she questions her relationship to the young women she teaches, as she sheds the traditional habit and experiences the other outreaching reforms of the convent, and as she travels in the United States seeking a more meaningful way to realize her Christian faith. They arise, too, in the development of the original student group's most conservative member, who eventually comes to criticize the Catholic hierarcy and to lead a lay movement to make the Church more open and accountable; in the spiritual journeys of those who cease to consider themselves Catholics; and in the troubled marriages, divorces, and love affairs (adulterous and otherwise) of most everyone in the novel. Such is the efficiency of Lodge's method here, and the resulting capacity of *Souls and Bodies* to accommodate meaningful narrative and commentary, that the same questioning about human love, about spirituality, and about the efficacy of Catholic doctrine within an often inimical social and economic order occurs even in the brief but pointed accounts of the novel's second generation, the children of some of the original group members.

Bernard Bergonzi has noted what a rarity David Lodge is, as a "cradle Catholic" who became a novelist yet remained a practicing Catholic (Bergonzi 1995, 29). Certainly his novels about Catholics and Catholicism carry a different tone from the fiction of Greene, Joyce, and other Catholic writers he has admired, partly because of the perspective of unprecedented change both inside and outside the Church from which he writes. At a crucial point in *Souls and Bodies,* just after revealing the

second misfortune to hit Angela and Dennis, Lodge reminds us, "I
didn't say this was a comic novel, exactly" (SB, 112). Comments like
this, as well as the whole complex of narrative self-reflection and intrusion, have contributed to some readers' view of this novel as "chilly."[25]
But such strategies clearly relate to a serious intellectual purpose transcending realism. They relate, too, to *Slaughterhouse Five,* which Lodge
identified as a prime influence in terms of the "jokey, oblique, digres-
sive" manner in which Vonnegut wrestles with a subject impossible to
treat adequately in fictional terms (Haffenden, 156). While *Souls and
Bodies* contains many amusing, even farcical moments—mostly in relation to the awkward sexual fumblings of its 1950s-vintage young
adults, augmented by the droll tone the narrator often takes—any claim
that it is comic is open to serious challenge.

For all of the novel's didactic appearance, and especially the sense of a
dominant authorial presence it imparts, to detect in it a sustained stance
on any of the several issues raised is difficult. In this connection Morace
and others have charted the twists and turns—the positionings, coun-
terpositionings and repositionings—marking the narrative persona,[26]
and Gerald Parsons has labeled the novel "calculatedly ambiguous"
(Parsons, 185).

Particularly interesting is the link drawn between the novel's mix of
realistic and antirealistic devices and the situation of contemporary
Catholics it portrays. In the voice-over to the film of the Paschal Festival, the speaker invokes a parallel between religious belief and literary
convention by insisting, "We must not only believe, but know that we
believe, live our belief and yet see it from outside, aware that in another
time, another place, we would have believed differently. . . . Just as
when reading a novel, or writing one for that matter, we maintain a
double consciousness of the characters as both, as it were, real and fictitious" (SB, 240–41). A novelist may "break frame" in a story to remind
us we are reading fiction, but on some level we know this anyway. Earlier, reflecting on our will to believe, if only in stories, Lodge observes
the irony of "[p]eople who find religious belief absurd [being] often
upset if a novelist breaks the illusion of reality he has created" (SB, 143).

This particular observation occurs within the description of a meeting
of would-be Church reformers attended by many of the novel's original
group of characters. Given the differences between their mode of wor-
ship in this setting and what they grew up with, and given the considerable damage done recently to the old metaphysic on which their earlier
faith was constructed, a "certain theological ambiguity" marks the occa-

sion. They are said to have started life with an excess of beliefs ("useless answers to non-questions") and to have shed many of them after recognizing their uselessness (*SB,* 143). The challenge facing them now is to sustain a double perspective (to "live [their] belief and yet see it from outside") without feeling belief itself to be useless or invalid, to know "how far you can go in this process without throwing out something vital" (*SB,* 143).

"Catholicism happens to be the ideological milieu I grew up in, that I know and write out of," Lodge has said (Haffenden, 152). Presumably the writing of novels about contemporary Catholics and Catholicism while feeling "hustled by history" has helped him work out his own evolving relationship with a religion and a Church that have changed radically in his lifetime and no doubt will continue to change (*SB,* 243). Altering somewhat the self-descriptive formula Graham Greene used in his later years, Lodge describes himself as an "agnostic Catholic" regarding any reality behind the Church's liturgy or the Bible (Bergonzi 1992, 71). Even so, the move away from the orthodoxy of his youth has not emptied religion of its meaning for him.

The difficult question of "How far can you go?" is raised, often directly, throughout this novel (beginning with the cover and title page in the British editions) in relation both to the abandonment of established moral and social practices and to the dismantling of traditional religious beliefs. Like most of the other questions raised here, this one receives only a cacophonous chorus of provisional responses, with very little in the way of a definitive answer. In the compassion he shows for his characters even as he imposes misfortunes on them, Lodge resembles the decidedly non-Catholic John Updike, whose work he has admired.[27] One reviewer has compared the feeling *Souls and Bodies* evokes to that of Philip Larkin's celebrated poem "Church Going," in its attention to the religious needs of the human soul in a secular and seemingly soulless age and in the nondogmatic manner of its appeal to skeptics and nonbelievers.[28] (It seems significant that Lodge includes in a conversation between Angela and one of the novel's other wives the permutations of "[un]true" and "[un]kind" talk explored in another Larkin poem, "Talking in Bed," and that he has cited Larkin in other novels, as well [*SB,* 222].) Unquestionably *Souls and Bodies* deserves to be counted along with "Church Going" and along with the reformist theologian Hans Kung's *On Being a Christian,* from which Lodge took the novel's epigram, as belonging among the last half-century's most forthright and provocative reflections on the challenge of religious belief in modern life.

Chapter Five

Postacademic Developments

In 1987 David Lodge retired from teaching at the University of Birmingham. How much the work he has completed since then represents an advance is difficult to say and is partly irrelevant in the case of a writer who has been so productive for so long and with such distinction. During the 27 years he taught at Birmingham he wrote or edited almost 20 books plus dozens of uncollected literary essays, reviews, and journalistic pieces. What seems easier to say—and what probably suggests an advance—is that his more recent projects represent changes in direction, as well as extensions of directions only begun previously, for which the freedom from teaching and other professional duties has obviously been conducive. At the very least, the move to a full-time writing career has afforded Lodge a perspective on education, the university, the academic life, and the discipline of English studies, which, even as he was moving toward it before 1987, could not have been achieved or sustained so fully had he remained on the inside. Even recent work that in terms of mode or format resembles his earlier writing shows signs of this altered perspective.

Critical Writings

Lodge reports that since giving up his academic career he has most enjoyed writing the kind of criticism that "tries to demystify and shed light on the creative process, to explain how literary and dramatic works are made, and to describe the many different factors, not always under the control of the writer, that come into play in this process" (*WP,* ix). The popularity of theory in the university, he suggests, seems to have "exhausted the energy and interest of even its devotees" (including him) and may be giving way to a more "practical" approach to writing and literature, to which he hopes his own criticism will contribute (*PW,* x). Relatedly, not long after he quit teaching at Birmingham he predicted that his future critical writing would not be "academic" in the way it had been (*AB,* 8).

Presumably this newer criticism would address the larger audience outside the university that, as Lodge has frequently pointed out, has become more distant with the rise of literary theory. While the same qualities of mind and style his earlier criticism suggests—clear argument and pointed evidence, crisp syntax and avoidance of jargon, lightness of tone and ready wit—have persisted in these latest writings, a shift is clearly evident. To the extent that collections can represent a critic's work (admittedly a risky proposition with someone so productive as Lodge), the very differences in titles and subjects between the essays in *After Bakhtin* (1990) and those in *The Practice of Writing* (1996) suggest such a shift. It is unlikely that readers outside the universities, even well-educated ones with an interest in books and writing, would as readily seek out what Lodge has to say about Bakhtin's theory or its applications, interesting though it is, as they would the essays in the more recent collection, most of which seek to illustrate how writers, including Lodge himself, move through the process of writing their fiction, poetry, and drama.

On the surface the stated intention of *The Practice of Writing* to "demystify and shed light on the creative process" resembles that of much poststructuralist theory in that it eschews the romantic notion of artistic genius operating beyond ordinary human understanding. (Relatedly, Lodge admits that writers cannot always take credit for what they do; he has often cited luck as a factor in his own writing.) The difference, of course, is that where many poststructuralists have tended to attribute literary accomplishment to impersonal social and institutional forces (economic, political, educational) and to resort to theoretical argument as a principal way of taking the wraps off the "creative process," Lodge chooses to approach writing as a practice and the writer as a practitioner (terms that blend into *practicality* and *praxis*).

Some of his most theoretical writing in the 1990s—although he might not regard it as theoretical at all—insists that theory be tied to what writers actually do. Both "Fact and Fiction: An Author's Note" (1990) and "Joyce's Choices" (1993) revisit a question of long-standing interest to Lodge. The first of these, in terms of its reliance on literary history, resembles his much earlier writing about the factuality of fiction. Like *Language of Fiction,* written a quarter century previously, this newer essay cites Ian Watt on the eighteenth-century novel's claims to truth telling. And certainly the novels it mentions represent as wide a range as those discussed in *Language of Fiction,* although interestingly the newest writer from that earlier discussion, Kingsley Amis, has been supplanted by his son Martin.

But such resemblance, stemming from what Lodge calls his essay's "occasional flourish of scholarly jargon and allusion," he attributes to its having been written originally for an academic collection. In the context of *The Practice of Writing,* he suggests, it is to be taken as "an essentially personal and anecdotal essay" (*PW,* 21). While perhaps intended to put the general reader at ease, this statement belies the essay's theoretical significance. "Fact and Fiction in the Novel" begins and ends with extensive discussion of *Small World,* and it is as useful a source of information about the origins of that novel as one could wish for. But while it can clearly be put to such use (as shown earlier in the present study), this is not its principal thrust. Rather, it ultimately concerns the much more significant question of how novelists integrate facts into basically fictional constructs (which, according to Lodge, are "founded . . . upon the reconciliation of the irreconcilable" [*PW,* 28), with his own writings and experiences as a writer, as well as those of others, providing illustrations.

That this essay has wider appeal than *Language of Fiction* relates in part to its concern, largely overlooked in Lodge's early criticism, with how actual readers often relate to writers (or at least to "inferred authors") and to its tacit recognition that on reading something that moves or otherwise interests them, most readers may wonder, "What sort of person would write something like this?" or "Did it really happen?" The essay's appeal relates, too, to its inclusive rhetoric. At one point Lodge comments, "When you are working on a book, everything that happens to you is considered for possible exploitation in the work-in-progress" (PW, 31). While such indefinite use of the second-person pronoun here and elsewhere in "Fact and Fiction" simply may be a part of the essay's relaxed tone, it connects with Lodge's concept of creative-writing study as the site where the "practice of writing" can be learned "both for its own sake and as a tool to enhance critical skills" (*PW,* x). His use of *you* implies, intentionally or not, that the readers of novels are themselves potential novelists and that they must acquire, at least vicariously, something of the novelist's skill and judgment if they are to experience a high degree of discrimination or pleasure in their reading. This is why Lodge has urged the inclusion of creative writing as part of literary education at every level (*PW,* 176).

"Joyce's Choices" likewise illustrates the level of theoretical engagement and significance in Lodge's later critical writing that its relaxed

manner and personal reference sometimes camouflage. And as the latest
of his many pieces on Joyce, this one reflects his determination to write
about novelists who have especially influenced or inspired him (*PW,* ix),
an intention even better demonstrated by several recent articles, some of
them uncollected, concerning Graham Greene, Anthony Burgess, and
Kingsley Amis. The longest single essay in *The Practice of Writing* deals
with Greene and pulls together the two parts of a lengthy review-essay,
written in 1995 for the *New York Review of Books,* concerning recent
Greene biographies, plus most of a *TLS* piece ("Graham Green: A Personal View") originally published in 1991, not long after Greene died.
To the latter Lodge attaches an exchange of letters, also first published
in the *New York Review,* that he had with the most hostile of Greene's
biographers.

While he notes a decline in Greene's later fiction, and while he might
find the Catholic novels of the middle period somewhat dated theologically, Lodge nevertheless acknowledges how Greene's work has been
"more closely entwined with my own pursuit of a literary career than
that of any other contemporary writer" and reminds those disappointed
by things they learn about Greene's personal affairs from various biographical accounts that "[r]evelations about a writer's life should not
affect our independently-formed critical assessment of his work" (*PW,*
70, 78). Lodge paid tribute to his friend Anthony Burgess in a 1987
TLS review of the first volume of Burgess's autobiography and in a piece
contributed to the *Tablet* at the time of Burgess's death. Compared with
Greene's autobiographical volumes ("masterpieces of self-concealment,"
Lodge calls them), Burgess's autobiography impresses him as "a fascinating and remarkably courageous book, self-critical but not falsely
modest" (*PW,* 143, 144). The same could be said of Burgess himself,
whom Lodge admires for having been "a Renaissance man, polyglot and
polymath, born into an age of specialization, where such energy and ver-
satility is suspected and sometimes sneered at," and for having remained
to the end "his own man, rebellious, irreverent, irrepressible."[1] As for
Amis, Lodge's obituary in the *Independent* recalled him as not only the
most gifted among the so-called Angry Young Men of the 1950s but
"the one with the most stamina and capacity for development,"[2] while
his introduction to the 1992 Penguin reissue of *Lucky Jim* pointed out
the precision and complexity of both the social history and the comedy
in Amis's most famous novel.

Among Lodge's recent critical writings, the most striking, and
arguably the most representative of his revised agenda as a critic, came

with the 50 weekly columns written for the *Independent,* beginning in
May 1991 and published, in somewhat altered form, as *The Art of Fiction*
in 1992 (some appeared in the *Washington Post* as well). Intended as a
sequel to similar columns on poetry that James Fenton wrote for the
Independent, this project appealed to Lodge's sense that despite his disin-
clination to write for an academic audience, a weekly newspaper column
might provide "an ideal platform" for addressing a more general audience about the art and history of fiction (*AF,* ix). Each piece, devoted to
a different aspect of fiction, begins with a sizable passage from a novel
(or occasionally from more than one novel), followed by Lodge's discussion of that aspect of fiction and fiction writing the passage is said to
illustrate.

Taken together, the pieces offer a remarkably wide survey of "the practice of writing," ranging from the commonplace topics of guides to reading and writing fiction (examples include "Point of View," "Time-Shift,"
"Irony," and "The Unreliable Narrator") to the seemingly whimsical
("Lists," "Weather," "The Telephone") and including such up to date
pieces as "Defamiliarization," "Intertextuality," and "Metafiction." The
series began with "Beginning" and ended with "Ending," and other pair-
ings among individual essays are possible, especially in those instances
where one literally led to another (notably "A Sense of the Past" and
"Imagining the Future"). But as Lodge notes, there is nothing systematic
or progressive about the overall sequence or movement here (*AF,* x).

Sometimes his discussion consists almost entirely of close analysis of
the passage initially quoted in terms of the technique or principle it
illustrates. "The Stream of Consciousness" and "Interior Monologue,"
for instance, start with passages from *Mrs. Dalloway* and *Ulysses,* respectively, and pretty much stay with them. More often, though, the discussion moves away from the initial quotation to range across other titles
and passages, as in "The Sense of Place," which opens with two paragraphs from Martin Amis's *Money* describing Los Angeles but soon
moves to passages from *Tom Jones* and *Oliver Twist* concerning London.
Lodge also makes references to T. S. Eliot and J. D. Salinger, to put into
historical context Amis's general method of creating a sense of place as
well as the particular language with which he exercises it.

Lodge always suggests, with characteristic conciseness and clarity, the
location and function of the cited quotation within the novel from which
it is taken. Always, too, he works to give it and the topic it illustrates
some grounding in literary history. The examination of the Joyce selections involves passing reference to the French originator of interior

monologue and to its other modern masters, Faulkner and Beckett, and
a comparison of the techniques and functions of the three *Ulysses* monologues from which the brief extracts are taken. With Woolf, Lodge notes
briefly but pointedly the shift from the high realism of the nineteenth-
century novel, with its greater attention to the social context of character, to the increased emphasis on interiority in the modern period. Additionally he offers a useful comparison between the feelings generated
toward Clarissa Dalloway in the novel named after her and in her earlier
appearance in the more straightforward *Voyage Out* to suggest the kinds
of effects possible with stream of consciousness.

   These pieces, none of which exceeds a few pages, bring together
intentions and tendencies exhibited more separately in Lodge's other
recent writings. They tend to take as their raw material the work of
those novelists who have meant most to him and to insist on the continuity—even in instances of seeming rebellion—between the English-
novel tradition as he values it and the most recent fiction. Not surprisingly, the most frequently mentioned writers here include Austen,
Fielding, and Sterne, as Lodge in essay after essay traces the roots of
contemporary practice back to the eighteenth century. His discussion of
the telephone in fiction typifies his way of noting how changes in technology that we take for granted have presented the novelist with new
resources, which in this instance extend to a very new American novel
based on telephone sex. The frequent references to film in these essays—
whether to suggest the cinematic implications (or variants) of a technique or a passage or to discuss the filmed adaptation of a particular
novel—point to an interest that connects the period when Lodge was
beginning to write *The Picturegoers* with his most recent involvement in
screenwriting and filmmaking. Where his own experiences as a writer
seem pertinent, he brings them in, as when he places his principles for
dividing his novels into chapters alongside those of Scott and Eliot or
when he shows how his own difficulty in choosing acceptable titles for
his books has been shared by novelists for centuries. Because the intention is "to suggest new possibilities of reading—and, who knows, even
writing" (*AF*, xi), revelations about the titling of *The British Museum Is
Falling Down* or the alternate title given the American edition of *How
Far Can You Go?*, like Lodge's confession that he couldn't "imaginatively
inhabit" the character of Robyn Penrose until her name was fixed (*AF*,
39), are of interest for would-be novelists as well as readers.

   Given its origins in newspaper columns that can stand independently,
The Art of Fiction seems more a book for browsing and skipping around

than for reading straight through—hence the irrelevance of one
reviewer's complaints about its lack of organization and the overlap
among individual pieces.[3] It seems a much more postmodern text, a
much freer read, than any of Lodge's other critical writings. In combining a journalistic format with the penchant to instruct evident in much
of Lodge's other writing (including parts of his novels), plus his desire to
reach an audience beyond the university, *The Art of Fiction* especially
resembles the film that Lodge helped put together for Channel Four
television at about the time he left teaching.

Ostensibly a documentary about a conference entitled "The Linguistics of Writing" held at the University of Strathclyde in Glasgow in the
summer of 1987, *Big Words: Small World* quickly becomes an examination of the nature of discourse, the state of contemporary theory, and
academic conferences in general. Coming as it did between *Small World*
and *Nice Work,* it relates to each. While offering scarcely a hint of the
kinds of carnivalesque activity common among confreres in the earlier
novel (which, Lodge later admitted, was exaggerated [*PW,* 30]), the film
does reveal an intensity and passion in the reception and discussion of
papers similar to that described in *Small World* (and concerning many of
the same theoretical issues), plus the participation of international jet-
setting academics from the United States (Stanley Fish, Mary Louise
Pratt, and others) and elsewhere (including Michael A. K. Halliday and
even Jacques Derrida). The social and political concerns of *Nice Work*
find their way into the conference and the film, as young participants
complain of their colleagues' apparent indifference to the malaise of
Thatcherite Britain and their failure even to notice the contiguous
squalor in Glasgow.

Lodge assumed several roles here, as planner and writer, as presenter
and narrator, and even as conference participant (we see him delivering
the paper that became the title essay of *After Bakhtin* and sitting jeans-
clad in the audience while others deliver their papers). One of the film's
many postmodern moments comes near the end of the first day of the
conference, with the interruption of Lodge's description of ongoing
events by Colin McCabe, who proposes, over Lodge's halfhearted
protest, that the narrative mode be broken by further interruptions of
speakers from outside (Stuart Hall, Terry Eagleton, Frederic Jameson,
and others) taking issue with Lodge's views or with various aspects of
the conference.

While such ensuing gaps in the film's narrative necessarily have a
somewhat staged feel, the conference itself takes on a more restive and

less predictable character as the fairly abstract debate over language purported to be at its center gives way to more heated disagreement over the discourse and intellectual honesty of the conference. The final section of the film focuses on participants complaining about all sorts of things, from the intrusiveness of the television cameras (a medium that, rather than being blandly neutral, is shown to have its own distinctive features)[4] to the privileging of main speakers (who, Lodge points out, are much more hesitant when deprived of the power given them by their written texts) and including the apparent inescapability of time-honored professional protocols (including the ritual of getting fed up at conferences).

Dramatic Writings

In showing an academic community struggling to retain (or to shed) its shared objectives and methods and a documentary medium struggling to confront its own emergent issues, *Big Words: Small World* often creates a sense of high drama. Although this was Lodge's first venture into large-scale television production, his involvement with stage drama dates back to his collaboration on satirical revues with Malcolm Bradbury and others during his early days in Birmingham, an experience Lodge credits with having freed up his comic gifts.[5] His interest in film, of course, dates back even further, and he worked on screenplays based on *Out of the Shelter* and *How Far Can You Go?*, though neither made it into production.

Lodge's greatest strengths as a writer of fiction have seemed to rest in talents central to writing for the stage and for film—namely his ability to imagine situations, mostly funny ones, and to write pungent dialogue. This is not to say that other aspects of his fiction, notably its narrative style, are not carefully crafted or effective but simply that the talk among his characters and the dilemmas in which they get caught stand out. (As Merritt Moseley remarks, Lodge is "not one of the writers one thinks of as a word-magician, or the possessor of an immediate style" [Moseley, 15].) Lodge has speculated on whether "that little eighth of Jewish blood in me" (his father's grandmother was Jewish) may explain his seemingly congenital liking for comedy and the absurd. No doubt his father's career as a saxophonist in London nightclubs, which introduced young David to a number of people in show business and the theater (such as Kenneth Tynan), encouraged this interest (Haffenden, 148). "There's a bit of Morris Zapp in me," he has confessed: "I have to use self-discipline, because I am sometimes tempted to use a wisecrack which isn't right in context, but I feel a glow of satisfaction when I can work in a one-liner which is contextually appropriate" (Haffenden, 165).

The ITV adaptation of *Small World,* broadcast in 1988, tested the transferability of Lodge's skills as an inventor of comic situations and dialogue to a more dramatic medium. In general, they more than passed this test, as in the especially funny episode in which Morris, bound and gagged by Fulvia Morgana at her villa, endures her husband's arrival and in certain scenes between Persse and Angelica. In some instances the television medium permitted the novel's comic potential to be enhanced, as with the prolonged kidnapping of Morris or the double casting of Hilary-Joy and Fulvia-Désirée. Not surprisingly, though, not even six hour-long episodes proved adequate to accommodate fully all of the material taken from the novel, even though many elements were excised and many others were downplayed.

Although Lodge's involvement in the production of *Small World* was limited, undoubtedly he learned a great deal from what he observed in both the production process and the finished product. This seems evident from the BBC adaptation of *Nice Work,* which appeared as a four-part serial in April 1989 and for which he wrote the script. His agreement to do so had come a year earlier, before the novel had even been published, although he delayed writing the screenplay until the novel text was "irrevocably fixed" and ready for publication. "It was as if the story was having two different 'lives,' " he recalls, "and I wanted the first to be over, as far as I was concerned, before the second one began" (*PW,* 219).

Because, as Lodge observes, turning a novel into a film even several hours long inevitably becomes "a process of reduction, condensation and deletion, rather than expansion" (*PW,* 213), *Nice Work,* with its relatively limited focus, seems a more appropriate choice for television adaptation than the much busier and more crowded *Small World.* Even so, many scenes (and even a couple of characters) of some significance in *Nice Work* had to be left out of the screen version. Also, because writing for the screen necessarily becomes a collaborative effort, in contrast with the relatively solitary pursuit of writing novels, there were outside forces and considerations that repeatedly impinged on the script as Lodge had planned and written it, especially in relation to the production's serial format, and that necessitated several rounds of rewriting (*PW,* 219–21). Despite such frustrations, the BBC's *Nice Work* represents an intelligent and highly effective transformation and illustrates how participation in the work of adaptation can, as Lodge says, be "very rewarding when it leads to the discovery of new meanings and effects in familiar material."[6]

No one fond of *Nice Work* can help but appreciate not only how much the television adaptation retains from the novel but also how much it compensates for what is missing. The basic characterization and plotting from the novel remain, and the screen version depends almost entirely on the novel for dialogue. But much of the narrative content is revealed or reinforced by the camera, and such techniques as rapid cross-cutting and the split screen permit the dramatic contrasts central to the novel's "shadow scheme" premise and its exposure of basic divisions in British society to be sped up and intensified, especially in key telephone conversations and in the ongoing comparison of Vic Wilcox's private life and work situation with Robyn Penrose's. The camera affords telling aerial views of the Birmingham equivalent of Robyn's university and the expressway system she and Vic negotiate each day, and the soundtrack augments photography to give the viewer something of the shock Robyn experiences when she enters the foundry with Vic for the first time. The production was generally fortunate in its casting, and not just in the roles of Vic and Robyn, and in a musical score that helps sustain the emotional effects of plot and script.

Probably most noticeable among the many additions in the adaptation, and especially illustrative of Lodge's contention about "new meanings and effects in familiar material," is the series of dreams Vic has of Robyn. This change originated in a passage from the novel in which Vic has just learned from Robyn that she has a boyfriend and wonders at his own surprise: "He hadn't supposed she was a virgin, for God's sake, not the way she talked about penises and vaginas without so much as a blush; nor that she was a lezzie, in spite of the cropped hair. But there was something about her that was different from the other women he knew" (*NW,* 158). After pondering this puzzle a bit more, he realizes that her independent spirit has caused him to think of her as "somehow unattached and—it was a funny word to float into his mind, but, well, *chaste*" (158). He traces this idea back to a painting he saw on a school excursion to the local art gallery 30 years before. Lodge recalls how Vic's rather detailed memory of the painting's contents but not its subject—Diana, the goddess of chastity, surprised by Acteon—was intended to produce "a very literary kind of irony at Vic's expense, appealing over his head to the educated reader to supply the missing information that explains why Vic associates Robyn with chastity and with the painting" (*PW,* 228).

He also recalls how the production's director saw in the rather brief passage, which Lodge had discarded as "antithetical to the film" and otherwise inessential, a way of rendering "the turmoil of Vic's inner emotional life as he becomes romantically infatuated with Robyn" (*PW,* 228). As a result, the televised adaptation shows Vic dreaming (and day-dreaming) of the painting, with Robyn in the role of Diana bathing with her nymphs and himself as Acteon spying on her. This dream fantasy, which is connected to other voyeuristic incidents in the story, occurs more than once and climaxes with Vic's nightmare of himself, like Acteon, being hunted down by dogs and by the archeress Robyn-Diana, from which he awakes sweaty and distraught. Like the fantasies them-selves, the subsequent flashback through which Vic is allowed to figure out their origin went far beyond anything in the novel and required elaborate technical resources (*PW,* 229), but it contributes significantly to his character as we see it.

Not surprisingly, Lodge's first full-length stage play was a comedy. Actually, the beginnings of *The Writing Game*, originally titled *The Pres-sure Cooker,* predate all of his television projects, including *Big Words: Small World,* as the first draft was written in the summer of 1985 (*PW,* 288). But because in its present form *The Writing Game* was not per-formed until 1990, and because Lodge based the television adaptation of it on that version, a discussion of the play seems most appropriate between those of *Nice Work* and *Martin Chuzzlewit.*

At the play's center is the premise of a course for amateur writers held in the British countryside and the comedy featuring three instruc-tors: Leo, a 50ish divorced American on leave from his university posi-tion in the states; Maude, somewhat younger, attractive, and married, and the author of nine best-sellers; and Simon, a much younger writer of journalism and fiction, with one blockbuster success to his credit. While the main interest revolves around Leo's pursuit of Maude and his rivalry with Simon, which have a professional as well as a sexual aspect, the play, particularly as it was revised over time, exhibits another strength evident in Lodge's fiction, namely his ability to present serious and com-plex issues and ideas in a pleasing and accessible manner.

The Anglo-American dimension of the ongoing debate Leo has with Maude and Simon connects directly with *Changing Places* and *Out of the Shelter.* When Simon asks Leo how much he knows about English liter-ary life, he replies: "You only have to go to a few publishers' parties, read the book pages in the newspapers, to understand how it works. The log-rolling, the back-scratching, the back-biting."[7] As a consequence, Leo claims, British writing is marked by a "dreadful thinness" and "glib, self-satisfied prattle" (*WG,* 87). A bit later, when Maude asks what "metafictional" means, Simon responds with an attitude similar to what Lodge himself might have been feeling in the late 1980s:

> "It's a bit of American academic jargon, Maude. Remember, Leo works in a university English Department. He can't open his mouth to breathe without inhaling a lungful of words like *metafiction, intertextuality, deconstruction.* They dance like dustmotes in the air of American classrooms." (*WG,* 88)

Other issues connect the play not only to Lodge's academic satires but to the reexamination of writing and literary theory with which his recent critical work has been increasingly concerned. Here the "practice" of writing is scrutinized as a "game," as Leo comes to reflect seriously on what has been driving him to write a new novel and as the one pupil he encounters who shows much promise gratefully acknowledges his encouragement but decides not to pursue writing. ("It seems to me that writers are a bit like sharks," she tells him. "They have to keep moving, devouring experience, turning it into writing, or they would cease to be recognized, praised, respected and that would be death for them" [*WG,* 112]). The topic of "fact and fiction in the novel" is treated extensively, as the three writers interrogate, and sometimes taunt, each other about the autobiographical origins of their novels. And Lodge skillfully weaves into their discussions and disagreements the competing claims for high culture and the literary marketplace and for the respective kinds of fiction each has produced. Simon, for instance, observes how the Aristotelian virtues of reversal and discovery have "rather lost their cutting edge, now that every TV commercial has them," and Leo complains that the "cheap tricks" of the new literary technology only work once." To this Simon responds: "Another reason why they require courage. Experimental fiction burns its bridges behind it, while the realistic novel goes trudging up and down the same, boring old highway" (*WG,* 93).

Lodge termed his participation in the Birmingham production of *The Writing Game* "the most intensely interesting experience of my literary career to date" and attributed the special gratification he had felt to the fact that "[i]n no other medium can the writer observe and measure the reception of his work so closely and intimately" (*PW,* 329, 327). Yet he also recorded the disappointments and frustrations of the process (especially if one was hoping for a London production) and the relatively small audience and financial compensation for a play compared with a novel or a script for film or television.[8] But if writing for television offers less fascination than writing for the stage, apparently Lodge has found it at least a sufficiently interesting collaborative activity to replace "the collegiate activity of university teaching" (*PW*, 216).

In the case of adapting *Martin Chuzzlewit* for the 1994 BBC production that won high praise in the United States as well as in Britain—and for Lodge an award by the British Writers' Guild in 1996 for the best adapted screenplay—there was the added interest of working from a text by a classic novelist whom he much admired. As with most film and television adaptations, and certainly those to which Lodge had been a party (including *The Writing Game*, in which its standard two acts had to be reduced by a third and reconfigured into four segments), the relatively inflexible constraints of time and division the medium imposed proved to be overriding considerations. With *Martin Chuzzlewit*, this meant first having to revise the script to include considerable additions the director requested and to adapt to the extra viewing time (and an extra episode) the BBC authorized to accommodate those additions. Then much later, when the production was proving too long even for the expanded format, Lodge had to shorten it considerably and redo climaxes and breaks between episodes that had been planned carefully. "I wondered if television drama was *ever* transmitted in the form in which it had originally been commissioned," he recalls (*PW*, 252).

Lodge has written extensively about this and other aspects of the process that resulted in the final version of the script and the finished production of *Martin Chuzzlewit*, particularly the (largely useful) disagreements between him and the director.[9] Once again he was struck by how much dialogue and narrative description the camera allowed him to dispense with in writing the script (*PW*, 213). Again, too, he had the singular pleasure of having his work read and discussed by a professional cast ("like a literary seminar at which every participant was committed one hundred per cent—something I never experienced as a university teacher" [*PW*, 251]). Among the many difficulties he faced in adapting this particular novel to television was Dickens's handling of time, which in *Martin Chuzzlewit* is as vague and implausible as in *Great Expectations* and many of his other novels. Because what the writer could put over on the reader in a 900-page novel was not likely to get past the viewer of a serial less than six hours long, Lodge had to revise and tighten up the original to fit the new medium (*PW*, 241–44).

One of the most significant examples of how he and the director, Chris Pedr, collaborated for a heightened effect concerned the casting of Paul Scofield as both old Martin Chuzzlewit and his brother Anthony. While the idea to place Scofield in both roles was Pedr's, it was inspired by a bit of dialogue Lodge had invented for a scene late in the novel, when old Martin enters the house of his dead brother's son Jonas to confront him with evidence that he killed his father. Because Dickens notes a "ghastly change" in Jonas as he sees his uncle, Lodge surmised that this might be caused by a family resemblance leading Jonas to think he is seeing his father's ghost, and so Lodge added both a line to that effect spoken by Jonas and a relevant reply from old Martin. As a result, Lodge recalls, "Reflecting that this would mean casting an Anthony who looked reasonably like Paul Scofield, it struck Pedr that, since the two brothers never appeared in the same scene, Paul could play both" (*PW,* 250).

The pleasure that Scofield's performance (one of many in the production that were nominated for major acting awards) gives viewers owes in part to this assignment of the two roles. Just as giving the same actress the parts of Philip Swallow's wife, Hilary, and his lover, Joy (or those of Désirée Zapp and Fulvia Morgan), in the adaptation of *Small World* leads not so much to the illusion that a different woman is playing each role but to pleasure at recognizing the same actress playing both even as she effects noticeable differences between the two characters (plus amusement at how literally consistent is the taste in women of both Philip and Morris Zapp), so it is with Scofield in *Martin Chuzzlewit.* While the difference in motive and manner between the two elderly brothers emerges immediately in the production, early on we suspect that the same actor is playing both, a suspicion that is soon confirmed. But ironically, even as we cease to be fooled by Scofield, we admire all the more his masterful portrayal of both the nasty Anthony and the more elegant Martin, such is the self-congratulatory pleasure we feel on having recognized him in both roles—a feeling of complicity in the production itself, somewhat analogous to the effect produced by many devices of metafiction.

Paradise News

Lodge has claimed that his roots in the English realistic tradition and his generally "orderly, sedate and protected" life have made him cautious regarding extreme experimentation (or any other extreme) in his writing. "I am not like Joyce or Beckett," he admits, "who would follow their own sense of artistic logic—indifferent to or defying the literary institution or the public." It is in this context that he has viewed *Souls and Bodies,* for example, as "quite a risky book" (Haffenden, 157).

But even by such a modest standard, *Paradise News* is decidedly not risky. In its formal appearance and in the way it generally pulls back from the kinds of radical stances frequently suggested in Lodge's academic satires, as well as in *Souls and Bodies,* it is his most realistic, least complicated, and least experimental fiction since *Out of the Shelter.* Indeed, in some respects it is even more straightforward than *Out of the Shelter,* as it lacks even the modest degree of stylistic experimentation found in that earlier novel (particularly its revised version). And while Lodge's next four works of fiction tended to avoid a single central character, through either the opposition of dual protagonists (*Changing Places* and *Nice Work*) or the unfocused effect produced by a large cast of characters (*Small World* and *Souls and Bodies*), *Paradise News* returned to the practice of his earliest fiction by emphasizing a main line of action featuring one character.

It might even be argued that *Paradise News* exceeds the early novels in its stress on a traditional protagonist. There is no secondary figure or subplot here given a degree of interest or complexity comparable to that of Clare Mallory, Mike Brady, Barbara Appleby, or Timothy Young's sister Kate or to what happens to each of them. To be sure, Yolande Miller, as both the driver of the car that accidentally hits Bernard Walsh's father and the woman with whom Bernard subsequently falls in love, represents an interesting twist, but it is a twist that focuses our attention mostly on the personal problems of Bernard himself. As a personality Yolande commands much less independent interest than does Clare, Mike, or Kate, partly because each of them is made into more of a puzzle and an object of suspense—for the central figures with whom they are connected as well as for the reader. The closing soliloquy of *The British Museum* permits Barbara Appleby to upstage her husband, something Lodge never allows to happen to Bernard Walsh, and it reinforces that novel's parodic structure, which, among other things, detracts from any conventionally realistic agenda of plot and characterization, whether the author's or the reader's.

As for Bernard's Aunt Ursula, whose wish to see her brother before she dies motivates father and son to travel to Hawaii, the imminence of her death, rather like the two-week travel package on which Bernard and his father visit her, operates as one of the novel's framing assumptions—so much so that the scene of her dying need not be shown directly but only described afterward, in a lengthy letter from Yolande to Bernard that itself mostly concerns the funeral and ultimately focuses on their relationship. Of course, Lodge's portrayal of the terminally ill Ursula raises the question of how to approach death and offers a thoughtful answer, but that question (along with its corollary, how to live) seems transferred to most of the other characters, especially Bernard, and to the artificial earthly paradise affected by Hawaii. Like Yolande, and like Bernard's father and his sister Tess, Ursula offers Bernard a relationship in which he can ponder and explore the fuller and more rewarding responses to life that prior circumstances and conditioning have discouraged him from cultivating.

This centrality of Bernard is produced and sustained by a narrative point of view that is almost exclusively his. Only for brief interludes, and mostly for the satire afforded by glimpses at the package tourists accompanying him and his father from London to Honolulu, does the narrative abandon his perspective. Furthermore, very little of Lodge's capacity for elaborate reversals and twists of sequence is to be found here. The few flashbacks, such as the second chapter (which explains how Bernard and Mr. Walsh came to be at Heathrow, where the first chapter is set), are clear and direct. The chief way in which Lodge enlivens the novel's otherwise linear structure is by shifting its format, so that halfway through, third-person narration gives way to 60 pages of detailed journal entries by Bernard, followed by 20 pages of letters and postcard messages to and from members of the tour group.

Such conservative devices only confirm the novel's realistic tendencies. Perhaps the antirealistic elements in the three academic satires and *Souls of Bodies* resulted in part from Lodge's discouragement at the failure of *Out of the Shelter*. If so, his reversion to realism in *Paradise News* suggests not so much a rejection of experimentation or a return to traditional practice as an attempt to create something of value by relying on the resources of realism and on his judgment of their appropriate use, a judgment sharpened by having written four highly successful novels. Seen in this light, the nonexperimental *Paradise News* itself constitutes a sort of experiment, somewhat like that of a composer reverting to tonal composition after having succeeded with atonality. Of course, this comparison is undercut by the formal tension between realistic and antirealistic practices seen even in Lodge's most experimental writing and by his use of realism in some of his critical and theoretical writings as an analog to liberal humanism (and to religious belief in *Souls and Bodies*). Because in both his theory and his practice he had continued to value realism, especially as he found it affirmed by Bakhtin, a Lodge novel relying almost exclusively on the techniques of realism had never ceased to be a real possibility.

In the case of *Paradise News,* realistic conventions seem tied to the nature of the protagonist and his story and to the tone they are designed to command. The novelist Jane Smiley has insisted that while less complex than *Small World* and less profound than *Souls and Bodies, Paradise News* is nevertheless "a working comic machine, and a pleasure to read." Her concept of comedy does not necessarily involve funniness but rather points to a formal structure proposing "the possibility of integration" (such as marriage or something like it), which in *Paradise News* takes the form of Bernard's match-up with Yolande and the two brother-sister reconciliations (his father's with Ursula, paralleled by his own with Tess).[10] As Lodge conceives of them, these are relatively gentle matters, and certainly Bernard is depicted as a gentle person. Apparently, in presenting them Lodge saw little need for the antitraditional techniques employed in his other, less gentle novels. And while this is not a "funny" novel per se, his confidence in such a venture is no more evident than in the handling of humor here, from the satirical sketches of the tourists to the insightful images used to cast Bernard's situation—as when his inability to forget a painful episode is explained by the narrator's calling the mind a "capricious and undisciplined creature" and observing that "[y]ou couldn't always keep it on a lead, and it was for ever dashing off into the undergrowth of the past, digging up some decayed bone of memory, and bringing it back, with tail wagging, to lay it at your feet" (*PN,* 25).

One element of the story that permits, and perhaps demands, more or less exclusive attention to Bernard is the singularity of his situation. Smiley describes him as "the man the boy in *Out of the Shelter* might have become had he merely been visited rather than carried off to Germany by his glamorous female relative,"[11] and it is indeed interesting that both novels are premised not just on the change of location or the international travel so common with Lodge but on the beckoning of a faraway older woman to whom the central character is related. But if Bernard's story seems a milder version of Timothy Young's, in some important respects it is much more extreme.

So rich is the bildungsroman tradition, and so strong the anxiety of influence it might cause, that a principal concern in writing a novel like *Out of the Shelter* surely must be the avoidance of cliché. But Lodge hardly faced this problem with Bernard Walsh. Not that other novels have not dealt with ex-priests trying to make their way in the world, but the shelter out of which Bernard must climb is an especially deep one. As the novel opens, he is in his mid-40s, having served first as a teacher in a seminary and later as a parish priest before having a brief affair with a female parishioner caused him to leave the priesthood and the Church. In the few years since, he has been earning a scant living teaching theology part-time in a small nondenominational college in Rummidge (the same Birmingham-inspired setting used in the academic satires). The repression caused by his lower-middle-class London upbringing, which from the beginning marked him to be a priest, has been augmented by severe self-doubts, stemming largely from the disaster of his only sexual encounter, his parishioner having been only slightly less inexperienced than he.

Lodge helps (indeed, forces) Bernard out of this stifling environment and mind-set, first by transporting him into the commercialized hedonist culture of contemporary Hawaii, which invites him to become a more complete person than England ever did; then by consigning his fussy father to a prolonged hospital stay, thus freeing up Bernard to attend more to his own desires; and finally by providing him with an irresistible incentive to enjoy himself in the social and sexual way he has come to regard as unobtainable, in the form of the kind and perceptive Yolande.

In the 1991 documentary *Profile of David Lodge* produced for ITV, Lodge noted how in *Nice Work* he had sought to avoid the conventional depiction of sex by having the woman initiate the man. Certainly Robyn Penrose is able and willing to instruct the relatively naive Vic Wilcox and to reassure him about a problem like impotence ("If it happens, it doesn't matter, OK?" [*NW,* 208]). A similar situation, in which the less experienced male is aided and comforted by the more knowing female, occurs near the end of *Out of the Shelter,* when the American teenager Gloria calms the shame-stricken Timothy Young after he has ejaculated prematurely into her hand:

—I'm sorry, he said hoarsely, keeping his head turned away from her.
—What for? (*OS,* 241)

But Lodge takes this dynamic much further in *Paradise News.* The single incident of sexual instruction is made plural, is spread over several days, and mostly is not shown directly. As with the Robyn-Vic and

Gloria-Timothy relationships, this one moves toward a physical encounter only gradually, though the prior stages (initial meeting, telephone conversations, dinner at Yolande's, dinner out) necessarily cover a
shorter time span. Though both dinners go well, each ends abruptly
when Bernard is overcome by the fear that things will get physical and
he will again fail. After the evening at Yolande's, when she recounts her
life but he is afraid to talk much about his, he begins a journal that ultimately includes all the things from his past that he wishes he could
share with her. After he leaves her at the end of their evening at a
restaurant, the realization of how strange his behavior must have
seemed prompts him to deliver the journal ("or confession, or whatever
it was") to her mailbox as an explanation.[12]

Fortunately it happens that besides being attractive and sexually
knowledgeable, Yolande is also a professional counselor experienced in
sex therapy and generous with her expertise. Because Bernard's problems go far beyond Timothy's or Vic's, more than a well-meaning Gloria
or Robyn is required to rescue him. Yolande's skill at reading troubled
personalities, plus her immediate access to Bernard's past through his
journal, allows the subsequent short-circuiting of their relationship to
remain well within the novel's realistic frame. She immediately becomes
his guide. When he refers to his fear of lovemaking, she replies: "I could
teach you. I could show you how. I could heal you, Bernard, I know I
could" (PN, 214). After she describes his journal as a "cry for help" and
confesses her own need for some loving, he agrees to begin his tutelage:

> It was as if all his life he had been holding his breath, or clenching his
> fist, and now at last he had decided to exhale, to relax, to let go, not car-
> ing about the consequences, and it was such a relief, such a violent meta-
> bolic change, that he felt momentarily dizzy. He swayed on his feet and
> staggered slightly as Yolande hugged him. (PN, 215)

Things proceed smoothly between them, and if Bernard's idea that
he loves Yolande and that they ought to marry echoes what Vic mistak-
enly tells Robyn after they have had sex, Yolande's more mixed response
signals that Bernard may be less mistaken. Jane Smiley observes that
one of the principal pleasures of Paradise News ("in lieu of funniness") is
the "satisfying and believable integration of Bernard with his body," and
Lodge has insisted on the contemporary novelist's obligation to treat
sexuality, in all of its wonder and complexity, as an essential part of
being human.[13] The self-awareness and self-confidence Bernard gains
with Yolande's assistance prepare him to establish a deeper, more satisfy-

ing relationship with his sister Tess when she comes to Hawaii to check
on their father. He is also able to facilitate more capably the reunion of
his father and aunt, who parted on bad terms decades earlier.

Repeatedly Yolande cites honesty as Bernard's most salient virtue. "I
could tell you were an honest man," she says to him early in their relationship. "There aren't so many left" (*PN*, 139). Later, when the husband
from whom she has been separated seeks a reconciliation, she explains
her refusal by saying, "Lewis is all right, but he's not an honest man"
(*PN*, 292). But if Bernard is honest when Yolande first meets him, he is
also fearful, guilt ridden, and wracked by a sense of helplessness, emotions that relate to his sexual hang-ups and impede fully honest behavior.
While in a sense Yolande does not need to make him honest, in a sense
she does, and this seems to hinge on helping him feel more comfortable
about his body and about his sexuality. Being honest is what allows him
to get closer to his sister, but that occurs only after Yolande has helped
him be other things as well. In this, Lodge demonstrates the interdepen-
dence of all spheres of human feeling and activity, the connectedness of
the sexual sphere to all the others, and by implication, the severe short-
coming—even dishonesty—of any contemporary fiction that has the
opportunity to deal openly with sex but fails to do so.

In its simple design, and especially in the story of Bernard and
Yolande, *Paradise News* perhaps merits Smiley's description of it as "a
satisfying doodle more English than worldly."[14] Most everybody gets
together by the end. And even if Bernard and Yolande may not marry,
or at least not right away, they may, and they certainly will be together,
thus offering another instance of the conciliatory endings so common in
Lodge's fiction, which some critics consider overly sentimental. The discovery of a long-forgotten 1950s share of IBM stock in a drawer at
Ursula's apartment, which assures her financial security and a healthy
sum for each of her relatives when she dies, would probably also dissat-
isfy purist critics. But like the windfall inheritance Robyn receives near
the end of *Nice Work* or the marriage of Austin Brierley to the woman
with whom Dennis has had an affair in *Souls and Bodies*, such a device
serves mainly to facilitate closure while leaving the novel's ethical and
psychological realism intact.

To view *Paradise News* as only or even as mainly a love story or a novel
about relationships is to ignore many of its principal elements. Perhaps
most significant, such a view fails to consider the religious terms and
indices that frequent and at times take over the text. Late in the novel,
after Bernard has returned to Rummidge, we see him lecturing on the

question of what can be salvaged from the "eschatological wreckage" of traditional Christianity (*PN,* 280), particularly without the concept of an afterlife. Moving through a number of related issues and arguments and alluding to many sources reflecting his (and Lodge's) reading— mostly theologians, of course, but perhaps also some critical theorists[15]— he ends up by citing the apocalyptic passage from Matthew on the sepa- ration of sheep from goats at the Second Coming and comments, "It's as if Jesus left this essentially humanist message knowing that one day all the supernatural mythology in which it was wrapped would have to be discarded" (*PN,* 283). In similarly detailed fashion, theology often enters into Bernard's dealings with his dying aunt Ursula. In the scene in which she asks him whether he believes in an afterlife, for instance, he in turn asks her whether she wants to live forever, and Lodge devotes five pages of dialogue to their exchange of responses and insights (*PN,* 205–9).

But religion operates here also on a simpler yet in some ways more pervasive level than that of explicitly theological speech or dialogue. In the very first scene one of the Heathrow travel agents tells a colleague that they are like "guardian angels" for their customers, and the narra- tor notes how one of the travelers possesses a "halo of fine light curls" (*PN,* 7, 8). The same page initiates the elaborate pattern of paradise-talk that will extend to the novel's end (a pattern already suggested by its title and epigraph), as the young woman with the "halo" remarks that Hawaii is said to be "like Paradise" (*PN,* 8). This connection between Hawaii and paradise, in turn, is reinforced by an anthropologist travel- ing with the tour group who, in his research on the idea of tourism as the new world religion, searches for as many uses of the word *paradise* as possible during his time in Hawaii, a formidable task given the readiness of local businesses to include that word in their names and advertising. In recounting his experience as a parish priest, Bernard pulls many of these terms and ideas together and reverses the connection established earlier when he asserts that "[t]he Good News is news of eternal life, Paradise news" and recalls how "[f]or my parishioners, I was a kind of travel agent, issuing tickets, insurance, brochures, guaranteeing them ultimate happiness" (*PN,* 153).

Given its preoccupation with religion, a case might be made for including *Paradise News* among Lodge's novels about Catholics and Catholicism, and indeed Bernard Bergonzi has discussed it in a chapter titled "Catholic Questions" (Bergonzi 1995, 29–59). Obviously Cathol- icism figures heavily in Bernard's story, and not just in his past. Because

Ursula's troubles with her brother's family stemmed from her having married a divorced American, she hopes that the news that she has returned to the Church will place her in a better light with them. Religious observances figure prominently in developments connected with her, especially her reunion with her brother, which is climaxed by communion and the Sacrament of the Sick (or Extreme Unction, as it was formerly called) administered by a priest in her hospital room, with Bernard, his father, and Tess present.

But certain factors mitigate against classifying this as a novel about Catholics and Catholicism in the same sense as Lodge's others and suggest instead a broader orientation. In his 1959 M.A. thesis on the Catholic novel since the Oxford movement, Lodge traced the overall shift that had occurred in Catholic fiction from an intellectual to an imaginative and emotional interpretation of religion in relation to life, concluding with Graham Greene. Later he would note a move away even from the "high-cultural equivalent of the Catholic ghetto" represented by Greene's novels (quoted in Bergonzi 1980, 177), presumably as the Catholic ghetto itself had begun to disappear from English life. Although Bergonzi has credited Lodge's novels through *Souls and Bodies* with "faultless precision" in describing recent changes in the Church, he insists that Lodge's fiction has been part of the fall of Catholic fiction from the "dangerous peaks" where carnal and divine passion could become confused to "the flat, populous plain where most of us live our daily lives" (Bergonzi 1980, 186–87).

Paradise News represents both a continuation of this trend and a departure from it. Because in a sense Bernard Walsh is a post-Catholic, to the extent that the novel centers on him it too merits that label. Where Austin Brierley in *Souls and Bodies,* for all of the changes his beliefs have undergone, seems determined to remain a Catholic of some sort and to locate at least on the rebellious fringes of the institutional Church, such a stance would be unthinkable for Bernard. He had lost his faith—he had become "an atheist priest, or at least an agnostic one" (*PN,* 154)—long before the crisis with the parishioner forced him to leave the priesthood. When during his crisis period he sought to be laicized (a plan he would later term "naive and ill-thought-out"), it was only to avoid hurting his parents, whose simple faith was "as vital to them as the circulation of their blood" (*PN,* 168, 169). They were predictably shocked when he resigned from the priesthood without being laicized (thus in effect ex-communicating himself), and his mother prayed for the return of his faith until her death. Bernard Bergonzi insists that despite their piety the Walsh family had been "permeated by self-deception and bad faith," and he sees in the contrast between the depiction of them and the way the Mallory family in *The Picturegoers* is portrayed a measure of the distance Lodge had moved from his earlier concept of Catholic fiction (Bergonzi 1995, 40).

The seminarians Bernard once taught have been replaced by a mix of students at the college, most of them non-Catholics, and his approach to theology, though informed and sincere, is essentially secular and unmarked by any passion of assent. There seems to be no question of his returning to the Church or to his earlier belief system, which makes up part of his "baggage of guilt and failure" (*PN*, 77). He tries to avoid religious topics with his father, and in trying to help his dying aunt he approaches the Church warily, to the point of uncertainty over accepting a kindly priest's blessing.

And yet, post- (or ex-) Catholic though he is, Bernard troubles over broadly religious issues when he troubles over the failures of his life. At one point during their flight to Honolulu, his father gives voice to some of Bernard's feelings by citing his unrealized potential and concluding, "But he threw it away. A wasted life I call it" (*PN*, 46). (Similarly, Tess judges Bernard's life "a mess" [*PN*, 32].) As Bernard dozes during the flight, he dreams a distorted version of the Penny Catechism (Who made you? Why did God make you? etc.), which ends with his answering the question as to whether he is "religious" in a disinterested sense (for the sake of being religious), "No. I would like to be. I thought I was, once. I was wrong" (*PN*, 48). Such is the fatalistic sense of being at a loss that he projects that, prior to their discussion on the afterlife, Ursula is prompted to ask, "Do you believe in anything at all?" (*PN*, 205).

One thing that assuredly does not satisfy Bernard's itch to believe is the very subject he teaches, especially in its more extreme forms. Reminiscent of Lodge's comments about poststructuralist literary theory is Bernard's view that "the discourse of much modern radical theology was just as implausible and unfounded as the orthodoxy it had displaced, but nobody noticed because nobody read it except those with a professional stake in its continuation" (*PN*, 29). For this reason the escape to Hawaii from the narrow academic path on which he has been moving, and the leap into the quotidian it entails, is singularly fortuitous. The unfortunate episode with the parishioner had been an alert (even now he admits, "I felt more alive than I had done for years" [*PN*, 167]). The unexpected telephone call from his long-estranged aunt halfway around the world leads him to the experience of being loved and of loving far beyond anything he has known previously. The chance to be served by Yolande and the chance to serve Ursula (as well as his father and sister) complete him in ways his cramped background had never allowed.

What Bernard is seeking emerges in an epiphany inspired by the surfers off Waikiki beach:

> Tensed and balanced, knees flexed, backs arched, hands grasping the curved steel bows that harnessed their bellying sails, they careened toward the shore under the curling crests of the rollers and then . . . leaped like salmon through the spume of the oncoming waves. . . . They seemed to have discovered the secret of perpetual motion. They seemed, to Bernard, like gods. (*PN*, 210)

An equally crucial recognition occurs when, while searching for keys lost in the sand, he makes use of the twilight, so that "something gleamed and glinted, something reflected back the light of the setting sun, like a tiny star in the immensity of space" (*PN*, 165)—an incident Yolande interprets as emblematic of bending good fortune to advantage. "Life is full of surprises," she tells him, but she adds, "[W]e have to make our own heaven on this earth . . . [a]nd answer our own prayers" (*PN*, 220).

The lure of an earthly paradise is, of course, what motivates tourists who come to Hawaii—whom the anthropologist in the group calls "pilgrims," in keeping with his thesis that "sightseeing is a substitute for religious ritual" ("The sightseeing tour as secular pilgrimage. Accumulation of grace by visiting the shrines of high culture. Souvenirs as relics. Guidebooks as devotional aids" [*PN*, 61]). Lodge's pilgrims include honeymooners, second honeymooners, working women on holiday, and families. Such transference of the pilgrimage concept from the international scholarly conferences of *Small World* to the group tour extends the satire of academic pretentiousness and self-promotion begun in earlier novels.

However, Lodge does propose a more serious connection between the quest of such contemporary secular pilgrims, as well as the banal appropriations of the term *paradise* throughout the world (including his own city of Birmingham, which boasts a Paradise Circus and a Paradise Plaza), and the traditional preoccupation of theologians and other religious persons with the idea of heaven. At the very least, the novel suggests that to be meaningful, religion and theology must offer us news about paradise that accords with our concerns and needs as earthly creatures.

Therapy

Near the end of David Lodge's 10th novel, the main character, a highly successful 58-year-old television sitcom writer named Lawrence "Tubby" Passmore, and his first teenage sweetheart, with whom he has been reunited, look up at the Milky Way. When he tells her about the attitude of the ancient Greeks toward that particular galaxy and about pre-Christian pilgrimages organized to follow it as far as possible, she asks, "Goodness, how do you know all these things, Tubby?" He answers, "I look them up. It's a habit."[16] Throughout *Therapy* we see Tubby looking up all sorts of things (mostly strange words but sometimes more extensive information he wants or needs to find)—his way, he claims, of compensating for the formal education he lost out on by doing poorly on exams and leaving school at the age of 16.

Readers have often commented on the peculiar power of David Lodge's fiction to deliver information on a variety of subjects. While his ability to clarify for his mostly non-Catholic readership the intricacies of Catholic beliefs and practices or to formulate concisely the often obscure positions and arguments advanced by contemporary literary theorists is especially impressive, the same ability to inform and instruct, usually while maintaining a light tone, extends also to many small matters that arise in establishing a setting or developing a character. Sometimes his novels acknowledge the help of individuals with certain bits of information—such as those related to the military matters dealt with in *Ginger, You're Barmy* or the world of business and industry in *Nice Work*—and one of them (*Small World*) even cites particular books that proved especially helpful.

Such clarity and precision seem indicative of Lodge's own propensity for looking things up. But he has expressed skepticism as to whether they necessarily indicate a deep knowledge, as he recently noted how "[r]eaders of novels often assume that the knowledge of a particular subject displayed in its pages must be the visible tip of a submerged iceberg of information, when in fact there is no iceberg—the tip is all there is."[17] No doubt it is usually true that information about an unfamiliar subject that a writer seeks and finds does not go beyond what the immediate writing task requires and is displayed entirely in the completed piece of writing. This seems the case, for example, with the details of the air travel industry presented in *Small World* and *Paradise News,* or the brief but useful description of the arthroscopic knee surgery that Tubby Passmore undergoes in the first part of *Therapy.*

But sometimes a writer's knowledge comes out of extended background exposure—Lodge's familiarity with Catholicism or with the South London or Birmingham settings he renders so suggestively are prime examples—or from experiences that initially have nothing to do with any fiction he might write (what he noticed about America during his trips in the 1960s, or about Hawaii from his own visit to a dying aunt, or even his grasp of literary theory, acquired through years of study, teaching, and academic writing). His novels offer many examples of an authorial understanding about esoteric subjects that extends far beyond those few particulars that happen to get mentioned.

One such subject is the pilgrimage to the shrine of St. James at Santiago de Compostela, in the most northwestern corner of Spain, which figures prominently in the final section of *Therapy*. When Tubby and his newly rediscovered sweetheart, Maureen, gaze up at the Milky Way, three days have passed since she completed the grueling 800-kilometer walk from southwestern France to Santiago. They have driven out to the coast for their last evening together before they must return, separately, to England. This final part of the novel has been describing the gradual reawakening of their love 40 years after they last saw each other and after Tubby has been hard pressed to find Maureen on her pilgrimage. Included in his rather lengthy account of tracking her down is what amounts to several pages of detailed information on the nature and history of the pilgrimage, which carries independent interest even when its fictional context is disregarded.

Virtually all of this information is taken, sometimes verbatim, from a Lodge piece concerning the Santiago pilgrimage that appeared in the *Independent on Sunday* in December 1993 and that, like the corresponding portion of the novel, describes such things as the symbology of the scallop shells attached to pilgrims' rucksacks, the dubious origin of James as Spain's patron saint and of the shrine itself, and the cultural and commercial factors behind the centuries-old pilgrimage and the recent burst of interest in it. Reversing the tour-as-pilgrimage formula proposed by the anthropologist in *Paradise News*, Lodge insists that "the analogy works both ways," as he points out how medieval pilgrims resemble today's package tourists. Both the newspaper piece and the novel sort out the various types of pilgrims, old and new, as well as their motives for making the difficult journey, to suggest that both recently and in the past, "There is no doubt that for some the pilgrimage was a life-changing experience; but for many it was an excuse to see the world and have a good time."[18]

But that newspaper article was hardly the ultimate source for the depiction of the Santiago pilgrimage in *Therapy*. In this instance "looking it up" for Lodge meant searching out the actual route pilgrims took, exploring Santiago and the cathedral housing the St. James shrine, and turning out a documentary on the entire business. His *Independent on Sunday* piece was published on the same day the BBC broadcast his film *The Way of St. James*. The article refers to the abbreviated manner in which Lodge made his way to Santiago, almost entirely by automobile and in the company of a camera crew. His actual walking along the pilgrims' route, like Tubby Passmore's, was confined mostly to the very last stretch, from the village closest to the cathedral city, a painless experience compared with that of Maureen and the mass of other pilgrims described in *Therapy* and shown in the documentary.

Lodge turns this into an inside joke with a prefatory note to the novel referring to a not entirely fictitious writer-presenter of a television documentary whom the reader will encounter in the final section. Sure enough, at one point during Tubby and Maureen's slow progress toward Santiago, they come upon a BBC unit making a film about the pilgrimage, just when the director needs an English pilgrim to be interviewed. After Maureen refuses and Tubby is selected, things come to a halt while crew members search for the writer-presenter, whose name happens to be David. According to the director, who ends up having to do the interview himself, "[David]'s probably sulking because he had to actually *walk* a bit this morning" (*T,* 304). A further extension of Lodge's experience in making the Santiago film came when he discovered, in a 1994 book on travels in Catholic Europe, a description of himself with the BBC crew in Galicia during the summer of 1992. (He said that this discovery was "like catching sight of yourself on a TV monitor.")[19] And just as Lodge himself was recognized by the author of the travel book, he similarly makes sure that a member of the film crew in *Therapy* recognizes Tubby Passmore.

Of course, the extensive treatment of Santiago de Compostela in the novel, in the newspaper pieces, and in the documentary represents only a part of Lodge's larger interest in modern pilgrimages generally, an interest that directly connects *Therapy* with *Paradise News*. To be sure, such connections are readily detectable in the work of any writer as prolific as David Lodge. His early novels easily can be seen as forerunners of the later ones, and sometimes he creates connections rather gratuitously, as when he identifies one of the package tourists in *Paradise News* as

Brian Everthorpe, the same character who carried on an affair with Vic Wilcox's secretary in *Nice Work* and conspired against Vic.

Even so, *Therapy* seems especially rich in links with Lodge's other fiction. Like Timothy Young and the students portrayed in *Souls and Bodies*—and like Lodge himself—Tubby Passmore was born in 1935. Like Dennis and Angela, the older Maureen and her husband have been shaken recently by the death of a child. Like various characters from the three academic satires as well as Bernard Walsh in *Paradise News* (and Brian Everthorpe, too), Tubby lives in Rummidge, though his work frequently takes him to central London, where he maintains an apartment, rather like the latter-day David Lodge (hence the frequent and reliable-seeming renderings of the London-Rummidge train commute). Tubby's wife, Sally, teaches at Vic Wilcox's alma mater, Rummidge Polytechnic, recently upgraded to university status. And not surprisingly, Tubby's recollection of National Service in the 1950s replicates, though much more briefly, the overall experience and sentiment of Jonathan Browne in *Ginger, You're Barmy*.

But such things suggest only a relatively superficial overlap among the novels. More significant, and more suggestive of integral interests and issues accruing in Lodge's fiction through the years and consolidating in *Therapy*, is the relationship between Tubby and Maureen as teenagers. Although both were South Londoners from working-class backgrounds, Maureen was a Catholic. In fact, her family attended the same church, Our Lady of Perpetual Succour (Brickley), as the Mallorys in *The Picturegoers*. Tubby's memoir of Maureen traces in detail his romantic feelings for her, their gradual coming together, and their abrupt parting, developments that occurred over a period of roughly two years.

Although when he first met Maureen he was somewhat younger than Dennis is at the opening of *Souls and Bodies*, the non-Catholic Tubby was just as indifferent to religion. Like Dennis's church-related activities, Tubby's membership in the parish youth club and his participation on the church football team were intended primarily to please his girlfriend and to keep other boys away from her. While the account of Tubby and Maureen's increasing physical intimacy recalls that of other young couples in Lodge novels—Mark and Clare in *The Picturegoers*, Jonathan and Pauline in *Ginger, You're Barmy*, and Adam and Barbara in *The British Museum Is Falling Down*—it especially resembles that of Dennis and Angela in terms of its emphasis on their generation's innocence.

For the older Tubby the paradoxes and hypocrisies of the earlier period are encapsulated in one of the approved ways in which young men and women could relate physically at that time:

> Dancing meant that, even in a church youth club, you were actually allowed to hold a girl in your arms in public, perhaps a girl you'd never even met before you asked her to dance, feel her thighs brush against yours under her rustling petticoats, sense the warmth of her bosom against your chest. . . . Of course you had to pretend that this wasn't the point of it, you had to chat about the weather or the music or whatever while you steered your partner around the floor, but the license for physical sensation was considerable. Imagine a cocktail party where all the guests are masturbating while ostensibly preoccupied with sipping white wine and discussing the latest books and plays, and you have some idea of what dancing was like for adolescents in the early nineteen-fifties. (*T,* 235–36)

In wondering at the current contrast "between the eroticism of the ambiance . . . and the tactile impoverishment of the actual dancing" (*T,* 235), Tubby carries some authority, having been a skilled dancer when he was young (and before he was tubby). Indeed, despite their considerable piety, Maureen, Angela, and probably most of the young women he knew then would have been happy to dance with him, and in the manner he describes. The pique with which he describes it is informed in part by the memory of how he was often moved by physical and psychological stimuli such as dancing to greater intimacy with the innocent but readily acquiescent Maureen once they were alone together, until fear of the consequences of sin (a fear encouraged in the same church where they were encouraged to dance) set in, and she retreated. It is informed, too, by the recollection of his response to her rebuff: he hurt her by breaking off the relationship and flirting with another girl without any explanation, and he never tried to see her again—a decision he has come to regard as the determinant mistake of his life.

Tubby comes to realize this only after he has been wrestling for some time with an inexplicable bout of depression, to which he believes a mysterious recurring pain in his knee is related. Lodge has stated that the most important starting point for this novel was the idea of depression, both personal and societal, coupled with the related notion of therapy ("If the 'sixties were about politics, the 'seventies about sex, and the 'eighties about money, then [it seems to me] the 'nineties are about therapy" [Kierkegaard, 36]). Through the experiences of Tubby and some of his friends, the novel pokes fun at the contemporary therapeutic culture. Tubby tells us:

> I have a lot of therapy. On Mondays I see Roland for Physiotherapy, on Tuesdays I see Alexandra for Cognitive Behavior Therapy, and on Fridays I have either aromatherapy or acupuncture. Wednesdays and Thursdays I'm usually in London, but then I see Amy, which is a sort of therapy too, I suppose. (*T,* 14–15)

More seriously, *Therapy* updates the social critique of *Nice Work* through Tubby's frequent reflections on the malaise of British society in the early 1990s. Referring to the kidnap and murder of the two-year-old James Bulger by older boys in early 1993, he asks in what sort of society such things can happen and answers, "A pretty sick one" (*T,* 72). The relevance of emotional illness emerges explicitly when he reflects on the economic recession that Britain is undergoing and on the high incidence of psychological depression in a time of increasing unemployment, business collapse, and home repossession. At one point he discovers that the unresponsiveness of an audience of workers brought in for the taping of an episode of his sitcom is probably due to their having just learned that their factory will be shut down and they will lose their jobs. Having read that John Major, too, has a bad knee, he comments, "Explains a lot, that" (*T,* 37).

One of the running gags in Tubby's narrative concerns the acronym IDK. After his knee fails to respond to surgery, his physiotherapist informs him that he has Internal Derangement of the Knee and also notes the bit of medical code this disguises: "Internal Derangement of the Knee. I.D.K. I Don't Know" (*T,* 13). Tubby goes on to modify this formula to fit various problems of contemporary Britain: the royal family's dysfunction ("Dianagate, Camillagate, Squidgey tapes, Charles's tampon fantasies, Fergie's toe-sucking. Internal Derangement of the Monarchy" [*T,* 92]); the rise of mortgage rates, depression in the housing values, and the resulting "negative equity" ("when your mortgage is more than your home is worth . . . a kind of internal derangement of the property market" [*T,* 104]); and the crisis of confidence in the government and in Britain's future ("Internal Derangement of the National Psyche" [*T,* 103]).

Of course, such observations, like his preoccupation with the decline of the railroads under privatization or with England's demise as a football power since the 1960s, cross the imperceptible line between social commentary and characterization. Partly because there is no omniscient narrator here, because *Therapy* relies wholly on Tubby to tell us the story, it hardly approaches *Nice Work* as a state-of-England novel, and it is totally lacking in the "essay" feeling many readers have reported with

Souls and Bodies. Significantly, Tubby's comments on British society, like his knee complaints, largely cease once he begins to focus on finding Maureen.

Much of the impetus of his search for her comes from an initially unpredictable source. While early on he occasionally recalls Maureen in passing, not until after he has discovered the nineteenth-century existentialist philosopher Søren Kierkegaard does Tubby determine to find her. The plausibility of the detailed attention given Kierkegaard's life and writings in *Therapy* (which to Lodge may have seemed risky but to some readers might seem merely strange) depends on our accepting it as a crucial part of Tubby's solution to his puzzling depression and of his consequent escape from it. Tubby feels depressed but can't understand why. He draws up a list of the many reasons why he shouldn't feel this way (successful career, financial well-being, good health, happy marriage, etc.), he thinks of people obviously much worse off than he (which, he notes "only makes you despise yourself more and thus feel more depressed" [*T,* 107]), and of course he pursues his various therapies. But nothing seems to be working until, after a friend happens to ask him how his angst is, he wonders about that word and proceeds to "look it up," which, in turn, leads him to existentialism and Kierkegaard. If Kierkegaard is not initially predictable in Tubby's story, the likelihood that Tubby will look him up if curious is, thanks to the planting of this trait early and often, before the plot openly demands it.

The process by which Lodge came to include the Danish philosopher in the novel was itself almost as much a fluke as the way Tubby finds him. Early in the writing of *Therapy* Lodge realized that relying on Tubby's viewpoint alone, and indeed solely on the language Tubby provides as narrator, would likely prove monotonous: "I felt the need of another discourse, another perspective, another (parallel) story" ("Kierkegaard," 38). Then he remembered having written somewhere in the notebook he was keeping for *Therapy* that maybe Tubby Passmore should read Kierkegaard, who also suffered from intense depression. (Lodge knew this from having read a biography of the philosopher while preparing to write *Paradise News,* in which Kierkegaard gets brief mention as a religious thinker in connection with Bernard Walsh's dilemma as an unbelieving priest (*PN,* 154]). Lodge also remembered that Kierkegaard had "a strange, poignant, unhappy, obsessive relationship" with a young woman to whom he was for a time engaged, which led to the suspicion that "in Kierkegaard's depression and life-long obsession with Regine I would find what I wanted: an intertextual structural idea for *Therapy*, a parallel story to Tubby's, yielding a different perspective on his plight and a different language for talking about it" ("Kierkegaard," 38–39).

And so Lodge did indeed arrange to have Tubby "read Kierkegaard," so that Tubby might work through his depression and so that the inherent disadvantage of the novel's narrative mode might be offset. As in most of his other novels, Lodge here sought a sense of similarity-within-difference (and difference-within-similarity). But whereas in some cases such a sense comes through the opposition of characters within the novel—Mark and Clare in *The Picturegoers*, Jonathan Browne and Mike Brady in *Ginger, You're Barmy*, Philip Swallow and Morris Zapp in *Changing Places*, or Vic and Robyn in *Nice Work*—here it is created through a comparison of a character with his literary antecedent, somewhat similar to what happens in *The British Museum Is Falling Down*, *Small World*, and even, though to a lesser degree, *Out of the Shelter*. Yet where Lodge succeeds with Adam Appleby or with the various scholarly "knights errant" in *Small World* only to the extent that the reader knows *Ulysses* or the romance tradition—a problem partly solved in *Small World* through overdetermination—in *Therapy* he makes the probably unfamiliar antecedent familiar by having Tubby exercise extensively his penchant for "looking it up," for us as well as for himself. There is a good deal of direct quotation from Kierkegaard here and a good deal of hashing over what the philosopher may have meant in his more opaque passages and terminology, but it all occurs in the context of Tubby's hunch that in Kierkegaard lies the solution to his personal difficulties, a hunch analogous to Lodge's own about structuring his novel.

Tubby's Kierkegaardian interests shift gradually from the philosophical to the biographical and ultimately require a mecca to Copenhagen. Initially drawn by the very titles of the Kierkegaard books (*Fear and Trembling, The Sickness unto Death, The Concept of Dread*) that seem to name his condition "like arrows thudding into a target" (*T,* 65), he increasingly takes pleasure in finding in such texts the terms with which to define and analyze his own feelings and in sensing an implied author who understands his pain. Such pleasure is carried to a higher plane when the suspicion that despite frequently employing fictional personae Kierkegaard was really talking about himself is confirmed by the study of his journals and his life, so that eventually Tubby feels justified in calling him "the thin man inside me that has been struggling to get out" (*T,* 209). Lodge has noted, too, how once it was established the Tubby-Kierkegaard relationship soon took on a life of its own, yielding connec-

tions with relatively little effort or anticipation on his part ("Kierkegaard," 42).

When, shortly after beginning his investigation of Kierkegaard,
Tubby is shocked at the news that his wife wants to leave him and that
he may lose his job, the Danish philosopher provides perspective on his
misfortunes as well as on his outlandish subsequent behavior. At an earlier point he comments on how much time the preoccupation with
Kierkegaard and the writing of a journal increasingly occupied with
thoughts of Kierkegaard has been taking—this when Tubby is beginning to read the lengthy journals that Kierkegaard himself wrote.

Through a slightly circuitous path of association involving both his
aroma therapist and Kierkegaard, Tubby comes to focus on Maureen as
the key to both his basic problem and its solution. "She's been flitting in
and out of my consciousness ever since I started this journal," he notes,
"like a figure glimpsed indistinctly at the edge of a distant wood":

> The smell of lavender drew her out into the open—the lavender and
> Kierkegaard. I made a note some weeks ago that the symbol for the dou-
> ble *aa* in modern Danish, the single *a* with a little circle on top, reminded
> me of something I couldn't pin down at the time. Well, it was Maureen's
> handwriting. She used to dot her *i*'s that way. (*T*, 221)

Once her reentry into his daily thinking has led him to remember Maureen by writing a memoir of their relationship and to regret the way he
treated her ("callously, selfishly, wantonly" [*T*, 261]), he realizes what a
"very Kierkegaardian story" he has written. After comparing their relationship with Kierkegaard and Regine's, he becomes obsessed with
tracking Maureen down and seeking her forgiveness.

Though Lodge recognized the "incongruity" of pairing Kierkegaard
with someone like Tubby Passmore, he figured that this was precisely
what would make them interesting, especially as he was determined to
write "a novel about depression that would not be depressing" ("Kierkegaard," 39). Apparently his plan succeeded, at least to the extent that
reviewers' complaints concerned more the credibility of Tubby's depression or the novel's conclusion.[20] Lodge has argued that it doesn't matter
that he or Tubby fully understand Kierkegaard, not even the particular
passages quoted, since for purposes of the novel "[t]he criterion is not
what does Kierkegaard mean, but, what does Kierkegaard mean for
Tubby?" By this logic, even a misunderstanding of Kierkegaard would
be acceptable as long as it occurred in "an interesting and instructive
way" ("Kierkegaard," 39). But while Lodge was free to remain, along

with Tubby, an amateur reader of Kierkegaard, Tubby's role as professional television writer demanded an insider's familiarity with the technicalities of film and television production that postacademic experience equipped Lodge to provide.

For all of the Kierkegaard strategy's effectiveness, though, it is but one of the several tactics with which Lodge sought to forestall tedium in *Therapy*. Most required a departure from having Tubby, Lodge's only first-person narrator besides Jonathan Browne in *Ginger, You're Barmy*, tell his story in a standard linear fashion. One such departure involves the daily journal Tubby writes over several months at the suggestion of his therapist, which constitutes roughly one-third of the novel. Lodge arranged the journal material in three separate parts, the first being divided from the second by a series of monologues spoken by several people who encounter Tubby after his wife, Sally, announces she is leaving him, and the second from the third by the memoir about Maureen. While technically the novel's final section constitutes an additional part of the journal—a single long entry written several weeks after Tubby and Maureen return from Europe and purportedly designed to pull together into a coherent form his chaotic notes concerning their reunion—in its more straightforward movement and narrower focus it approximates conventional first-person narration much more closely than do the others.

Probably the most striking attempt to diversify the novel's format—and certainly the occasion for its most hilarious episodes and situations—is the sequence of monologues, which contain an impressive array of voices, viewpoints, motives, and formats. Starting with the court deposition given by Sally's tennis coach, with whom Tubby suspects she has been having an affair, they present a broad picture of his often manic behavior after she asks for a separation, particularly once he begins seeking sex with most any woman he thinks might be interested. Presented to a variety of auditors in a variety of circumstances, the statements often express puzzlement over Tubby's rambling philosophical references, as when the beautiful young woman who accompanies him to Copenhagen, ostensibly for a weekend of sex, tells how he ignores her because of his fixation with Kierkegaard.

But among the many surprises that the monologues give us, perhaps the biggest is that they turn out to have been written by Tubby himself (another exercise proposed by his therapist). The carping of critics about this being an unfair and inartistic trick on the reader rests on questionable grounds. Certainly Lodge thought so, and he defended his practice in this instance with a logic comparable to that of his justification of his, Tubby's, and the novel's ignorance of Kierkegaard and reminiscent of the formalist stance he first took in *Language of Fiction*. Because the monologues represent Tubby's surmise about what people have been thinking about him, they reflect a hard-won perspective, not just on others but on himself, which is confirmed in those journal pages in which he reflects on having written the monologues and on the experiences they recount. Taken together, they measure his progress through a difficult and painful process of discovery and self-discovery.

Any claim that some sort of reader-writer contract is being violated here is largely invalidated by the considerable pleasure produced not only by the monologues themselves but by Tubby's reflections on them. Such a complaint relates to Lodge's observation in *Souls and Bodies* about how some who are most skeptical about religious beliefs can themselves be unduly credulous and literal minded when they read fiction. Taken as Lodge has intended them, the monologues function in part as evidence of Tubby's talents as a creator of comic character and speech, which surely need demonstration in light of the high reputation among television professionals that, we are asked to believe, he commands throughout the novel.

One of *Therapy*'s reviewers wrote that "[t]he sheer amiability of the author's style should not confuse the reader as to the novel's ambitions."[21] Surely if Tubby Passmore emerges as a writer of widely ranging talents, even more obviously does David Lodge, and from the very beginning of the book. One of the many things he accomplishes here is *skaz* ("a type of first-person narration that has the characteristics of the spoken rather than the written word" [*AF*, 18]). The examples of this technique cited in *The Art of Fiction* were chosen from *Catcher in the Rye* and *Huckleberry Finn* to illustrate its teenage variety. The creation of middle-age *skaz* in *Therapy* amusingly (and functionally) depends on Tubby Passmore's occupational habits. So accustomed has he become to writing lines and speeches for television dialogue that the self-description he writes for his therapist turns out to be three pages long (a thousand words) with no paragraphing. Tubby explains that he's "out of practice" writing paragraphs. "I can only write as if I'm speaking to someone" (*T*, 21). He can write his journal only as if to a listening "you" ("I've no idea who 'you' is. Just an imaginary sympathetic ear" [*T*, 22]). In this respect his journal differs markedly from Bernard Walsh's in *Paradise News*, which is ironic in light of how specific a "you" Bernard had in mind as he composed his journal.

Part of the fun of reading *Therapy* comes out of the free and engaging manner in which Lodge has Tubby not only recount his experience but range speculatively and philosophically, and unpretentiously, over many things that trouble and excite a man of his age, temperament, and background. In this he is allowed gradually to win the reader's "sympathetic ear." Combined with the various other discursive modes employed here—a variety for which Lodge found precedent in Kierkegaard ("Kierkegaard," 46)—the *skaz* of the novel encourages a heightened sense of the various ways in which we try to record and communicate our experiences. Noting how the novelist, unlike the scriptwriter, must describe everything ("the whole boiling") in detail, Tubby says, "I take my hat off to book writers, I do honestly" (*T,* 18). By having Tubby engage in some informal literary theory along the way to becoming a "book writer" and by tracing in reverse the course he himself has taken in his own career, Lodge suggests how both reading and writing can lead to self-discovery and self-actualization. In this way *Therapy* itself becomes a valuable resource, a place to "look it up."

Conclusion

To appraise the overall work of a living writer, especially one as active as David Lodge has continued to be even after four decades, is difficult and risky. Even so, given his considerable accomplishments to date, it seems appropriate to review them, to suggest what other directions his work may take, and to speculate about how he might be regarded in the future. With 10 novels to date, an equal number of critical works, occasional essays, hundreds of reviews, critical anthologies, several screenplay adaptations, and two professionally produced plays to his credit (the second, *Home Truths,* having premiered in early 1998), David Lodge can look back on a distinguished and varied career. He has contributed singularly to literary and cultural life, especially in Britain but really throughout the English-speaking world—and even farther, if one considers the broader audience that translation has found for his works.

Lodge's writings have been translated into more than 20 languages, several of which contain a body of criticism and commentary on his work corresponding to that in English. His novels have achieved best-seller status in Italy, France, and Germany. In December 1997 he was recognized by the French Ministry of Culture by being made a *Chevalier dans l'Ordre des Arts et Lettres* at a ceremony at the Institut Français in London. Most of the several awards given his novels in Britain have been noted, the most recent being the short-listing of *Therapy* for the 1996 Commonwealth Writers Prize. (It was judged the best book in the Eurasian region at the first stage of this competition.)

For over 20 years Lodge's novels have been best-sellers in Britain, appearing on the same lists as the writings of Tom Clancy, Jackie Collins, and Jeffrey Archer. Thus the *Guardian* ranked *Nice Work* 29th among its "fastsellers" for 1989, with almost 300,000 paperback copies sold, while in 1992 the Great Britain sales figures for *Paradise News* exceeded those of the latest Colin Dexter release and of every other title published by Penguin that year and came near those for books by Ken Follett and Joanna Trollope.[1] While Lodge's popularity in the *United States* has never approached this level, a source of some concern to him,[2] his books are in steady demand here, as evidenced by several of his titles being stocked regularly by American bookstores of any appreciable size, and not just on the East and West Coasts. Where he is known in Great

Britain as simply a "popular novelist," the designation of "literary novelist" American critics and readers have given him suggests a more limited though substantial popularity, though this may also reflect differences between the two reading cultures.

Lodge's worldwide reputation seems to have resulted from certain qualities in his writing already described. It rests, of course, on the supreme wit evident in the hilarious situations of his novels and the energetic pace and telling specificity with which they are narrated, as well as in exchanges between characters. But it rests, too, on his ability not only to write serious fiction but to make serious use of the amusing and absurd materials he develops in his comic novels, to shift at appropriate points in his narratives to a serious, even moral tone. Among the countless hilarious situations in his novels, perhaps none is funnier than the brief scene in *Small World* in which Philip Swallow, asleep in an Ankara hotel room after a comically inept arrival, awakens to find himself at the mercy of diarrhea and one of the city's frequent power outages. After making his way slowly to the bathroom ("tightening his sphincter muscle . . . [shuffling] along the wall like a rock-climber" [*SW,* 190]), he is able finally to relieve himself—only to discover, when the lights come on, that what he thought were sheets intended as toilet paper hastily grabbed from his briefcase are, in fact, pages from the lecture he is to deliver the next day for the British Council. Despite the high comedy of the scene, which Lodge characteristically exploits in full, it serves as a prelude to Philip's reunion with Joy, to the resumption of their affair, to the hard choices he will be forced to make, and to the existential issues of aging, death, and acquired loyalties that surround such choices. Similarly, though Tubby Passmore seems fully attuned to the mores of sexual liberation permeating late-twentieth-century England, and though his quest for sexual satisfaction occasions as many funny moments as similar quests by other Lodge characters, repeatedly it occasions searching questions about Tubby's and about society's sexual behavior.

During a 1991 ITV profile, Lodge admitted to being terribly interested in sex. Clearly his fiction adheres to the novel's traditional interest in sexual matters and in the comedy of sex. But also in keeping with that tradition, it does much more, as Lodge's novels seem designed not only to describe sexualized individuals and a sexualized society but to ask whether some reconsideration might not be in order. Besides reveling in the carnivalesque aspect of contemporary sexual behavior—as in the account Tubby writes of the young woman's experience in accompanying him to Copenhagen, or Fulvia Morgana's capture of Morris, or Vic Wilcox's excitement over Robyn—Lodge's fiction traffics in the messiness and complexity that the sexual revolution seems hardly to have alleviated. One critic has called Lodge "always a writer with an eye for the less alluring aspects of sex . . . something of a trailblazer," citing the attention given the question of how *not* to have children, especially in *The British Museum Is Falling Down,* as a prime example of his treatment of subjects of considerable public interest that novelists generally neglect.[3]

As many critics have noted, the question "How far can you go?" permeates Lodge's writing. It frames his portrayals of commercial society, of university education and the academic profession as they have evolved since World War II, and of contemporary Britain generally—especially its tendency toward commodifying everything and toward regarding profitability as the main criterion of all enterprises. Not that Lodge is being reactionary in such portrayals, since his depiction of the past is hardly nostalgic and since he recognizes the advantages afforded by new goods and services, as well as by reformed institutions and liberated behavior. But his fiction insists that such improvements and gains rarely occur without exacting a cost of some sort, so that some sort of weighing of such trade-offs, for the individual as well as society, becomes essential.

It is in terms of the broad topics of sex and religion that such concerns have been addressed in his novels, and it is for his treatment of these topics that his fiction is likely to be read in the future—both as a thoughtful sociological record of late-twentieth-century society and behavior and as a frequently amusing but sometimes deeply moving consideration of human problems hardly unique to our time. In this regard Lodge's latest novel, *Therapy,* is both illustrative and encouraging, since it brings together a variety of issues and techniques that for a long time remained largely separated in his writing and since it adds to them in terms of his recent interest in television and drama. Along with *Souls and Bodies, Small World,* and perhaps *Nice Work, Therapy* seems to be the work he has written that will be most read in the future.

But such things are difficult to predict, especially as Lodge is pursuing new projects, including new fiction. His second play, *Home Truths,* concerns some of the same issues raised in *The Writing Game* and examines in particular the relationship between writers and the press. The success of *Therapy* suggests his ability to juggle the writing of fiction with other projects and makes a new novel likely before too long, along with further work for television and film. And if *Big Words: Small World* and *The Art of Fiction* are indicators, David Lodge has just begun his project of bridging the gap between readers and writers and of bypassing academia in the process.

Lodge has said that the ultimate incentive for writing is the chance to "defy death" by leaving behind "some trace of oneself, however slight" (*WO*, 78). In a time when books and reading face increasing competition from newer forms of entertainment, he has managed to reach a large and loyal audience and to give them a special kind of pleasure and meaning—and there is no evidence of either his productivity or the reading public's responsiveness to his work letting up. In a time when the publishing trade seems increasingly obsessed by a bottom-line mentality, Lodge continues to write fiction that both challenges received attitudes and behaviors and appropriates them for comic, satirical, and other literary purposes. In a time when tradition of every kind, including the literary, is being increasingly ignored or tossed away unthinkingly, Lodge remains a voice, in his creative writing as well as in his criticism, that insists on the indispensability of the past and the need for acknowledging continuity even as society and artistic fashions change.

Although he is still negotiating between novel writing and the writing of scripts and plays, there is every indication that each of these activities will be reinforcing and enhancing the others for some time to come. While his legacy is already a rich one, his recent work suggests that it will expand and even find new forms and directions. For those who have found David Lodge entertaining and worthwhile, and for those who will be discovering him in the future, this is good news indeed.

Notes and References

Chapter One

1   Arthur Marwick, *British Society Since 1945* (London: Penguin, 1982), 75.
2.   David Lodge, *Out of the Shelter,* rev. ed. (Harmondsworth, England: Penguin, 1986), 274; hereafter cited in text as *OS.*
3.   John Haffenden, "David Lodge," *Novelists in Interview* (London: Methuen, 1985), 148; hereafter cited in text.
4.   David Lodge, *The Practice of Writing* (New York: Allen Lane/The Penguin Press, 1997), 127; hereafter cited in text as *PW.*
5.   Robert Morace, *The Dialogic Novels of Malcolm Bradbury and David Lodge* (Carbondale: Southern Illinois University Press, 1989), 150; hereafter cited in text.
6.   For example, "Anglo-American Encounter," *TLS* (9 October 1970): 1155; hereafter cited in text as "Encounter."
7.   Dennis Jackson, "David Lodge," in *British Novelists since 1960,* vol. 19, part 2 of *Dictionary of Literary Biography,* ed. Jay L. Halio (Detroit: Gale, 1983), 474; hereafter cited in text.
8.   Park Honan, "David Lodge and the Cinematic Novel in England," *Novel* 5 (1972): 172–73; hereafter cited in text.
9.   Christopher Hawkins, "Guiness Tints," *TLS* (31 May 1985): 599.
10.   Bernard Bergonzi, "David Lodge Interviewed," *Month* 229 (February 1970): 112–13; hereafter cited in text.
11.   David Lodge, *Ginger, You're Barmy* (London: Penguin, 1984), 217; hereafter cited in text as *GB.*
12.   David Lodge, *Graham Greene* (New York: Columbia University Press, 1966), 36; hereafter cited in text as *GG.*
13.   David Lodge, *Write On* (London: Secker and Warburg, 1986), 64; hereafter cited in text as *WO.*

Chapter Two

1.   Alfred E. Havighurst, *Britain in Transition: The Twentieth Century,* 4th ed. (Chicago: University of Chicago Press, 1985), 422.
2.   Edward Royle, *Modern Britain: A Social History, 1750–1985* (London: Edward Arnold, 1987), 384.
3.   Ibid.
4.   Marwick, *British Society Since 1945,* 182.

5. Malcolm Bradbury, "Campus Fictions," in *University Fiction,* ed. David Devan (Amsterdam: Rudopi, 1990), 54.

6. Peter Hennessy, *Never Again: Britain 1945–1951* (New York: Pantheon, 1993), 321.

7. David Lodge, *Changing Places* (New York: Penguin, 1978), 10; hereafter cited in text as *CP.*

8. David Lodge, *The Modes of Modern Writing* (Ithaca, N.Y.: Cornell University Press, 1977), x; hereafter cited in text as *MM.*

9. Published originally in *Modernism 1890–1930,* ed. Malcolm Bradbury and James McFarlane (Middlesex, England: Penguin, 1974), 481–96. Parts of this essay reappeared at different points in *The Modes of Modern Writing.*

10. David Lodge, *The Art of Fiction* (New York: Penguin, 1994), 227; hereafter cited in text as *AF.*

11. Steven Connor, *The English Novel in History, 1950–1995* (London: Routledge, 1996), 69–72; hereafter cited in text.

12. See "The People's Park and the Battle of Berkeley," *WO,* 17–27. Originally published in the Birmingham University publication *Alta* in the fall of 1969.

13. John Sutherland, *Fiction and the Fiction Industry* (London: Athlone, 1978), 158.

14. David Lodge, *Small World* (Harmondsworth, England: Penguin, 1985), 43; hereafter cited in text as *SW.*

15. *Twentieth-Century Literary Criticism: A Reader,* ed. David Lodge (London: Longman, 1972), xvii.

16. *Modern Criticism and Theory: A Reader,* ed. David Lodge (London: Longman, 1988), x.

17. Ibid., xi.

18. Lodge has acknowledged that Norman Mailer inspired at least the rhetorical flourish of Morris Zapp (quoted in Joan Marecki, "David Lodge," *Contemporary Authors,* n.s., 19 [1987]: 300; hereafter cited in text), and in the 1987 documentary *Big Words: Small World,* he refers to the widespread notion that Stanley Fish was the model for Zapp.

19. Siegfried Mews, "The Professor's Novel: David Lodge's *Small World,*" *Modern Language Notes* 10 (1989): 722; hereafter cited in text.

20. Paul Gray, "Gypsy Scholars," *Time* (15 April 1985): 101.

21. Alastair Fowler, "The Life and Death of Literary Forms," in *New Directions in Literary History,* ed. Ralph Cohen (Baltimore: Johns Hopkins University Press, 1974), 90–91.

22. Allan H. Gilbert, *Literary Criticism: Plato to Dryden* (Detroit: Wayne State University Press, 1961), 700.

23. Patricia A. Parker, *Inescapable Romance: Studies in the Poetics of a Mode* (Princeton, N.J.: Princeton University Press, 1989), 220.

24. See, for example, Morace, 205.

25. Marguerite Alexander, *Flight from Realism: Themes and Strategies in Postmodernist British and American Fiction* (London: Edward Arnold, 1990), 122.

26. Michael Billington, "Leading Three Lives," *New York Times Book Review* 17 (March 1985): 7.

27. David Lodge, *After Bakhtin* (New York: Routledge, 1990), 178; hereafter cited in text as *AB*.

28. David Lodge, *Nice Work* (New York: Penguin, 1990), author's note; hereafter cited in text as *NW.*

29. This passage is referred to in a textbook discussion of "feminist bashing"—see Keith Green and Jill LeBihan, *Critical Theory and Practice* (London: Routledge, 1996), 6–7.

30. See Connor, 74–76, and Patricia Waugh, *Harvest of the Sixties: English Literature and Its Background, 1960 to 1990* (Oxford, England: Oxford University Press, 1995), 34–36; hereafter cited in text.

31. See Mary Jo Salter, "Only Connect," *New Republic* (18 and 25 September 1989): 46, and Lawrence Lerner, "The Return of the Signified," *Spectator* (24 September 1988): 38.

32. Terry Eagleton, "The Silences of David Lodge," *New Left Review* (November/December 1988): 99; hereafter cited in text.

33. Eden Ross Lipson, "Liberated by Thatcher," *New York Times Book Review* (23 July 1989): 20.

34. Lerner, "The Return of the Signified," 38.

35. [David Lodge et al.], "Thinking about Women," *TLS* (March 1988). 615.

36. Salter, "Only Connect," 47.

Chapter Three

1. David Lodge, *The Novelist at the Crossroads* (Ithaca, N.Y.: Cornell University Press, 1971), 247; hereafter cited in text as *NC.*

2. David Lodge, *Language of Fiction* (New York: Columbia University Press, 1966), x, hereafter cited in text as *LF; Twentieth-Century Literary Criticism,* 386.

3. David Lodge, [review of Wayne Booth, *The Rhetoric of Fiction*], *Modern Language Review* 57 (1962): 580–81.

4. See *LF,* xi, and Lodge's review of K. Graham's *English Criticism of the Novel, 1865–1900* in *Modern Language Review* 61 (1967): 713–14.

5. For those that found them superior, see, for example, Martin Price, "Theories of the Novel," *Yale Review* 56 (1966–1967): 248; for those that found them inferior, see, for example, Ronald Paulson, [review of *LF*], *JEGP* 66 (1967): 248.

6. Laurence Lerner, [review of *LF*], *Review of English Studies* 18 (1967): 357–58.

7. Malcolm Bradbury, "The Language Novelists Use," *Kenyon Review* 29 (1967): 132; hereafter cited in text.

8. Lodge, [review of *The Rhetoric of Fiction*], 581.

9. *Twentieth-Century Literary Criticism,* 592.

10. Malcolm Bradbury, "Toward a Poetics of Fiction: An Approach through Structure," *Novel* 1 (1967–1968): 47.

11. Graham Hough, "Just a *Soupçon* of Paris," *TLS* 26 (June 1981): 275.

12. *Modernism 1890–1930,* ed. Bradbury and McFarlane, 481–96.

13. Thus the reprinting of Lodge's entire discussion of Larkin in *Philip Larkin: The Man and His Work,* ed. Dale Salwak (Iowa City: University of Iowa Press, 1989), 118–28.

14. Tony Tanner, [review of *LF*], *Modern Language Review* 62 (1967): 708.

15. Terrence Hawkes, "Where the Vertical Meets the Horizontal," *TLS* (13 January 1978): 28.

16. Garrett Stewart, [review of *MM*], *JEGP* 78 (1979): 276.

17. Phyllis A. Roth, [review of *MM*], *Comparative Literature* 32 (1980): 215.

18. Nicola Bradbury, [review of *Working with Structuralism*], *Review of English Studies* 35 (1984): 428; Terrence Hawkes, "Critics in Their Castle," *New Statesman* 101 (1981): 19.

19. David Lodge, *Working with Structuralism* (London: Routledge & Kegan Paul, 1981), viii; hereafter cited in text as *WS.*

20. David Lodge, "This Way to Folly," *TLS* (30 May 1980): 605–6.

21. See David Lodge, "From Don Juan to Tristan," *TLS* (25 May 1984): 568; "Outrageous Things," *New York Review of Books* 35 (1988): 25–26; and "Hermits and Fools," *New York Review of Books* 36 (1989): 35–36.

22. See David Lodge, "Before the Deluge," *Tablet* 225 (October 1971): 1024, and "Closing Time," *New York Review of Books* 34 (1987): 15–16.

Chapter Four

1. Billington, "Leading Three Lives," 7.

2. Edward Norman, *Roman Catholicism in England from the Elizabethan Settlement to the Second Vatican Council* (New York: Oxford University Press, 1985), 115.

3. Ibid., 115–18.

4. Royle, *Modern Britain: A Social History,* 337.

5. David Martin, *A Sociology of English Religion* (London: SCM Press, 1967), 39.

6. David Lodge, *The Picturegoers* (London: Penguin, 1993), 173–75; hereafter cited in text as *P.*

7. Maurice Richardson in *New Statesman,* quoted in Marecki, "David Lodge," 298.

8.   Bernard Bergonzi, "A Religious Romance: David Lodge in Conversation," *Critic* 47 (1992): 70; hereafter cited in text.

9.   Park Honan, "David Lodge before *Changing Places*," in Honan, *Authors' Lives: On Literary Biography and the Arts of Language* (New York: St. Martin's, 1990), 230.

10.   Bernard Bergonzi, *David Lodge* (Plymouth, England: Northcote House, 1995), 31; hereafter cited in text.

11.   David Lodge, "Writing without Art," *Sunday Times* (22 May 1982): 46.

12.   Edward T. Wheeler, "The Machinery of Illusion and Effect," *Commonweal* 117 (1990): 538.

13.   David Lodge, *The British Museum Is Falling Down* (New York: Penguin, 1989), 174; hereafter cited in text as *BM*.

14.   Morace, 132–41, and Robert Burden, "The Novel Interrogates Itself: Parody as Self-Consciousness in Contemporary English Fiction," in *The Contemporary English Novel*, ed. Malcolm Bradbury and David Palmer (New York: Holmes and Meier, 1979), 140; hereafter cited in text.

15.   David Lodge, "Graham Greene: A Personal View," *TLS* (12 April 1991): 10.

16.   Daniel Amman, *David Lodge and the Art-and-Reality Novel* (Heidelberg, Germany: Carl Winter Universitats Verlag, 1991), 130; hereafter cited in text.

17.   See Peter Widdowson, "The Anti-History Men: Malcolm Bradbury and David Lodge," *Critical Quarterly* 26, no. 4 (Winter 1984): 23–29.

18.   As noted earlier, the title of this novel in its first edition, published in London by Secker and Warburg, was *How Far Can You Go?*. Its American publisher persuaded Lodge to change the title to *Souls and Bodies* for the first American edition (1982), fearing that otherwise it would be shelved in American bookstores under how-to books ("a silly argument to which I have always regretted yielding," Lodge has commented [*AF*, 195]. This difference in titles has continued to be retained between British and American paperback editions. Because citations here are to the Penguin edition published in New York in 1990, the American title is being used, and hereafter the novel will be cited in the text as *SB*.

19.   Jeremy Treglown, "Where Shall Wisdom Be Found?" *TLS* (1 May 1980): 487; Nicholas Shrimpton, "Conjugal Rites," *New Statesman* 99 (1980): 749, and Paul Ableman, "Rock 'n Roll," *Spectator* (3 May 1980): 23.

20.   John Podhoretz, "How Far Can You Go?," *New Republic* (7 April 1982): 37.

21.   Gerald Parsons, "Paradigm or Period Piece? David Lodge's *How Far Can You Go?* in Perspective," *Journal of Literature and Theology* 6 (1992): 172; hereafter cited in text.

22.   David Lodge, "Pilgrim's Noughts and Crosses," *Independent on Sunday* (16 October 1994): 33.

23. Chris Walsh, "David Lodge Interviewed," *Strawberry Fare* (Autumn 1984): 4–5.

24. Bernard Bergonzi, "The Decline and Fall of the Catholic Novel," in *The Myth of Modernism and Twentieth-Century Literature* (Brighton, England: Harvester, 1986), 183; hereafter cited in text.

25. Lodge's term for the view of some of his readers (Walsh, 7).

26. "At every turn of the narrative screw, Lodge undermines the logic of both the old morality and the new (and, one might add, of the old novel and the new fiction, as well)" (Morace, 180).

27. See "Post-Pill Paradise: John Updike's *Couples*," in *NC*, 237–44.

28. Podhoretz, "How Far Can You Go?," 38.

Chapter Five

1. David Lodge, "A Renaissance Man," *Tablet* 247 (1993): 1586.

2. David Lodge, "Sir Kingsley Amis," *Independent* (23 October 1995): 16.

3. Peter Kemp, "Holding the Floor," *TLS* (23 October 1992): 7.

4. Stuart Laing, "The Three Small Worlds of David Lodge," *Critical Survey* 3 (1991): 330.

5. Merritt Moseley, *David Lodge* (San Bernardino, Calif.: Borgo Press, 1991), 15; hereafter cited in text.

6. David Lodge, "Adapting *Nice Work* for Television," *Novel Images: Literature in Performance,* ed. Peter Reynolds (London: Routledge, 1993), 192.

7. David Lodge, *The Writing Game* (London: Secker and Warburg, 1991), 86; hereafter cited in text as *WG*.

8. See "Playbacks: Extracts from a Writer's Diary," *PW,* 286–333.

9. David Lodge, "Three Weddings and a Big Row," *Independent* (4 November 1994): 13, and "Adapting *Martin Chuzzlewit*," *PW,* 230–59.

10. Jane Smiley, "Fiction in Review," *Yale Review* 81 (1993): 152–53.

11. Ibid., 152.

12. David Lodge, *Paradise News* (New York: Penguin, 1993), 188; hereafter cited in text as *PN*.

13. Smiley, "Fiction in Review," 153; David Lodge, "The Mystery and Misery of an Orgasm," *Guardian* (1 January 1992): 25.

14. Smiley, "Fiction in Review," 153.

15. One example is Frank Kermode, whose *Sense of an Ending* (1966) influenced the writing of more than one Lodge novel (see Walsh, 9).

16. David Lodge, *Therapy* (New York: Penguin, 1996), 317; hereafter cited in text as *T*.

17. David Lodge, "Kierkegaard for Special Purposes," *Kierkegaard Studies* 1 (1997): 34; hereafter cited in text as "Kierkegaard."

18. David Lodge, "A Pilgrim's Package," *Independent on Sunday* (16 December 1993): 84.

19. David Lodge, "Pilgrim's Noughts and Crosses," 33.

20.   See, for example, John Banville, "Nice Work," *New York Review of Books* (10 August 1995): 24–26.

21.   Anita Brookner, "The Story of a Knee," *Spectator* (6 May 1995): 40.

Conclusion

1.   "Guardian Fastsellers," *Guardian* (11 January 1990): 28; (12 January 1993): 17.

2.   Marecki, "David Lodge," 303.

3.   D. J. Taylor, *After the War: The Novel and English Society Since 1945* (London: Chatto and Windus, 1993), 230.

Selected Bibliography

Primary Sources

Fiction (First British and American publication plus significant later editions)

The Picturegoers. London: MacGibbon and Kee, 1960. With introduction by David Lodge, Harmondsworth, England: Penguin, 1993.

Ginger, You're Barmy. London: MacGibbon & Kee, 1962. First U.S. publication, Garden City, N.J.: Doubleday, 1965. With introduction by David Lodge, London: Secker and Warburg, 1982.

The British Museum Is Falling Down. London: MacGibbon & Kee, 1965. First U.S. edition, New York: Holt, Rinehart & Winston, 1966. Introduction by David Lodge, London: Secker & Warburg, 1981.

Out of the Shelter. London: Macmillan, 1970. With new introduction by David Lodge, London: Secker & Warburg, 1985. First U.S. publication (with afterword by David Lodge), New York: Viking Penguin, 1989.

Changing Places. London: Secker & Warburg, 1975. First U.S. publication, Harmondsworth, England, and New York: Penguin, 1978 (published simultaneously in England and in the U.S.)

How Far Can You Go? London: Secker & Warburg, 1980. First U.S. publication (as *Souls and Bodies*), New York: Morrow, 1982.

Small World. London: Secker & Warburg, 1984. First U.S. publication, New York: Macmillan, 1984.

Nice Work. London: Secker & Warburg, 1988. First U.S. publication, New York: Viking, 1989.

Paradise News. London: Secker & Warburg, 1991. First U.S. publication, New York: Viking Penguin, 1992.

Therapy. London: Secker & Warburg, 1995. First U.S. publication, New York: Viking Penguin, 1995.

Drama and Screenplays

Nice Work. Four-part television-adaptation broadcast. BBC, 10 April–10 May 1989.

Martin Chuzzlewit. Six-part television-adaptation broadcast. BBC, 7 November–12 December 1994.

The Writing Game. London: Secker & Warburg, 1991. Television-adaptation broadcast, Channel 4, 28 December 1995.

Home Truths. Birmingham Repertory Theatre, February–March 1998.

Criticism

About Catholic Authors. London: St. Paul Press, 1957.
Graham Greene. Columbia Essays on Modern Writers, no. 17. New York: Columbia University Press, 1966.
Language of Fiction: Essays in Criticism and Verbal Analysis of the English Novel. London: Routledge and Kegan Paul; New York: Columbia University Press, 1966. Rev. ed. (with afterword by David Lodge), London: Routledge and Kegan Paul, 1984.
Evelyn Waugh. Columbia Essays on Modern Writers, no. 58. New York: Columbia University Press, 1971.
The Novelist at the Crossroads. Ithaca, N.Y.: Cornell University Press, 1971.
The Modes of Modern Writing. Ithaca, N.Y.: Cornell University Press, 1977.
Working with Structuralism. London: Routledge & Kegan Paul, 1981.
Big Words, Small World. Channel Four, 2 November 1987. Documentary.
After Bakhtin. London and New York: Routledge, 1990.
The Practice of Writing. London: Penguin, 1996. First U.S. publication, New York: Allen Lane/The Penguin Press, 1997.

Essays

Write On: Occasional Essays, '65–'85. London: Secker & Warburg, 1986.
The Art of Fiction. London: Secker & Warburg, 1992. First U.S. publication, New York: Viking Penguin, 1993.
"Kierkegaard for Special Purposes," *Kierkegaard Studies* 1 (1997): 34–47.

Edited Collections

Jane Austen, "Emma": A Casebook. London: Macmillan, 1968.
Twentieth-Century Literary Criticism: A Reader. London and New York: Longman, 1972.
Modern Criticism and Theory: A Reader. London and New York: Longman, 1988.

Secondary Sources

Bibliography

An authorized bibliography of David Lodge is currently in preparation by Elizabeth Harrison.

Books

Alexander, Marguerite. *Flights from Realism: Themes and Strategies in Postmodern British and American Fiction.* London: Edward Arnold, 1990.

Ammann, Daniel. *David Lodge and the Art-and-Reality Novel.* Heidelberg, Germany: Carol Winter Universitats Verlag, 1991. Helpful on literary allusion in Lodge's fiction.

Bergonzi, Bernard. *David Lodge.* Plymouth, England: Northcote House, 1995. A useful introduction by a critic close to Lodge and to his work.

Connor, Steven. *The English Novel in History, 1950–1995.* London: Routledge, 1996. Presents a useful context in which to view Lodge's writings.

Morace, Robert A. *The Dialogic Novels of Malcolm Bradbury and David Lodge.* Carbondale: Southern Illinois University Press, 1989. Lodge's novels through *Nice Work* analyzed in terms of Bakhtin and poststructuralism.

Moseley, Merritt. *David Lodge: How Far Can You Go?* San Bernardino, Calif.: Borgo, 1991. A brief survey of Lodge's writings through *Nice Work.*

Waugh, Patricia. *Harvest of the Sixties: English Literature and Its Background, 1960 to 1990.* Oxford, England: Oxford University Press, 1995.

Articles and Essays

Bergonzi, Bernard. "David Lodge Interviewed." *Month* 229 (February 1970): 108–16.

———. "The Decline and Fall of the Catholic Novel." In *The Myth of Modernism and Twentieth-Century Literature.* Brighton, England: Harvester, 1980, 172–87.

———. "A Religious Romance: David Lodge in Conversation." *Critic* 47 (1992): 69–73.

Bradbury, Malcolm. "Campus Fictions." In *University Fiction,* ed. David Bevan. Amsterdam: Rudopi, 1990, 49–55.

———. "The Language Novelists Use." *Kenyon Review* 29 (1967): 123–36.

Burden, Robert. "The Novel Interrogates Itself: Parody as Self-Consciousness in Contemporary English Fiction." In *The Contemporary English Novel,* ed. Malcolm Bradbury and David Palmer. New York: Holmes and Meier, 1979, 113–56.

Durrant, Sabine. "An Oral Exam with the Prof." *Guardian* (21 February 1998): 3.

Eagleton, Terry. "The Silences of David Lodge." *New Left Review* (November/December 1988): 93–102. Sharply critical of Lodge.

Haffenden, John. "David Lodge." In *Novelists in Interview.* New York: Methuen, 1985, 145–67. Contains much useful information.

Honan, Park. "David Lodge and the Cinematic Novel in England." *Novel* 5 (1972): 167–73.

———. "David Lodge before Changing Places." In *Authors' Lives: On Literary Biography and the Arts of Language.* New York: St. Martin's Press, 1990, 220–30.

Jackson, Dennis. "David Lodge." In *British Novelists Since 1960,* vol. 14, part 2 of *Dictionary of Literary Biography,* ed. Jay L. Halio. Detroit: Gale Research, 1983, 469–81. Very helpful.

Marecki, Joan. "David Lodge." *Contemporary Authors.* New Revision Series, no. 19. Detroit: Gale Research, 1987, 297–303.

Mews, Siegfried. "The Professor's Novel: David Lodge's *Small World.*" *Modern Language Notes* 10 (1989): 713–26.

Parsons, Gerald. "Paradigm or Period Piece? David Lodge's *How Far Can You Go?* in Perspective." *Journal of Literature and Theology* 6 (1992): 11–90.

Walsh, Chris. "David Lodge Interviewed." *Strawberry Fare* (Autumn 1984): 3–12.

Wheeler, Edward T. "The Machinery of Illusion and Effect." *Commonweal* 117 (1990): 538–42.

Widdowson, Peter. "The Anti-History Men: Malcolm Bradbury and David Lodge." *Critical Quarterly* 26, no. 4 (Winter 1984): 5–32.

Film

Profile of David Lodge. Produced and directed by David Thomas. ITV: 29 September 1991. Extremely informative documentary.

Index

Note: pages for the main discussion of individual books by David Lodge will be indicated in boldface.

10 (film), 36

Aberfan disaster, 120–21
About Catholic Authors (Lodge), xi
Abrams, M. H., 87
academics and academic life, treatment of: in *The British Museum Is Falling Down*, 107; in *Changing Places*, 24, 37–38; in *Ginger, You're Barmy*, 21; in *Nice Work*, 62–64, in *Out of the Shelter*, 6; in *Small World*, 40, 42, 44–45, 49
Adventures of Huckleberry Finn, The (Twain), 162
"Affective Fallacy, The" (Wimsatt and Beardsley), 72
After Bakhtin (Lodge), 82–86; compared with David Lodge's earlier critical books, 82; reaction against poststructuralism in, 85–86; sense of excited discovery in, 83–86
Ambassadors, The (James), 26
Amis, Kingsley, 24; David Lodge compared with, 1, 7, 14, 21; David Lodge's critical treatment of, 87, 130, 131
Amis, Martin, 130, 132
"Anglo-American Attitudes. Decorum in British and American Fiction" (Lodge), 26
Anglo-American contrast: David Lodge's fascination with, 25–26; in *Changing Places*, 35, 38; in *Out of the Shelter*, 5; in *Stepping Westward* (Bradbury), 25; in *The Writing Game*, 139–40
Angry Young Men, 44, 123, 131
antirealism: in *The British Museum Is Falling Down*, 142; in *Changing Places*, 31, 33; in *Small World*, 51, 53
Archeology of Knowledge, The (Foucault), 40
Ariosto, 54, 55
Armies of the Night (Mailer), 77
Arnold, Matthew, 71
Art of Fiction, The (Lodge), 167; as a postmodern critical book, 133–34; methodology, 132–33; range of sources, 133; range of topics, 132
Austen, Jane, 27, 42, 47, 61, 133

Bakhtin, Mikhail, 55, 82–86, 88
Barth, John, 26, 81, 87
Barthelme, Donald, 81
Barthes, Roland, 32, 77, 88; and *After Bakhtin*, 84, 85; and *The Modes of Modern Writing*, 78; and *Small World*, 40, 53, 54
Beardsley, Monroe, 72
Beast in the Jungle, The (James), 110
Beckett, Samuel, 56, 81, 133
Bellow, Saul, 26
Bergonzi, Bernard, 96, 125, 149
Berkeley, University of California at, and David Lodge, 6, 26, 27, 29, 38
Big Words: Small World (David Lodge documentary), 134–35, 167
bildungsroman, 5, 144
Biographia Literaria (Coleridge), 71
Birmingham, University of, x, xv, 6, 24–25
birth control, as issue: in *The British Museum Is Falling Down*, 107–9; in *Out of the Shelter*, 92; in *Souls and Bodies*, 120–21, 124–25
Bleak House (Dickens), 80
Blithedale Romance, The (Hawthorne), 25
Book of Laughter and Forgetting, The (Kundera), 85
Booth, Wayne, 72, 83, 86
Bowen, Elizabeth, 3
"Bowling Alley and the Sun, The" (Lodge), 30
Bradbury, Malcolm: as campus novelist, 24; friendship and early collaboration with David Lodge, 25, 135; on campus fiction, 25; reaction to *Language of Fiction*, 77
Brighton Rock (Greene), 100
British Museum Is Falling Down, The (Lodge), 104–15; absurdist elements in, 105–7; academics satirized in, 107; birth control as issue in, 107–9, 113–14; character development in, 108–9; comic elements in, 105–9, 114; compared with *The Picturegoers*, 104–5, 109; completed in U.S., 26; conservative resolution of, 114–15; link with *Language of Fiction*, 112; literary allusions in, 106–7; Malcolm Bradbury and, 25; New Critical orientation of, 88; parallels with *Ulysses*, 47, 105, 107–8; problem of parody in, 34, 47, 109–12 ; reflection of David Lodge's "anxiety of influence," 112; regarded by David Lodge as his first

188

The Author

Bruce K. Martin is professor of English and Endowment Professor of Humanities at Drake University, where he has taught since 1967 and where he served as department chair from 1983 to 1989. He received his graduate training and degrees from the University of Cincinnati. From 1986 to 1987 he was Visiting Fulbright Lecturer in the Department of English Language and Literature at the National University of Singapore, where he returned in 1991–1992 as Visiting Professor of English. In 1995–1996 he was Visiting Fulbright Professor of English at Kwangju University (South Korea). His scholarly interests center on British literature of the nineteenth and twentieth centuries and on literary theory. Besides essays on various British and American writers and on aspects of teaching and literary theory, he has published two books, *Philip Larkin* (1978) and *British Poetry Since 1939* (1985).

The Editor

Kinley E. Roby is professor emeritus of English at Northeastern University. He is the twentieth-century field editor of Twayne's English Authors Series, series editor of Twayne's Critical History of British Drama, and general editor of Twayne's Women and Literature Series. He has written books on Arnold Bennett, Edward VII, and Joyce Cary and has edited a collection of essays on T. S. Eliot. He makes his home in Naples, Florida.